D0557965

YALE STUDIES IN ENGLISH

Yale Studies in English publishes books on English, American, and Anglophone literature developed in and by the Yale University community. Founded in 1898 by Albert Stanburrough Cook, the original series continued into the 1970s, producing such titles as *The Poetry of Meditation* by Louis Martz, *Shelley's Mythmaking* by Harold Bloom, *The Cankered Muse* by Alvin Kernan, *The Hero of the Waverly Novels* by Alexander Welsh, *John Skelton's Poetry* by Stanley Fish, and *Sir Walter Ralegh: The Renaissance Man and His Roles* by Stephen Greenblatt. With the goal of encouraging publications by emerging scholars alongside the work of established colleagues, the series has been revived for the twenty-first century with the support of a grant from the Andrew W. Mellon Foundation and in partnership with Yale University Press.

CALEB SMITH

THE Prison
AND THE American
Imagination

YALE UNIVERSITY PRESS   NEW HAVEN & LONDON

Published with the assistance of the Frederick W. Hilles Publication Fund of Yale University.

Copyright © 2009 by Yale University.
All rights reserved.
This book may not be reproduced, in whole or in part, including illustrations, in any form (beyond that copying permitted by Sections 107 and 108 of the U.S. Copyright Law and except by reviewers for the public press), without written permission from the publishers.

Set in Scala type by Westchester Book Group.
Printed in the United States of America.

The Library of Congress has cataloged the hardcover edition as follows:

Smith, Caleb, 1977–
    The prison and the American imagination / Caleb Smith.
        p.   cm.
    Includes bibliographical references and index.
    ISBN 978-0-300-14166-5 (hardcover : alk. paper)   1. American literature—History and criticism.   2. Imprisonment in literature.   3. Prisoners—United States—Intellectual life.   4. Prisons in literature.   I. Title
    PS169.I47s65 2009
    810.9'9206927—dc22   2009002868

    ISBN 978-0-300-17149-5 (pbk.)

A catalogue record for this book is available from the British Library.

10 9 8 7 6 5 4 3 2 1

For J. M.

CONTENTS

ACKNOWLEDGMENTS

I BEGAN WRITING THIS BOOK with the suspicion that the enclosed, often obscure space of the prison, the great instrument and symbol of captivity in America, might contain some secrets about our modern ways of imagining freedom. I wondered if its solitary cells, in particular, might be the most concrete manifestations of certain deeply held beliefs about the character of the self. As I conducted my research and wrote the ensuing pages, I came to see how the prison condemns offenders to a kind of living death as a precondition for their resurrection into the community of the living; the cell is both a tomb of abjection and the birthplace of a new humanity. These are fascinating but harrowing subjects, and my inquiry into them over the past several years has been made grimmer, at times, by the ongoing bad news from the American prison— the scandals of Guantánamo, Abu Ghraib, and other war prisons abroad; the rapid expansion of the world's largest carceral system at home. I've been sustained, meanwhile, by the generous counsel and conversation of many fellow travelers. I'm grateful to all of them.

The book has been watched over by two guardian angels. Marianna Torgovnick, my dissertation adviser at Duke University, helped me to conceive of the project in the first place and was wonderfully helpful in teaching me how to write it. Jennifer Banks, my editor at Yale University Press, patiently worked with me on the final stages of revision. Along the way, many others kindly offered their time and thoughts. Tom Ferraro was the splendid teacher I often imagined as an interlocutor as I wrote in solitude. Michael Hardt and Mark Antliff helped me to think through some basic problems of interdisciplinary criticism. Casey Jarrin was my favorite colleague in graduate school and my roommate in Danny Hoffman's house, a place full of talk about crime and punishment. Another old friend, Sarah Juliet Lauro, persuaded me to pay closer attention to the imagery of the undead. Nancy Kuhl was my guide to the archives at the Beinecke Library, and one or two of the best discoveries in this book are hers. I thank the friends and colleagues who read pieces of the manuscript and helped me to keep working on it: Colin Dayan, Benjamin Reiss, Houston Baker, Phil Barrish, Elizabeth Dillon, Wai Chee Dimock, Hsuan Hsu, Amy Hungerford, Rachel Kushner, Anne McClintock, Aaron Ritzenberg, Joe Roach. My father introduced me to the life of the mind, and my mother graciously enabled me to pursue it.

Some material from chapters 1 and 2 and the Epilogue was previously published, in an earlier version, as "Detention without Subjects: Prisons and the Poetics of Living Death," in *Texas Studies in Literature and Language* 50, no. 3 (September 2008): 243–267. Some portions of chapters 3 and 4 are revised from earlier versions first published as "Emerson and Incarceration" in *American Literature* 78, no. 2 (June 2006): 207–234. A selection from Judee Norton, "Arrival," copyright © Judee Norton, is reprinted with the permission of the publisher from *Doing Time: 25 Years of Prison Writing*, edited by Bell Gale Chevigny (New York: Arcade Publishing, 1999). Selections from Emily Dickinson are reprinted by permission of the publishers and the Trustees of Amherst College from *The Poems of Emily Dickinson*, edited by Thomas H. Johnson (Cambridge, MA: Belknap Press of Harvard University Press, copyright © 1951, 1955, 1979, 1983 by the President and Fellows of Harvard College). Selections from Jimmy Santiago Baca's *Immigrants in Our Own Land* (Baton Rouge: Louisiana State University Press, 1979) and Simon Ortiz's *from Sand Creek* (Tucson: University of Arizona Press, 1981) are reprinted with permission of the authors. I am also grateful to have received the support of the Yale Studies in English series, a Middlesworth Award from Duke University Special Collections, and a Hilles Publication Grant from the Whitney Humanities Center at Yale.

Introduction

THE POETICS OF PUNISHMENT

> Not so real
> The Cheek of Liberty—
>
> As this Phantasm Steel—
> Whose features—Day and Night—
> Are present to us—as Our Own—
> And as escapeless—quite—
>
> —EMILY DICKINSON, *"A prison gets to be a friend"* (652)

IN THE 1860S, Emily Dickinson slowly withdrew from the world, into her family's home in Amherst, Massachusetts. Outside was the sound and fury of a country reckoning with slavery, Indian Removal, and other horrors; in the enclosed, protected space of the homestead, Dickinson quietly tended her garden and wrote her thousands of letters and poems. As the years went by, her seclusion was more and more complete—in the last decades of her life, they say, Dickinson usually declined to receive even the visits of her closest friends. Instead, she might send a pressed flower or a few lines of verse downstairs: "The Soul selects her own Society," she wrote, "Then—shuts the Door."[1] Dickinson's poems, almost none of them published while she lived, record the exquisitely refined reflections of a mind long held in narrow confines.

In nineteenth-century Massachusetts, Emily Dickinson became a legend, the "nun of Amherst," shrouded in mystery and a white dress. After her death, when her poems began to circulate, readers and critics took up the legend. Dickinson came to represent a Romantic myth, the poet who, in a radical solitude, discovers a private and visionary sensibility.[2] Declaring that "Publication—is the Auction / Of the Mind of Man" (709), she stands for the genius that removes itself from, and finally

1

transcends, the public world of commerce and war and the man-made law. The legend is compelling, and almost any reader of Dickinson's poetry will testify to the feeling of encountering a most peculiar spirit. And yet, in recent decades, scholars have begun to doubt the perfection of Dickinson's solitude.[3] Even the sanctuary of the Dickinson homestead, it seems, was open to newspapers and literary movements, visited by lawyers and reformers and people of letters, among them the Philadelphia preacher Edward Wadsworth and the Concord sage Ralph Waldo Emerson. Many guests, many voices intruded upon Dickinson's private life. Listening closely to her verses, then, we might not hear only the musings of some new-world anchorite; we might also hear the sound and fury of the age. We might hear a culture's various and conflicting accounts of what it means to live a life confined.

As she explored her own removal from the world into the privacy of the home, Dickinson often imagined herself as a prisoner. She depicted the walls of her chamber as those of a cell, her seclusion as a kind of solitary confinement. Imprisonment, however, was an ambiguous condition for Dickinson, sometimes oppressive but also sometimes mysteriously liberating. Indeed, her verses present two apparently contradictory versions of the confined self. In "A prison gets to be a friend," Dickinson writes of "this Phantasm Steel—/Whose features—Day and Night—/Are present to us—as Our Own." Here, the poet takes up a trope with a long history in discourse about incarceration. According to the rhetoric of those who designed and defended the first great penitentiaries, the stone walls of the cell were not supposed only to confine the offender's body. Instead, the reformers imagined that the walls would become the mirrored surfaces of *reflection*, leading convicts to reckon with themselves and their crimes. The influential English minister and reformer Jonas Hanway, for example, was one of many who argued that the prisoner in solitary confinement would discover "the true resemblance of [his] mind, as it were in a mirror." The French magistrates Gustave de Beaumont and Alexis de Tocqueville, in their 1831 *Report on the Penitentiary System in the United States, and Its Application in France*, used the same imagery: "In solitude," wrote Beaumont and Tocqueville, "[the prisoner] reflects. Placed alone, in view of his crime, he learns to hate it."[4] (In the published works of the reformers who designed the prison, the inmate was almost always represented as a man; both the rigors of prison life and the power of self-discipline were assumed to be inappropriate for women.)[5] To the champions of reform who brought the penitentiary into being, solitary confinement provided an architecture of reflection, the first step toward penitence.

As if meditating on the meaning of solitary confinement, Dickinson in another poem depicts a soul divided against itself: "Since Myself assault Me—/How have I peace," the speaker asks, "Except by subjugating Consciousness [?]" (642). Split into two conflicting parts, the "self" becomes its own antagonist. It lives in a state of painful conflict, and it imagines that peace will come only when one side of the self, or "Consciousness," is subdued by the other. There is a misery in these lines, but the self suffers with the promise of a reconciliation: its "subjugating" discipline might lead to a redeemed integrity. Reflecting and self-conquering, it carries out its own correction. This is the poetry of what Michel Foucault, a century later, would call the disciplinary "soul." Through incarceration, reflection, and supervision, the various and unpredictable tendencies of the mind are forged into a unified subjectivity: "Captivity," as Dickinson writes elsewhere, "is Consciousness" (384).

But this vision of solitude is haunted by another. In poems like "Doom is the House without the Door," the fantasy of penitent self-correction meets the nightmare of live burial. "There is a pain—so utter," writes Dickinson, "It swallows substance up—/Then covers the Abyss with Trance" (599). Here, the cell does not inspire spiritual reflection; it imposes an alienating, deathlike captivity:

> There is a Languor of the Life
> More imminent than Pain—
> 'Til Pain's Successor—When the Soul
> Has suffered all it can—
>
> A Drowsiness—diffuses—
> A Dimness like a Fog
> Envelops Consciousness—
> As Mists—obliterate a Crag. (396)

The speaker doomed to captivity persists in a melancholy condition, bereft of the fullness of life. "The Nerves sit ceremonious, like Tombs," and "The Feet, mechanical, go round," but the soul seems already to have expired (341). "I have so much to do—" says Dickinson, "And yet—Existence—some way back—/Stopped—struck—my ticking—through" (443). The speaker of such stammering, dissolute lines is no reflexive, self-disciplining soul; she is an empty shell. Consciousness has been obliterated by a misty languor. Subjectivity has given way to a cadaverous inhumanity.

Dickinson's two versions of the imprisoned self—one reflexive and self-disciplining, the other reduced to a soul-numbed living death—might stand for two opposing accounts of the prison developed by critics over the past two hundred years, especially since the late twentieth century. According to the first, the prison is an exemplary institution of modern power structures that dominate subjects at the level of consciousness or the soul. The great theorist of this subject-making discipline is the French philosopher Michel Foucault, whose *Discipline and Punish* (1975) is easily the most important work on punishment for scholars in literary and cultural studies. To Foucault, the prison is an "apparatus for transforming individuals"—through isolation and surveillance, it trains its inmates to discipline themselves, turning its assembly of malefactors into a congregation of docile and submissive subjects.[6] The "spectacle of the scaffold" of the previous age exercised and dramatized sovereign power by mutilating the offender's body. The modern institution works, more subtly but perhaps more insidiously, on the soul, making prisoners responsible for the government of their own appetites and actions.

While the analysis of the prison as a subject-making institution is most readily associated with Foucault, it had been explored before his work, and it has been elaborated and expanded by many other writers. Some emphasize the place of the penal institution in the industrializing economy, showing how its architecture and timetables, reproducing those of the factory, train convicts to become alienated and obedient workers in a modern, capitalist system.[7] Others connect the prison to the changing political order, demonstrating how the solitary confinement cell creates the radically individuated and inward-looking citizens of liberal democracy.[8] They see the inmate as the "virtual image" of the free subject at large, and the "radical isolation" of the cell as "the specter which outlines the existence of man in the modern world."[9] For them, as for Foucault, the prison dominates by subjugating consciousness.

Against these interpretations of the prison as an exemplary scene of modern subject formation, a second critical tradition depicts its cells as brutal dungeons of torture and dehumanization. In the early 1840s, a Philadelphia prisoner-poet calling himself "Harry Hawser" depicted Pennsylvania's Eastern State Penitentiary—probably the most famous monument of enlightened prison reform in its day—as "a living tomb."[10] Over the past two hundred years, Hawser's vision has often recurred. The twentieth-century writer and activist Jimmy Santiago Baca describes his own descent, after a long period in solitary confinement in an Arizona penitentiary, into a living death—"I was empty," he writes; "I had no connection to this life."[11] The sociologist Erving Goffman depicts "total institutions" such as the prison as sites of a ritualized "mortification."[12] And the literary scholar Colin Dayan, whose illuminating recent work on the law has greatly informed my own, argues that the legal "fiction" of "civil death," which strips away the convict's human rights, finds its "materialization" in the solitary cells of the modern prison, a space of terror and ghostly half-life.[13]

Of course, Foucault and his followers are deeply skeptical about reformers' promises of "correction." They see the inmate's subjectivity as an effect of his subjection, of inescapable regimes of surveillance and control. But in the historical narrative they tell, the prison represents a new age, a modernity in which "the soul," in Foucault's phrase, becomes "the prison of the body." Critics belonging to the other group, meanwhile, tend to understand the prison not as a manifestation of modernity but as a remnant of uncivilized cruelty, a catacomb of abjection whose inmates are divested of rights, even of humanity, and persist in a shadowy living death. For them, the prisoner is not the counterpart of the citizen-subject but a figure of dehumanization or "bare life" akin to the other most famous captive in Jacksonian America, the plantation slave. While Foucault presents the prison as exemplary of mechanisms and techniques that are reproduced throughout society at large, the others argue that the prison is really a different world, excluded from or buried beneath the modern society of citizen-subjects. Their penitentiary has little in common with the school, the office, or other institutions of ordinary civil life, but it may help to explain the deep history of today's sprawling warehouse prisons, and the notorious violence at Guantánamo and Abu Ghraib. It may lead to the conclusion that the new war prisons and carceral warehouses are not "exceptions" to the rule of law and order but the most scandalous contemporary incarnations of what the American prison has been from the beginning.

In the literature and critical scholarship of the American prison, then, we confront two starkly opposed figures: a reflecting, self-governing soul and a cadaverous, dehumanized body. Each is fundamental to the carceral imagination of the past two centuries, yet the two seem almost irreconcilable. How can the prisoner represent the perfect subjectivity of the modern citizen and, at the same time, the abject body outcast from the circle of rights-bearing humanity? How, in other words, can the same captive stand at once for self and other? This book argues that the poetics of the penitentiary—developed by reformers, theorists, and literary artists in the late eighteenth and early nineteenth centuries—were organized around a narrative of rebirth, and that the narrative required, as a precondition, the convict's virtual death. The prison adapted ancient myths of resurrection to the demands of a post-Revolutionary social contract. It was a "living tomb" of servitude and degradation as well as the space of the citizen-subject's dramatic reanimation. Its legal codes divested the convict of rights; its ritualized disciplinary practices stripped away his identity; it exposed him to arbitrary and discretionary violence at the hands of his keepers; it buried him alive in a solitary cell. But it also promised him a glorious return to citizenship and humanity. It mortified the body, but it also claimed to renovate the soul. Its ideal subject was one who, in the words of one great Philadelphia reformer, "was dead and is alive."[14]

In search of the complex origins and far-reaching consequences of this ideal, I return to the era of the prison's conception and to the archive of texts that first gave it meaning. As the prison began to emerge from the ruins of older structures like the scaffold and the pillory, the new paradigm in punishment was an institution of ambiguous and contested significance. What exactly happened in the secluded space of the prison interior? Who was the new protagonist of punishment, the prisoner? Legal and political theorists, reformers and ex-convicts, novelists and poets all turned their attention to the prison's cells, developing a poetics of punishment for the modern age and creating a fascinating archive that records the long and often painful engagement between the hard realities of confinement and the transcendent dream of liberty in a new world.

To understand the prison's narrative of resurrection, we have to see how punishment in the age of the penitentiary remained, at a deep level, what punishment had already been in the earlier age of the scaffold and the pillory: a theater for the performance of its society's founding political myths. The modern prison was born in the late eighteenth century, when European and American authorities lost faith in openly violent punishments such as whipping and branding, humiliation and the gallows. These spectacles had once seemed to display the righteous power of princes over their subjects, and to teach the public the terrible consequences of crime. As many historians have shown, the scaffold was not merely an implement of bodily violence. It was a stage for the performance of a political allegory, a drama of domination and submission. Its exquisitely planned rituals, manifesting the "symbolic force of the law," had "bolstered the power of monarchs and magistrates and made it concretely visible" to the public.[15] The "spectacle of the scaffold" was "a ceremonial" designed "to make everyone aware, through the body of the criminal, of the unrestrained presence of the sovereign."[16] It involved a "dramaturgy" of "intense physical pain."[17] The execution in the seventeenth century was a kind of stage play, directed by the sovereign and by his magistrates, in which the condemned and the crowd must perform their assigned roles—the condemned as the sovereign's defeated antagonist, the crowd as the audience that reflected and appreciated the killing's allegorical lesson.

In the European capitals, the procession to the gallows moved through the most densely populated quarters while all the churches rang their bells. The scaffold was often ornately decorated, a deliberately crafted setting for the "theater of righteousness and repentance."[18] On many occasions, condemned criminals addressed the assembled spectators, reading confessions composed under the supervision of magistrates or clergymen.[19] Punishment in colonial America, importing English and European legal concepts, followed a similar script. The government of early eighteenth-century Virginia, for example, depended on the "public rituals" of whipping, branding, and the pillory to "warn the immoral" and fortify the "legitimacy" of power.[20] "The aim" of colonial justice, according to the legal historian Lawrence Friedman, "was not just to punish, but to teach a lesson," and "theatrical elements came out with special force at hangings."[21] State discipline, then, was not only an exercise of power against a condemned body but also a public spectacle with a carefully managed system of meanings and values. Surrounding the act of violence, even shaping it, were symbols of power and subjection, an elaborate *poetics of punishment.*

The execution was a political ritual, dependent on the obedient participation of the condemned and of the crowd. In this dependence, however, lay the potential subversion of the spectacle. Historians of punishment in Britain record that, by the mid-eighteenth century, "the procession to Tyburn had been turned into a travesty. Prisoners in the tumbril were no longer a dolorous and fearful spectacle but impious and brave."[22] Throwing off the mask of the defeated villain, convicts on parade adopted instead "the posture of heroes."[23] The drunken blasphemy of the condemned threatened the whole carefully produced scene, "distorting the dramatic meaning of public execution."[24] And worse—the raucous disobedience appeared to be a kind of contagion, spreading from the condemned to the spectators themselves. "Instead of taking a moral lesson to heart, [the crowds] approached the spectacle of execution with irreverence and sometimes even showed admiration for bold men who were about to die fearlessly." Spectators began to cheer the condemned, to offer them a drink and a word of encouragement, to join in "merriment" and "mockery of the law."[25] Execution day became a carnival, a holiday for drunks and pickpockets—the very authority that aimed to impress itself upon the people seemed instead to be suspended. When the crowd's sympathy for the convict was fortified by class solidarity or a common political cause, the menace of open rebellion swelled. In a few cases, minor uprisings took shape as crowds physically intervened to spare the lives of the condemned.

By the time of the Atlantic revolutions, authorities had begun to call for revisions in the art of punishment. In London, magistrates abolished the procession from Newgate Prison to the gallows at Tyburn in 1783; throughout Western Europe, public torture and maiming waned, and the death penalty was applied in a narrower range of cases.[26] In the newly independent United States, as the historian Michael Meranze notes, reformers "condemned public punishments for their uncontrollable and contradictory meanings and argued that public penalties disseminated violence and criminality."[27] Post-Revolutionary American critics associated the scaffold with the tyranny of the old world, and opposition took on a radical, patriotic tone. In 1787, the influential Philadelphia reformer

Benjamin Rush—physician, man of letters, and signer of the Declaration of Independence—argued that "public punishments, so far from preventing crimes by the terror they excite in the minds of spectators, are directly calculated to produce them."[28] The theater of punishment was in crisis.

Reformers and the scholars who study them have given many reasons for the decline of public punishments in the late eighteenth century. Perhaps the crowds of modernizing cities—places of industry and commerce, secularism and debauchery—were no longer suited to such solemn rituals. Perhaps the poor, in times of shortage or when revolution was stirring, were ever more inclined to feel their common cause with criminals hanged or burned or butchered by the agents of government.[29] Perhaps, in an American society increasingly dependent on plantation slavery and the racialized distinction between captive black bodies and free white minds, spectacular violence directed at white convicts looked more and more like a shocking offense against "humanity."[30] All of the various local outcries against torture and killing expressed aspects of a deeper common problem: the spectacle of the scaffold, perfected in the age of monarchies based on divine right, was unsuited to the modernizing political order. The all-powerful sovereign whose force was on display at the scaffold was giving way to the social contract and the citizen-subject. As the Italian legal theorist Cesare di Beccaria argued in his widely circulated *Of Crimes and Punishments* (1764), Enlightenment conceptions of humanity and natural rights required the reform of penal codes, from the foundations of the law's legitimacy to the techniques of correction. When criminals were dragged into the public square and exposed to open violence at the hands of the sovereign's magistrates, they were enacting an obsolescent ideal of political submission.

While the movement for reform was transatlantic, an important part of broad shifts in the political order of Euro-American modernity, the United States in the early Republican and Jacksonian periods became a central proving ground for new penal systems.[31] The founders of the U.S. political order—men of enlightenment including Rush, Benjamin Franklin, and Thomas Jefferson—felt that the new nation, with its social contract based on the liberty of the individual citizen-subject, required laws and punishments commensurate with its radical political vision. They called for a rational code that would coordinate the severity of punishments with the severity of crimes; that would respect the human and civil rights of accused offenders; and that would promise many convicts the possibility of being restored to citizenship in the body politic. Punishment, they supposed, should not only mark and mar the body of the transgressor—it should go deeper, to the soul. It should lead the fallen convict to penitence, and ultimately to redemption. To these ends, the reformers conceived of the "house of corrections," a secluded institution of chastisement and training from which, in time, a remade citizen-subject would emerge into the social world. It was Benjamin Rush who wrote that the redeemed convict would be greeted as one who "was lost and is found—was dead and is alive."

By the early nineteenth century, reform had ascended to authority in the United States. "Every day," Beaumont and Tocqueville observed during their tour of the country in the early 1830s, "punishments which wound humanity, become supplanted by milder ones."[32] Virginia and Pennsylvania were among the first states to build great model prisons, sentencing most convicts to a discipline of penitence in solitary confinement. In New York, solitude by night was joined to congregate labor by day in factory-like workshops. The two great penitentiary "systems" of Pennsylvania and New York took shape, and the rivalry between them became one of the defining controversies of the Jacksonian period, through which Americans contested the meaning of citizenship and humanity in the Republic.[33] The Pennsylvania reformers insisted that only full-time solitary confinement could lead the fallen convict through the purifying discipline of reflection and repentance to redemption. The New York faction argued that, with unblinking supervision and the strict enforcement of silence, solitude could be made compatible with collective labor in prison workshops modeled on the industrializing factory. Although much was made of the differences, however, the two systems were built on a common set of assumptions—about the corrective aims of punishment, about the human rights of criminals and the limits of state power, and especially about the character of the individual citizen-subject. The solitary confinement cell, the central unit of all modern penitentiaries, manifested in concrete a deeply held belief in the redeemable private soul.

The story of the passage from the scaffold to the penitentiary is familiar to any student of punishment, recounted by many historians and monumentalized in Foucault's *Discipline and Punish*. But as an account of the origins of the prison system in the United States, the story is incomplete. In reality, whipping, branding, and killing were not fading from the American social landscape as the penitentiary took shape. The Jacksonian age was a violent time of ongoing war and expanding slavery. Beaumont and Tocqueville, in their *Report*, simply declined to discuss the South at all. "In every place where one-half of the community is cruelly oppressed by the other," they wrote, "we must expect to find in the law of the oppressor, a weapon always ready to strike nature which revolts or humanity that complains. Punishment of death and stripes— these form the whole penal code for the slaves."[34] As a few critics have recognized, Foucault's periodization of "classical" and "modern" disciplines, attending mainly to the changing character of punishment in the metropole, seems to have overlooked the ongoing bodily violence that characterized power relations on colonial peripheries and plantations.[35] The difference between the spectacle of the scaffold and the privacy of the cell was, at least in the American context, a matter not so much of chronology as of race and geography.

The history of the American prison is not only an extension of European reforms, and its particular conditions may help to explain some of the contradictions that continue to haunt it. Since the first encounters between European colonists and the native peoples of the Americas, life in the new world had been imagined through stories and images of captivity. Indeed, the "captivity narrative" is often understood as the first distinctly American literary genre. In published accounts of their time as captives among Indians whom they saw as devils and savages, white colonists such as Mary Rowlandson had contributed to the development of the new world's conceptions of freedom and of civilization. Their tales of bondage, suffering, and redemption may have been among the many ideological sources for the penitentiary. By the Jacksonian period, when the prison was entering its golden age, Indian wars were again remaking the American landscape, as military campaigns and relocation programs drove out some of the last of the great Eastern tribes and confined the survivors on Western reservations. It was the period of the Trail of Tears and of several notorious massacres. Often, authorities conceived of Native Americans as sovereign enemies of the United States, foreign powers to be encountered in war, and their long-term captivity would be imagined and structured in militarized ways.

On the fertile lands confiscated through Indian Removal, and throughout the South and West, the slave plantation was rapidly expanded and refined. Slavery had of course been a part of the American economic and political order for centuries, but the plantation, with its spectacles of extreme violence, reached its fullest and most grotesque development in the United States in the 1830s.[36] Slavery was the great national scandal of the antebellum age, and the reformers who built the penitentiary—many of them sentimentalists and humanitarians who belonged to antislavery circles—defined their institution against the brutality of the plantation. They represented the discipline of slavery as a dehumanizing violence, and their own punishments, by contrast, as a set of refined chastisements that prepared the convict for freedom and self-governance. At the same time, however, the penitentiary systems depended on the legal power to strip away the convict's civil rights, and their programs of labor and silence were enforced with the lash and other weapons. Enduring their forms of living death, the convict approached "the condition of a Slave."[37]

Drawing from the sociologist Orlando Patterson, Toni Morrison's *Playing in the Dark* provides the best-known account of how the history of captivity enabled dreams of liberty in the United States. The "Africanist presence" of slaves, writes Morrison, "highlighted freedom—if it did not in fact create it."[38] From Jefferson's Enlightenment ideal of inalienable rights to Emerson's Romantic call for self-reliance, she suggests, the liberated American "self" emerged in opposition to a conspicuously bound and embodied "other," the black slave. Morrison develops a compelling poetics of American history and the forms of identity it produces: a stark, intractable opposition between light and shadow, white and black. But plantation slaves were not the only figures of unfreedom in Jacksonian America. The convict in the penitentiary was also shackled, chastised, and exiled from the body politic. Divested of rights, convicts were at the mercy of wardens and guards armed with whips. They labored with no hope of self-sufficiency or gain. Their ties to family and community were severed, and they lived in a dismal solitude. Their civil death, then, brought them very close to the "social death" of the slave.[39] The crucial difference was that many convicts, unlike slaves, were offered the promise of a new life in the world at large. Through an ascetic discipline of self-abasement and penitent reflection, they might pass from the darkness of abjection into the light of subjectivity. Unlike the savage enemy or the unredeemable slave, the convict bore a temporary abjection, imposed so that it might be transcended. He embodied *in a single figure* the opposition between bondage and freedom. The prisoner was neither only an ideal "self" nor an excluded "other"; he inhabited a threshold, a tunnel of passage. He performed the sacrifice of life through which the citizen-subject's transcendent humanity was born.

From one point of view, the myth of death and rebirth may seem to be an old-fashioned superstition with no place in the Enlightenment schemes of the penitentiary's founders. In contrast to the old theater of wounding and shame, the timetables and labor disciplines of the prison might appear to have done away with such dark, fantastic rituals. Some scholars interpret the decline of the scaffold and the rise of the prison as part of a larger story of progressive secularization.[40] As we shall see, however, the reformers drew explicitly from ancient and medieval Christian imagery, as well as from contemporary Protestant traditions, in their conception of the solitary cell. They adapted the old monastic chamber to the demands and ideals of their modernity. Penal law and policy did not abandon their claims on the soul or their power to unmake and remake humanity. Indeed, as the penitentiary became the great solution to the crisis of the scaffold, its proponents used a narrative of death and resurrection to understand the cell as the scene for a new political ritual, a drama of power and subjection for the modern social contract.

Jean-Jacques Rousseau, in *The Social Contract*, had written that the foundation of political society transforms each subject "from a stupid, limited animal into an intelligent being and a man."[41] In similar terms, the great English legal theorist Sir William Blackstone defined the entry into the social contract as a "sacrifice" of "wild and savage liberty" for the security of the civil state.[42] Attending to the symbols and imagery of these authors of the Enlightenment, we can begin to understand how the great epochal shift in the history of punishment, from the spectacle of the scaffold to the penitence of the prison cell, reflects a deeper shift in the political order. The social contract, as it was conceived in the enlightened and sentimental discourses of the late eighteenth and early nineteenth centuries, required the figurative sacrifice of natural (or animal) life as a precondition for the acquisition of the citizen's spiritual (or human) subjectivity. The civil state was founded through a process of mortification and reanimation. This was the new political myth that would be played out in the rituals of the new institution of punishment. The old scaffold had displayed the sovereign's control over the living and dying bodies of his or her subjects. In the modern age, the penitentiary would enact the abjection of the body and the birth of the citizen's refined, self-governing soul— it would sacrifice the "stupid, limited animal" and conjure, from its remains, "an intelligent being and a man."

Thus while the prison was emerging from the rubble of the scaffold and the pillory—or, rather, displacing them into other worlds—the function of punishment endured: it remained a ritual practice of performing the myths of submission on which the political order was founded. The difference, and the driving force behind the revolution in punishment, was that the new age required a new distribution of power and a remaking of the social imaginary. The philosopher Charles Taylor has analyzed how the social contract, originally a theory of political legitimacy, developed and expanded its range to become a "social imaginary" in the eighteenth and nineteenth centuries. "In the course of this expansion," writes Taylor, the idea "moved from being a theory, animating the discourse of a few experts, to becoming integral to our social imaginary, that is, the way our contemporaries imagine the societies they inhabit and sustain." What began as a controversial set of concepts becomes both more widely accepted and, in a sense, less visible as it is absorbed into the norms, common sense, and everyday practice of modern life. It undergirds our sense of "how we continuously stand . . . in relation to others and to power." Whether or not we acknowledge or subscribe to the theory of the social contract, then, it is there in our institutions and in our ways of understanding our world. Thus it "is not expressed in theoretical terms, but is carried in images, stories, and legends." It is the background, perhaps only dimly perceived, from which modern senses of the self and the community, of humanity and power, emerge into the imagination.[43]

Central to the conception of a new order and a new kind of citizen-subject were the penitentiary and the variously imagined, deeply contested figure at its center, the prisoner. The penitentiary was much more than an innovation in penal policy. It stood for a revolution in the relationship between the people and the powers that governed them. Developing his ideas in conversation with Taylor's theory of Western modernity, the anthropological theorist Talal Asad argues that the reformist narrative of a "progressive prohibition of cruel, inhuman, and degrading practices" that led to the prison is "part of a secular story of how one becomes truly human."[44] As I have already suggested, the penitentiary was not, in any narrow sense, a secular space. It often included a chapel and employed a chaplain, and its program of death and resurrection was a kind of modern, Protestant revision of ancient Catholic ideals. But the most sanguine humanitarians did believe that the institution represented a passage away from cruel tyranny, into enlightenment and civil society—a new age for "humanity" itself.

By the mid-nineteenth century, the American prison had captured the attention of reformers and writers around the Atlantic world. It was visited by such foreign dignitaries as Alexis de Tocqueville, Harriet Martineau, and Charles Dickens. It was promoted by such guiding lights as Margaret Fuller, Louis Dwight, and Francis Lieber. And in the writings of Emily Dickinson and Ralph Waldo Emerson, Herman Melville and Edgar Allan Poe, it helped to shape the literary imagination of the age. The work of defining the carceral institution at the heart of a new society devoted to liberty was not done by political theorists and penal reformers alone. It was undertaken by many other writers around the United States, as the living death and rebirth of penitentiary life was "carried in images, stories, and legends."

The narrative of the prison's founding, the passage from the spectacle of the scaffold to a secret discipline aimed at the soul, would be taken up in the most famous American literary depiction of punishment, Nathaniel Hawthorne's *The Scarlet Letter*. "The founders of a new colony," writes Hawthorne with a touch of irony in the novel's first chapter, "whatever Utopia of human virtue they might originally project, have invariably recognized it among their earliest practical necessities to allot a portion of the virgin soil as a cemetery, and another portion as the site of a prison."[45] The story of the outcast Hester Prynne, sentenced to wear a red badge of shame, is set in a colonial past, but Hawthorne uses it to explore the pressing issues of the penitentiary age: on the one hand, the vulnerability of public punishments to creative subversion by the offender; on the other hand, the secret and penitential turnings of a mind condemned to solitude.[46] Its deep and motivating problems arising from the history of penal reform, *The Scarlet Letter* can be understood as an allegory for the decline of the scaffold and the rise of the prison on the American scene.

In the opening pages of the narrative, the adulteress is paraded through the streets of Boston by magistrates who trust in the "venerable and awful" power of "public discipline" to instill shame in the sinner and righteousness in the assembled crowd. Indeed, some in the audience curse Hester Prynne and fantasize about inflicting worse harms than the pillory or the scarlet letter. Yet Hester is able, in Hawthorne's story, to turn the occasion of her humiliation into a show of controlled defiance. She emerges from the prison with an air of "natural dignity and force of character" (48–49). The scarlet A she has sewn for herself is elaborate and bright, suggestive of aesthetic sensuousness rather than ascetic penance. Hawthorne writes that the badge has "the effect of a spell, taking [Hester] out of the ordinary relations with humanity, and inclosing her in a sphere by herself" (51). Later, as she considers her life as an outcast, she recalls that the "procession and spectacle" of her ritualized shame were not so crushing as the prospect of unending toil and exile—in fact, she sees her performance on the scaffold as a "lurid triumph" over the Puritan magistrates who have tried to humiliate her (71). The worst nightmares of Benjamin Rush and his fellow reformers are realized, as the convict, with an artist's resourcefulness, subverts power and adopts the posture of a heroine.

The story of Hester's partner in crime, the young minister Dimmesdale, follows a different pattern. As the years go by, Hester regains a measure of respect and fellow feeling from the community (139–145). Dimmesdale, meanwhile, suffers through a slow and secret torment. He is preyed upon by the cuckold Chillingworth, recently redeemed from captivity among the Indians, a European-trained physician who claims to be his healer but who leads him through a "popish" discipline of ascetic self-mortification. Day and night punishing himself for a transgression known only to a few conspirators, Dimmesdale wastes away. His body grows thin and pale; his "nerve seem[s] absolutely destroyed"; there is a "morbid energy" in his speech and manner. His keeper "cause[s] him to die daily a living death," and the "terrible machinery" of his protopenitentiary regime turns him into a "ghost" (145, 139, 142). Dimmesdale needs no magistrate to drag him through the streets—he devotes himself to his own punishment, and, in the end, he climbs the scaffold steps burning with the desire to expose himself to shame. After years of regret and self-chastisement, his mortal body expires, but his soul is redeemed. Through the juxtaposed stories of Hester and Dimmesdale, Hawthorne dramatizes the failure of public punishments and the emergence of a private realm of "conscience" where a more intractable discipline can be instilled. The old spectacle of the scaffold is overturned by Hester's "lurid triumph," but Chillingworth, mixing modern science and the ascetic faith that Dimmesdale has learned in his study of Christian texts, introduces an alternative. He devises a punishment that leaves the body alone and, in private, goes all the way down to the soul.

Thus an institution conceived by jurists and political theorists and perfected by reformers becomes, in Hawthorne's novel, part of an origin myth of American society. In the capacious and contested cultural territory of the American imagination, the figure of the prisoner inhabits three major fields: legal and political treatises, the documents circulated by prison reformers, and literary texts. In the chapters that follow, I move among the three, exploring how each conceives of the prisoner's character. The criminal law is ordinarily understood as a code of crimes and consequences, but as many legal scholars have shown, the law also establishes a set of possible selves. "Law is a resource in signification that enables us to submit, rejoice, struggle, pervert, mock, disgrace, humiliate, or dignify."[47] It dictates who belongs to, and who is excluded from, the body politic, and it creates "characters in relation to each other," "roles and positions from which, and voices with which, to speak."[48] Undergirding the penitentiary system, it establishes how the convict may be divested of rights and exposed to discretionary violence—and, in some cases, how the redeemed criminal may be restored to law's protections.

The manifestos and pamphlets of prison reform, meanwhile, script the rituals of prison life: convicts' initiation into the dark and alienating tomb of the cell and the discipline of penitence through which they might hope to be resurrected from it. In the writings of such prominent reformers as Benjamin Rush, William Roscoe, and Beaumont and Tocqueville, we can follow the imaginative and rhetorical moves that blended the demands of a modern, rational, and humane penal system with religious, sometimes superstitious, visions of living death and spiritual rebirth. Often, reformers depict the prisoner's character according to a sentimental concept of humanity, presenting him as a wretched creature who needs the healing embrace of a benevolent authority. At other times, they depend on the circulation of gothic "tales" to create a public fear of punishment and obedience to the law, doing the work of representation and transmission that had once been performed by the spectacle of the scaffold. Their terms and tropes are drawn, in part, from the popular literature of their age.

In turn, a whole generation of authors—Dickinson, Hawthorne, Melville, Poe, Douglass, Emerson, Thoreau, not to mention forgotten prisoner-poets such as Harry Hawser—would take up the new subject of the prison. Much like the legal theorists and reformers, these writers are involved in imagining the prisoner, conceiving and circulating the language in which their culture will understand this crucial figure at the boundary between citizen and captive, between the community of the living and the exile of the living dead. Pursuing the project in a variety of genres—through fictional characterization, the creation of lyric subjectivities, and discourses on the shape of the soul—they invoke the prisoner in both his entombment and his resurrection.

Thus a complex of legal, material, and imaginative structures that emerged between the Revolution and the Civil War established the prison as a central institution for the remaking of humanity in America. The prison was a monument of a new age, but its architecture, practices, and representations also reworked older traditions. Indeed, just as it bridged abjection and subjectivity, it also stood at a boundary between ancient and modern. Its threshold position was articulated in narratives of progressive modernization, and also in spatial and racial terms, as the prison took shape in relation to other forms of captivity, especially the Indian reservation and the slave plantation, across the American landscape. Historians of the penitentiary's rise in the 1820s and 1830s have tended to align it with the insane asylum and other institutions that promised some form of rehabilitation and were commonly defined against the brutalities of war and slavery.[49] However, as the era of the penitentiary's rise was also the era of Indian Removal and of the full-scale plantation, we might better understand these three as mutually constitutive institutions—sometimes opposed, sometimes overlapping—that represented the extremes of captivity and helped to determine the meaning of freedom in the antebellum period.[50] Such a view reveals not only the deep history of civil death and solitary confinement behind the founding of the prison but also its peculiar afterlives in the twentieth century and beyond.

In the wake of the Indian Wars and the Civil War, the relations among prison, reservation, and plantation were recomposed—Emancipation and accelerating westward expansion provoked authorities to abandon some of the key oppositions that had previously defined the zones of captivity, and to develop hybrid forms. In the South, chattel slavery was followed by convict leasing and the "prison farm"; by the early twentieth century, penal plantations such as Angola in Louisiana and Parchman in Mississippi enforced a new version of the old labor discipline under the sign of criminal justice. Critics began to argue that slavery had endured and was thriving on the prison farms, and the work songs arising from their fields were heard as the living echoes of the slave music of the past.

In the West, the military structures of the Indian Wars were adapted to the purposes of long-term confinement. Relocation was followed by the reservation, and by the late twentieth century the old "frontier" was becoming the site of the largest and most advanced prison complexes in the world. The case of Colorado's Fort Lyon is exemplary. The army fort became famous after troops rode out from it to kill peaceful Cheyenne and Arapaho Indians during the Sand Creek Massacre of 1864. In the twentieth century, the institution was rebuilt to become a Veterans Administration psychiatric hospital, and in the early twenty-first century it was acquired by the state of Colorado's Department of Corrections for use as a prison. With a complex history that links the reservation, the asylum, and the modern prison, Fort Lyon might stand as a synecdoche for the various forms of violent displacement and captivity that have made it possible for some Americans to imagine the West as an open frontier, the space of rugged liberty.

Thus, from evolving notions of sovereignty and humanity, arose the penal farms of the South and the sprawling, semimilitarized prison system of the West. Each combined some of the penal logic of the penitentiary with the organized violence of other antebellum institutions, all of which were reshaped by evolving technologies and shifting codes of justice. Like the classic penitentiary before them, these hybrid institutions took on complex significance in the ongoing project of representing freedom and captivity. The final section of *The Prison and the American Imagination* traces some of the lines of continuity, with attention to their imaginative expression by prisoners and artists at large. The voices arising from the Southern prison farm can be heard in the haunting work songs recorded at Parchman and Angola by Alan Lomax in the 1930s and 1940s—and, perhaps more surprisingly, in the fiction of William Faulkner, with its careful handling of consciousness and voice, isolation and communion. Elsewhere, in the poetry of Jimmy Santiago Baca and another captive Native American writer, Simon Ortiz, who writes from within Colorado's Fort Lyon, the centuries-old genre of the captivity narrative is refashioned to represent the conditions of human life in the military and carceral institutions of the frontier West. These works connect imaginative writing about the penitentiary to such other traditions as the spiritual autobiography and the slave narrative; they also disclose some of the profound continuities between the classic penitentiary, with its ritualized mortifications, and the war prisons and domestic carceral network of our own age, zones of disappearance and incapacitation that seem to have abandoned any notion of redemption through penitence.

Since the 1970s, the riots and the rapid expansion of the American prison have provoked scholars to develop historical and theoretical accounts of this increasingly vast, menacing institution as one of both disciplinary subjection and brutal dehumanization. At the same time, literary and cultural critics have begun to explore the relations between punishment and the aesthetic imagination. Some, following Foucault, see the penitentiary as an apparatus of panoptic surveillance that exposes, and perhaps even creates, the inmate's private self; as such, it provides an interesting structural counterpart to the nineteenth-century novel, with its "omniscient" narrators and its views into the interior lives of its characters. In these accounts, the prison and the novel represent two parallel examples of how modern techniques of observation produced both subjectivity and knowledge about subjects.[51] Another school of critics, meanwhile, has turned to the writings of prisoners themselves, seeking a more authentic literature of survival and resistance.[52] For these critics, the unique voices of the incarcerated provide access to otherwise buried truths of violence and mortification. In my view, because the prisoner passes back and forth across the threshold between the ideal self and the abject other—and because so many people literally pass into and out of the modern prison—writings by inmates do not hold such a special status. Their authors are readers, often writing for audiences in the outside world. They do not only record the lived experiences of abjection or struggle. They also engage the ideological and even imaginative dimensions of the institutions that hold them. They belong to a common archive that includes the works of political theorists, penal reformers, and writers at large.

In assembling and interpreting a wider body of imaginative work, my readings attempt to move beyond the dilemma that ensnares so much criticism on texts representing scenes of violence and coercion, where the critic must choose whether a given work is "complicit" in, or "subversive" of, oppressive structures. Law, the rhetoric of prison reform, and literature are not separate spheres—they are intersecting, interdependent discourses, all involved in the project of imagining the human figure at the threshold between bondage and freedom. The gothic nightmares and sentimental dreams of literature, then, are not flights from the real world of law and power. They reckon with the defining political myths and institutions of their times. They attempt to imagine the prisoner as both an object of oppression and a subject of freedom. And reading them in relation to the history of the prison provides more than an underappreciated new "context" for the study of well-known authors such as Dickinson and Hawthorne: it opens a rich conceptual and imaginative archive for the critique of the long, tortured, and unfinished history of imprisonment in America.

Reflecting on the role of humanist critique in the twenty-first century, Judith Butler has suggested that "if critical thinking has something to say about or to the present situation"—that is, to the world in the age of Guantánamo, of a rapidly expanding U.S. regime of violence and captivity—"it may well be in the domain of representation where humanization and dehumanization occur ceaselessly."[53] The concepts of the human and of the inhuman, Butler observes, may appear to arise from the material world, but they become meaningful only in discourse, in acts of representation—acts which, in turn, reshape the real world of precarious life. Along similar lines, the political theorist and scholar Pheng Cheah argues that, in a globalizing age increasingly preoccupied with questions of human rights, only the humanities are able to critique the very ideological foundations of the human, a concept that other disciplines seem to take for granted as a universal article of faith. "If social-scientific solutions to the problems of globalization have always pre-comprehended an idea of humanity as the bearer of dignity, freedom, sociability, culture, or political life," writes Cheah, "and therefore as an ideal project that needs to be actualized, the task and challenge of the humanities today . . . may be to question this pre-comprehension of the human and, somewhat perversely, even to give it up."[54]

The deepest allure of the prison as an object of inquiry is not its place in the history of crime and punishment but its function as a central institution in modernity's redefinition of the human. In the original American penitentiaries, the inmate was divested of rights, social connections, and identity, stripped down to a bare life no longer recognizable as human; and then, through the rituals and disciplines of the prison, this bare life was ennobled with citizenship, a Christian soul, and the powers of reflection and self-governance—with the whole complex of qualities that constituted an ideal of humanity. The critical study of the prison, of its history but also of its many representations, is therefore in part a study of the material and imaginative conception of modern humanity. What it can offer is a look into the often obscure foundations of the social imaginary, a disclosure of the dehumanization that shadows the ideal of humanity—and, perhaps, an archive of alternatives.

In legal and activist circles, the most common and urgent language of protest against the exploding U.S. carceral system is today, as it was two centuries ago, the language of human rights. The prison-industrial complex is denounced as a new plantation or as a "domestic war zone" where human dignity suffers outrageous violations.[55] My research into the history and imaginative life of the American penitentiary—and into its ongoing afterlives—leads me to the conclusion that the human rights crusade, which has a vital role in remedying abuses and saving lives, will finally be limited if it is committed to the premises that brought the prison into being in the first place; it will tend to fold back into the project of the "reform," and thus the continuation, and even the expansion, of the prison system itself. The political work of human rights activists, then, might be joined to a kind of critique that explores what alternatives might appear beneath, or beyond, the limits of the human.

The problem of the prison does not end with a defense of the prisoner's human rights. Indeed, it begins there. Over the past two centuries, human rights claims have brought the convict back from monstrous exile, into the circle of juridical humanity. But the juridical humanity conceived with the founding of the United States and its penitentiary system was no human sanctuary. It involved a myth of sacrifice and a practice of dehumanizing penal violence. Prisoners are not beyond the embrace of the law; they are mortified by it. The critical challenge, then, is to pursue, perhaps to unmake, the harrowing concept of the human on which the prison rests. *The Prison and the American Imagination* therefore explores the place of a central institution in the building of the modern order, attending to the ways in which its narrative of death and resurrection helped to conceive a new ideal of humanity. It argues that the prison is not only a material structure or a matter of the law, narrowly defined, but also a set of images and narrative patterns; it is a language that enables expression and, at the same time, ensnares the subject in its designs. If the tradition of imaginative writing about the American prison opens some possibility of escape, it cannot be in the name of the inviolable humanity of the living entombed. It might, however, stall the narrative cycle that repeatedly absorbs the gothic inhumanity of the prisoner into a sentimental resolution. In the "cadaverous triumph" of Melville's Bartleby, or in Jimmy Santiago Baca's connection with "the dirt and the iron and concrete" of the inhuman world, we might discover a language that refuses both the prison's dehumanizing violence and its captivating vision of human redemption.

PART ONE BURIED ALIVE

He has ceased to be a citizen, but cannot be looked upon as an alien, for he is without a country; he does not exist save as a human being, and this, by a sort of commiseration which has no source in the law.

—P.-J.-J.-G. GUYOT, "Civil Death" (272)

He had contrived, or rather he had happened, to dissever himself from the world—to vanish—to give up his place and privileges with living men, without being admitted among the dead.

—NATHANIEL HAWTHORNE, "Wakefield" (156)

CHAPTER ONE

Civil Death and Carceral Life

"CAPTURE," wrote George Jackson from his cell in 1970, "is the closest thing to being dead that one is likely to experience in this life."[1] Jackson spent more than a decade in California prisons, much of the time in solitary confinement, before he was shot dead by a guard. While incarcerated, he educated himself in the prison library and became involved with the prisoners' rights movement and the Black Panthers. Jackson was an articulate voice from the prison interior, and his letters have been widely read for their elegance and rhetorical force. Jean Genet called them "a striking poem of love and of combat."[2] But Jackson's description of captivity as a deathly condition was more than the clever metaphor of a gifted writer. It was a deep insight into the history of punishment in America, arising from a long tradition of practices and representations.

Confined to Pennsylvania's world-famous Eastern State Penitentiary in the 1840s, the ex-sailor and poet using the pen name Harry Hawser also used the idiom of death-in-life:

> But fated to a living tomb,
> For years on years in woe to brood
> Upon the past, the Captive's doom
> Is galling chains and solitude.[3]

According to Hawser's poem, the captive in the penitentiary is violently arrested in time, painfully fixated upon the past while the years creep by. His penitence, enforced with chains and the walls of the solitary cell, is a form of "doom."

Composed in the American prisons of two centuries, the testimonies of George Jackson and Harry Hawser, like those of many other inmates, represent the prison as a catacomb, inhabited by cadaverous creatures exiled from the world of living humanity. For historians and other scholars of the prison system, such morbid visions present a challenge. In the prevailing critical narrative, the penitentiary has most often been understood as one of the great Enlightenment reforms, a humanitarian endeavor that replaced the gore and spectacle of public mutilation with a more rational, benevolent discipline of "kindness and proper instruction."[4] Even among critics such as Foucault, who are deeply skeptical about the prison's humanitarian promises, there is a consensus that it works to produce the inmate as a disciplined "subject," a kind of model worker or self-governing citizen for the modern age.[5] Suspicious as they may be about the secret oppressions of the penitentiary system and the ideological order it serves, such analyses must find it difficult to account for a dungeon-tomb whose inmates are not subjects at all but human lives divested of subjectivity, of humanity itself, persisting as ghosts or monsters in a carceral living death.[6]

And yet, for as long as the prison has defined punishment in the United States, it has been accompanied by the imagery of inmates as the living dead. The gothic tropes of Jackson and Hawser belong to a tradition of writing about carceral life that is as old as the American prison itself. Even the first great American penitentiaries, built as monuments to the prisoner's humanity and redeemable soul, were often depicted as places of living death. Nor did such imagery belong exclusively to the discourse of protest, used by prisoners and humanitarians to call attention to the abusive violence that often characterizes the hidden world of the prison. The very reformers who built the prison system understood it as a place of deliberate mortification.

Arising in a post-Revolutionary age of radical reform, the new prisons were devoted to the convict's resurrection as a citizen and a member of the human community, but they required, as a precondition, the virtual destruction of the self. In order to be born again, the offender had first to submit to sacrifice. Jurists and prison administrators invoked the ancient legal fiction of "civil death," divesting the inmate of rights and transforming him into a legal nonperson comparable to a slave. The initiation rituals and disciplinary techniques of the penitentiary system were scripted to enact a symbolic and material mortification. And, in the language of reformers, inmates, and literary artists at large, the prison was represented as the dark house of ghosts and monsters. Dehumanization, then, is no excess or exception; it is the very premise of the American prison. The inmate in the penitentiary is not only a subject in the making; he is also a figure of exclusion and decay, inspiring both pity and terror. To sentimental reformers, a virtual death was the first step toward the citizen-subject's glorious rebirth. To prisoners and others more suspicious of the penitentiary's designs, however, the gothic monstrosities of its interiors have sometimes seemed to destabilize the very foundations of sentimental humanity. The living dead threaten to rise. "This monster they've engendered in me," Jackson promised from his cell, "will return to torment its maker."

DEAD IN LAW

For centuries, Western criminal law has developed the gothic concept of civil death, a legal fiction indicating "the status of a person who has been deprived of all civil rights."[7] In the United States, civil death statutes have dictated that the felon may not vote or make contracts. He loses his property. In some states his wife becomes a widow, free to remarry without divorcing him. Thus the incarcerated convict retains his "natural life"—his heart beats on, he labors, and he consumes—but he has lost the higher, more abstract, civil life that made him fully human in the eyes of the law. Legal scholars trace the origins of civil death back to monasticism and to ancient and medieval criminal codes. In the Middle Ages, men and women who entered the cloister relinquished their possessions and their rights, leaving the political community for the city of God. Often, going into the monastery involved a ritualized passing away from the living world. Norman Johnston, in his history of prison architecture, notes that English anchorites "were installed during a solemn church service that included parts of the burial service, as the anchorite was literally bricked into his or her little prison."[8] Afterward, though his body lived on, the monk was "overlooked" by the law "as though he were no longer in the land of the living."[9]

The most violent and perhaps most haunting forms of civil death, however, belong to the traditions of punishment. In classical Greece, citizens who committed grave offenses were sometimes sentenced to political excommunication and "denied such fundamental rights . . . as the right to vote and to appear in court." In Rome, where the phrase "civil death" was first applied, the criminal could be branded with "infamia," a mark signifying moral corruption and banishment from public life.[10] In the medieval conceptions of crime and punishment that form the foundations of English common law, criminals were exposed to "outlawry," an expulsion from the protective sphere of the political community. The outlaw could be "killed with impunity"; he was "the legitimate prey of anyone anxious to satisfy a lust for cruelty."[11] Indeed, according to the nineteenth-century scholars Sir Frederick Pollock and Frederic William Maitland, the outlaw was a man turned into a menacing beast by the magic of justice: "He who breaks the law has gone to war with the community; the community goes to war with him. It is the right and duty of every man to pursue him, to ravage his land, to burn his house, to hunt him down like a wild beast and slay him; for a wild beast he is; not merely is he a 'friendless man,' he is a wolf."[12] Banishing the criminal from its protective circle, the community redefines him as a creature less than human. A "wolf" belonging to the state of nature and encountered in a state of war, he is exposed to unlimited violence.[13] Yet this human life divested of its humanity is never absolutely "a piece of animal nature without any relation to law"; as Giorgio Agamben writes in his discussion of medieval codes, the outlaw or bandit represents "a threshold of indistinction and of passage between animal and man."[14] The person "dead in law" dwells at the boundary between inside and outside, between the human and the haunting other.

The idea that the law can transform a person into a wolf or an animate corpse may seem to be an ancient and outmoded superstition, but civil death endured the Renaissance, taking on new meaning in the enlightened codes of the seventeenth and eighteenth centuries. Modern states, seeking to ground their power in something other than the divine right or the naked might of the sovereign, moved away from the warlike language of darker times. The new political models held that men were naturally free and had exchanged some of their freedom for the security of an ordered, collective existence. According to the emergent myth of the social contract—developed by a wide range of political philosophers including Thomas Hobbes, John Locke, and Jean-Jacques Rousseau—men were properly ruled only by their own consent. They were not the objects of conquest to be possessed by tyrants; they were the subjects of a commonwealth, a civil society that must recognize each as a citizen and a bearer of rights.

The myth of the social contract served, at least in theory, to restrain governments' powers over the lives and property of their subjects. In terms of criminal justice, it provided the theoretical premises for raising new questions about the infliction of bodily violence against offenders, and particularly about the death penalty. Perhaps the most rigorous application of social contract principles to the problem of punishment was made by Cesare di Beccaria, whose work was read and admired by reformers around the Atlantic world, including American authorities from Philadelphia to Virginia.[15] Beccaria argued that the social contract must limit the violence that could legitimately be done against criminal citizens. The convict was not an alien or a wartime enemy. He was a citizen-subject of the commonwealth. "By what right," demanded Beccaria, "can men presume to slaughter their fellows?" Given the doctrine that laws "represent the general will which is the aggregate of the individual wills," it seemed clear to him that the sovereign could claim no right over the lives of his subjects. His power depended on their consent, and of course nobody would "willingly [give] up to others the authority to kill him." If punishment was a legitimate violence exercised by the sovereign against subjects in the interest of the commonwealth, then killing was not punishment.[16] The death penalty is "not a matter of *right*," Beccaria concluded, "but is an act of war on the part of society against the citizen." When governments exercised an unrestrained force against the lives of their subjects, in other words, they violated the social contract, regressing from the civil state to a state of war.[17]

Beccaria's argument was that the natural life, the animate body, of the citizen had never been offered up to the community as part of the social contract, and therefore the community had no claim on that life. It could take from the criminal only the rights and privileges of citizenship: property, freedom, and the protection of the law. It was here, in the distinction between natural life and civil rights, between death and a not-quite-absolute deprivation, that the ancient idea of civil death found a place in the legal imagination of the Enlightenment.

Instead of the death penalty, Beccaria advocated a "permanent penal servitude," a "dreary and pitiable" condition in which the convict would be "deprived of freedom" and "become a beast of burden."[18] Imagining a figure "in manacles and chains, under the rod and the yoke or in an iron cage," he conceived of the convict as a marginal figure, lingering between the full humanity of the rights-bearing citizen and the monstrous, marked body of the enemy.[19] In the most extreme cases, he called for a "banishment" that would "sever all the ties between society and the malefactor," so that "the citizen dies and the man remains, and as far as the body politic is concerned, this should have the same effect as natural death."[20] Like many other theorists of the social contract, Beccaria began by conceiving of the natural person as a self-owning, rights-bearing sovereign, and by arguing that his natural rights were the origins of the civil rights he retained in the political state. But he ended by reducing the natural person to a minimum standard, the living thing that the state could bind and incapacitate but could not kill. Reasoning from the premise of the citizen's inviolable human rights, then, Beccaria had developed an argument for civil death.

In the same period, British and colonial authorities adapted versions of civil death to justify various forms of dehumanizing bondage. For them, as for Beccaria, penal servitude represented a marginal recognition of the offender's rights. Increasingly, this form of legal bondage became a substitute for capital punishment, a sentence by which rights-bearing people were cast out of the commonwealth and reduced to beasts of burden. In Britain and America, penal servitude helped to shape the policies and practices of colonialism. From 1617 forward, "transportation"—banishment from England, often including indenture or military conscription—was a legal punishment for felons. Sir William Monson praised the reform as a sign of rational, humanitarian progress, arguing that transportation would provide a useful class of "king's labourers" and "save much blood that is lamentably spilt by execution."[21] The felon, British lawmakers reasoned, might retain his natural life if he could be made to disappear from the kingdom he had wronged and put to work, elsewhere, in its service. The gallows were an emblem of tyranny, and even domestic penal servitude—recommended by Beccaria and adopted widely in Western Europe—offended a "free" English public with the sight of "manacled prisoners toiling like slaves" in its cities.[22] The English, one satirist wrote, "disdain that *Englishmen* should be Slaves on *English* land, and rather chuse *America* for the Theatre of our Shame."[23] Transportation would amputate the convict from the body politic, and it would remove the indignities of punishment from the view of polite society. It would exploit convict labor in distant territories like Maryland and Jamaica, where brutality and slavery belonged.[24]

In 1718, the Transportation Act dramatically expanded the use of penal banishment against those "who had forfeited their right to remain members of civil society," making it a central element of the British criminal justice system, a reform with enormous effects in the colonies.[25] After conviction, felons sentenced to transportation were declared legally dead.[26] They were detained temporarily in a local jail, then entrusted to a private merchant contractor who received a subsidy for deporting them. When the contractor's ship was ready to sail, the prisoners were marched through the city streets in shame, and it was "the privilege of bystanders to hoot at the convicts, and even on occasion to throw mud and stones."[27] From this point forward, they received a treatment that, as the historian Abbott Emerson Smith cryptically remarks, was like that of "other cargoes of servants."[28] Aboard the ship, they were chained together below the deck in the hold, a filthy space where disease spread quickly. More than one in ten died on the crossing.[29] Those "criminal outcasts" who lived to see America were sold into servitude on the plantations, where, according to A. Roger Ekirch, they "were forced to work as common field hands, much like slaves."[30] About thirty thousand men and women, the majority of English felons, were transported to America in the eighteenth century.[31]

Like others condemned to civil death and servitude, transported convicts devised strategies of escape and resistance, sometimes turning to violence. Many in the colonies raised loud cries against the infection of their communities by these monstrous cargoes. There were stories of contagious disease, of rampant crime and vagabondage.[32] Some transported convicts made their way back to England, though the law provided for their hanging if they were discovered in the metropole. Some, it was said, rose up against the crews who oversaw their passage, killing their captains and turning to piracy. The most famous cries of alarm, perhaps, came from Benjamin Franklin, in his pseudonymous polemics for the *Philadelphia Gazette*. The felons, wrote Franklin, were "*Serpents, and worse than serpents*"; the merchants who carried them were trafficking in an "abominable" business; and the whole transportation enterprise was a sign of England's contempt for her colonies.[33] In exchange, Franklin satirically proposed that the Americans should send ships full of rattlesnakes back to the mother country. For the planters of the Southern slaveholding colonies, meanwhile, transported felons carried an even more disturbing menace: Virginia's colonial council worried in 1749 that the convicts might be "wicked enough to join our Slaves" in insurrectionary "Mischief," a prospect that would "bring sure and sudden Destruction on all his Majesty's good Subjects of this Colony."[34] Civil death reduced convicts to a condition close to slavery, and the masters were haunted by visions of a revolutionary solidarity among the two classes of the living dead.

And yet, since arriving in the new world, the colonists had themselves enforced certain kinds of penal servitude and exile under the sign of civil death. The sentences of servitude (officially called "slavery") and banishment were available to colonial criminal courts in the seventeenth century: the former was often used to extend the term of indenture for offending servants; the latter was most notoriously applied to heretics.[35] During King Philip's War (1675), hundreds of Algonquian Indians—some prisoners of war, but also, it seems, many Christians and other captives who had not fought against the English—were sold into slavery, loaded into ships, and sent to the plantations of the West Indies. To justify their enslavement, English authorities resorted to a "confused and arbitrary" mixture of theological and legal reasoning.[36] They invoked what would come to be called the "just-war theory," which argues that those who commit unlawful aggressions against a state have forfeited their natural freedom and may rightfully be held in bondage.[37] A document carried by one of the slave ships outbound from Massachusetts declared that its cargo of "heathen Malefactors" had made war against the English "without any just cause." Guilty of "inhumane and barbarous crueltys[,] murder, outrages and villainies," they had reportedly "been Sentenced & Condemned to perpetuall Servitude" by "due and legall procedure."[38] Thus were the Indians subjected to what one of their few English defenders, the missionary John Eliot, called a "usage . . . worse than death."[39] Again, a judicial condemnation turned sovereign subjects into bandits and bonded laborers, as the ancient notion of civil death evolved to serve the more modern purposes of empire and slavery.

BURIED ALIVE

The movement that produced the penitentiary system may appear to have rejected the dehumanizing practices of civil death and servitude. The ascendant reformers of the late eighteenth and early nineteenth centuries held that discipline should not just harm the offender but also improve him; that open displays of violence were dangerous to the social order and should be replaced by an institutionalized regime of penitence and training; that the criminal should be prepared, upon release, for the sober task of self-government. Political philosophers developed the theory of the social contract, and legal theorists used the language of citizens' rights, but the popular reform movement preferred the idiom of Christian charity and sentimental "humanity." "Our object," wrote the English preacher and reformer Jonas Hanway in 1781, "is nothing less than the souls and bodies of the most miserable part of our fellow-creatures, our fellow-Christians."[40] The Philadelphia reformer George Washington Smith agreed: "Religion and policy alike dictate the adoption of mercy, of kindness and forbearance in the infliction of reformatory punishments."[41] By 1846, a penitentiary chaplain in Louisiana took it to be axiomatic that the convict was no "outcast" but "ought to be esteemed an object of sympathy."[42] The criminal was reconceived—no longer a predatory beast, he became a lost soul; no longer a monster, he was one of "our fellow-creatures" in need of benevolent attention. The "great moral justification of the reform movement," then, became the "*humanity* of the convict."[43] The whole enterprise of building the expensive new prisons, of providing clean air and water and the silence necessary for reflection, of teaching the prisoner how to read the Bible and how to earn his living through productive labor, was carried along by a legal recognition of the felon's human rights and by what Foucault calls the "cry from the heart"—a sentimental rhetorical mode that pledged its Christian charity and its enlightened sympathy to the miserable creatures living and dying in the shadow of the commonwealth.

At the same time, however, the gothic fiction of civil death was written into the law. In its modern form, as in its ancient one, the superstition of civil death depended on the legal distinction between the rights-bearing citizen-subject and unprotected "natural" life. In his monumental *Institutes of American Law* (1854), the jurist John Bouvier drew the line: "The enjoyment of civil rights is attached to the quality of citizen of the United States. This quality is subject to be lost by abdication or renunciation of the rights of citizen, or by civil death."[44] Bouvier went on to define the term: "Civil death is the state of a person who, though possessing natural life, has lost all his civil rights by a judicial condemnation, and is, as to them, considered dead."[45] Divested of citizenship and subjectivity, the condemned becomes a specter, an animate corpse in the eyes of the law.

What was the use of the ancient and supernatural legal fiction of civil death in a system expressly devoted to the rehabilitation of criminals and the making of proper subjects for the Republic? To many modern lawyers, civil death appears to be a "vestigial doctrine," a relic of older, more superstitious codes.[46] A 1937 *Harvard Law Review* article on the subject notes that, "with living men regarded as dead, dead men returning to life, and the same man considered alive for one purpose but dead for another, the realm of legal fiction acquires a touch of the supernatural under the paradoxical doctrine of civil death."[47] The U.S. Ninth Circuit Court of Appeals in 1972 similarly attacked civil death as a "quasi-metaphysical invocation" lacking "modern" justification.[48] In the age of normalized and normalizing punishments, of criminology and bureaucratic departments of "corrections," the notion that the law can turn a living citizen into an animate corpse seems like outdated wizardry.

However, "American political thought," especially as it encodes itself in the criminal law, "has always been characterized by paradoxes of inclusion and exclusion," and the ambiguous figure of the person dead in law persists even into modern times at "the boundaries of the body politic."[49] Colin Dayan, exploring what she calls law's "sorcery," argues that "the felon rendered dead in law" is no anachronism but an effect of a modern power that is "most instrumental when most fantastic and most violent when most spectral."[50] Civil death is neither a relic nor a fanciful metaphor. It is the legal "language" that finds its "materialization" in the modern prison.[51] Recognized as a legitimate legal possibility in the age of reform, civil death became a kind of script for the violence performed inside penitentiaries.

In *Asylums*, the sociologist Erving Goffman shows how social life in "total institutions" such as prisons enacts the "mortification" of the detained subject. Goffman, whose earlier work used the metaphor of the theater to explore "the presentation of self in everyday life," is closely attentive to the dynamics of ritual and performance. The legal fiction of civil death, he notes, is manifest in "various forms of disfigurement and defilement" that recast the inmate as a ghost.[52] The prisoner is severed from the social world in which his old identity was grounded; he loses his name and is called by a number; his clothes are confiscated and replaced by a uniform; his hair is cut or shaved. He is "shaped and coded into an object," often losing any identifying traits except those he "possesses merely because he is a member of the largest and most abstract of social categories, that of the human being."[53] Through "a series of abasements, degradations, humiliations, and profanations of self," the inmate is costumed for and directed through a ritualized death.[54]

Victor Hassine, confined to Pennsylvania's Graterford State Prison in the early 1980s, narrated his initiation this way: "My escort guard ordered me to 'get naked' and surrender my personal effects to an inmate dressed in brown prison garb. As I stripped down, I handed the silent inmate the last vestiges of my social identity. He tossed them impatiently into an old cardboard box. The guard conducted another 'bend-over-and-stretch-'em' search; I was given delousing shampoo and ordered to shower. Afterward, as I stood naked and shivering, I was assigned two pairs of navy-blue pants, two blue shirts, three T-shirts, three pairs of boxer shorts, three pairs of socks, a blue winter coat, a blue summer jacket, two towels, and a pair of brown shoes. Everything but the shoes and socks had AM4737 boldly stamped in black. This number was my new, permanent identity."[55]

For Hassine, incarceration begins with a loss of self. He narrates a routine, a ritual by which the new inmate is deliberately divested of his identity, becoming a creature of the institution. There is nothing extraordinary about Hassine's account, except perhaps its rhetorical restraint. Indeed, Hassine is careful and precise, reluctant to indulge in trope. The one phrase that might seem to invite sympathy—"I stood naked and shivering"—is, in this case, a literal description of a man stepping out of a shower, waiting for his captors to clothe him. The prisoner acknowledges his childlike helplessness in the moment between surrendering "the last vestiges" of his former, "social identity" and acquiring a "new, permanent identity" in dehumanizing code: AM4737. He trembles at the moment of rebirth. Hassine goes on to describe the "distorted . . . forms" of his fellow inmates and the "ashen gray pallor" of skin never exposed to sunlight. He wonders "whether it was the look of these men that led them to prison or whether it was the prison that gave them their look." His overwhelming impression is of monsters excluded from the community of the living: "None," he writes, "seemed human." There is a chill of recognition in the lines, as Hassine realizes that the prison's rituals are scripted to divest him of rights and identity, to turn him into one of these ghosts.[56]

Goffman and Hassine are contemporaries of Foucault who are mainly concerned with the institutions of the late twentieth century, but the ritualized "mortification" that appears in their accounts has been practiced in the American prison system since its origins. From 1829 forward, the new arrival at Philadelphia's Eastern State Penitentiary, after the usual surrender of possessions, shearing of hair, medical inspection, and numbering, was hooded and walked to his cell like a condemned man to the gallows.[57] Charles Dickens, who visited Eastern State in the early 1840s, was alive to the symbolism: "Over the head and face of every prisoner who comes into this melancholy house a black hood is drawn; and in this dark shroud, an emblem of the curtain dropped between him and the living world, he is led to the cell from which he never again comes forth until his whole term of imprisonment has expired. He never hears of wife or children; home or friends; the life or death of any single creature. He sees the prison officers, but, with that exception, he never looks upon a human countenance, or hears a human voice. He is a man buried alive; to be dug out in the slow round of years; and in the meantime dead to everything but torturing anxieties and horrible despair." For Dickens, Eastern State—a world-renowned monument to enlightenment, reform, and humanity—was in reality a dark chamber where the living dead awaited, despairingly, the day of their resurrection.[58]

The penitentiary, then, seems to be a paradox. Its founders declare their respect for the convict's humanity and their wish to lead him toward a new life, yet they invoke the legal fiction of civil death and the ritual practice of mortification. The object of these divided aims, the prisoner becomes a divided figure: a redeemable soul but also an offending body; a citizen-in-training but also an exile from civil society; a resurrected life but also an animate corpse. In the poetics of the penitentiary—the images and tropes that give meaning to the violence of incarceration—enlightened sentimentality is bound up with the violent and ghostly nightmares of the gothic. It is tempting, of course, to accuse the reformers of a flagrant hypocrisy, as if the promises of correction and "humanity" in punishment were just fig leaves covering a reality of dehumanizing violence. Jason Haslam's remarks on the "difference between the prisons' theoretical models and their practices" express such a view: "Rather than following through with the Protestant rhetoric of the possibility of the individual's reformation through meditation and reliance on conscience, these prisons in fact beat, brutalized, and killed more often than they rehabilitated."[59] The realities of prison life are often harrowing, but in the penitentiaries of the nineteenth century, dehumanization was no secret; it was written into the law, performed in the rituals of prison initiation, and discussed in well-publicized reform debates. It was, in short, an explicit part of reform's "theoretical models." "While confined here," a warden of New York's Auburn Prison openly announced to his inmates in 1826, "you are to be literally buried from the world."[60] Even eloquent theorists of the penitentiary such as Gustave de Beaumont and Alexis de Tocqueville sometimes described its inmate as one "dead to the world."[61] In order to understand the prison, we shall have to see how living death was neither an accident nor an excess but a fundamental part of the institution's design.

In the imaginative world of the penitentiary system, civil death—the legal and ritual processes that produced the figure of the prisoner as the living dead—played two roles. The two may have informed each other at times, but they were, in principle, distinct and opposed, resting on two different ideas about the status of the convict and the function of penitentiary discipline. First, civil death reduced the criminal citizen to the condition of an abject "other," the negative image of the citizen-subject. The citizen was free; the prisoner was bound and contained. The citizen was a transcendent spirit or a reasoning mind; the prisoner was an offensive body vulnerable to violence and deprivation. The citizen belonged to the human community; the prisoner was a monstrous exile, beyond the pale of humanity, without a claim to legal personhood. Divested of rights and exiled from the body politic, he was unprotected, infinitely vulnerable and pliable. He could be whipped or gagged, confined to solitude, deprived of food, or subjected to whatever other torments prison officials deemed necessary either to his correction or to the orderly functioning of the institution. This first use of civil death drew on ancient legal superstitions to depict the convict as an outlaw, and on the contemporary legal ideology of slavery to depict him as a degraded bondsman. Civil death justified a virtually unlimited exploitation and discretionary violence against the living entombed.

The excesses of exploitation and violence, however, were relentlessly attacked by the main line of prison reformers. Drawing from social contract theory and speaking a sentimental language of "humanity," they insisted that even convicts retained some human rights and some claim to the sympathy of those who punished them. To such reformers, the degradations of penitentiary discipline seemed to violate the liberal principles on which the institution was supposed to rest. They protested civil death as an obsolete piece of legal black magic; they decried the whip and other implements of torture as relics of a barbarous age. Their arguments about the anachronism of violence and dehumanization in modern America were in some ways disingenuous. After all, the United States in the Jacksonian period was actively pursuing Indian Removal and expanding plantation slavery. But the reformers were right to claim that the consignment of criminals to exile in a "living tomb" went against the guiding aims of the penitentiary's founders: a recognition of the convict's humanity and an effort to reclaim him as a responsible citizen-subject.

And yet their protest against civil death could only go so far. As much as they railed against excesses and abuses of power, as many pamphlets as they published in defense of prisoners' human rights, their movement was devoted to an ever-expanding prison system, and their institution could never quite dispense with the legal and ritual enforcement of civil death. The problem was that the kind of citizenship—the very humanity—into which they wished to conduct the convict, was itself founded on the sacrifice of life.

COARSE BEINGS

The creation of prisoners as the living dead—encoded in law and in the rhetoric of the reform movement, violently enacted in the rituals of prison initiation and discipline—drew from an old and complex punitive tradition. But such dehumanizing language and practices were not merely the latest manifestation of ancient punishments. Beyond its use in criminal justice, the penitentiary was one of several institutions in antebellum America through which the subjects of the young Republic established the crucial differences between free and unfree, citizen and exile. Indeed, the penitentiary was perfected between 1820 and the Civil War, alongside the plantation and the reservation, two other great institutions for the containment of figures without rights, condemned to a shadowy life at the margins of the human community.[62] In the political imagination of early nineteenth-century Americans, the "coarse beings" sentenced to civil death in the penitentiaries were the kindred of savages and slaves.

The directors of the Massachusetts State prison in 1823, for example, depicted the convict's initiation to penitence as a ritualized burial: "When a convict is received . . . he is stripped of his clothing, and dressed in the livery of disgrace; his hair is cut, and he is put, for a period of time, into a cell, where no sun ever shines. He is cut off from intercourse with society. He lives for twenty-four hours on eight ounces of coarse bread, with enough water to allay the fever which runs through his veins. He is removed into the workshops, and pursues a constant and laborious occupation for others' benefit, in the condition of a Slave."[63] Again, the prison is a scene of dehumanization, and the processes of initiation into its discipline invokes the symbolism of death. The prisoner is buried alive in a cell "where no sun ever shines." He loses his hair and clothes, markers of his identity. His nourishment is minimal and coarse, and his work is the possessed labor of the slave.

To get at the deeper meaning of civil death in the penitentiary, then, we shall have to attend to more than the institution's regimes of surveillance and discipline, its systems for training obedient subjects; we shall have to see how it was also a zone of internal exile from the body politic, a living tomb whose inmates were divested of rights and reduced to a kind of animal or undead life. With its legal exclusions, its violent drama of mortification, and its poetics of living death, incarceration reproduced the dehumanization of plantation slavery in the enclosed space of the prison. The civil death of the prisoner thus became a kind of counterpart to what the sociologist Orlando Patterson has described as the "social death" of the slave.[64]

Social death, as Patterson defines it, belongs to a larger set of images and symbols known as the "idiom of power." All social relations are, at least in part, power relations, but power is not merely the physical force that enables some people to harm or coerce others; it also shapes the terms in which they imagine and understand themselves as social beings. It helps to produce a language and a set of symbols, an "idiom" that, in turn, helps to shape the field of acts and identities where power works. In slave societies, where masters wield nearly absolute power, the "dominant symbol" is the slave's social death. "Because the slave had no socially recognized existence outside of his master," writes Patterson, "he became a social nonperson."[65] Slaves are not full members of the human community, embedded in nurturing familial and social relationships and bearing the rights and prerogatives of subjectivity; rather, they are suspended in a state of virtual lifelessness, infinitely manipulable and vulnerable.

It would be a mistake to assume that social death, however "dominant" such a symbol may have been in the antebellum United States, was simply accepted by all, particularly by slaves themselves. Alienation from family and community, the breaking of the will, the reduction of a human life to an implement of labor—all this could be accomplished only through a nearly relentless application of violence and terror. "To make a contented slave," as Frederick Douglass wrote, "it is necessary to make a thoughtless one. It is necessary to darken his moral and mental vision, and, as far as possible, to annihilate the power of reason. He must be able to detect no inconsistencies in slavery; he must be made to feel that slavery is right; and he can be brought to that only when he ceases to be a man."[66] Patterson considers Douglass "the most articulate" witness of social death in the antebellum United States, and indeed much of Douglass's autobiography is devoted to the processes by which, in his terms, "a man" is "transformed into a brute."[67]

Douglass records that children born into slavery usually had no knowledge of their birthdays, that they often could not name their fathers, and that it was a "custom" among slaveholders "to part [them] from their mothers at a very early age." The "inevitable result," writes Douglass, is "to hinder the development of the child's affection toward its mother, and to blunt and destroy the natural affection of the mother for the child."[68] The young Douglass finds himself unmoored from family and origins, adrift in what Patterson calls "the natal alienation of the slave."[69]

Of his mother's death, Douglass writes that he "received the tidings . . . with much the same emotions I should have probably felt at the death of a stranger."[70] As Douglass comes of age, he begins to show some signs of an unruly will, and his master sends him to the notorious Mr. Covey, a poor white farmer known for his ruthlessness in reducing slaves to submission. At Covey's farm, broken and brutalized, Douglass enters a period of what the political theorist Achille Mbembe, echoing Patterson, calls "death-in-life": he is "kept alive but in a *state of injury*, in a phantom-like world of horrors and intense cruelty and profanity."[71] Douglass himself uses the language of dehumanization: "I was broken in body, soul, and spirit," he writes; "the cheerful spark that lingered about my eye died; the dark night of slavery closed in upon me; and behold a man transformed into a brute!"[72] For Douglass, as for Patterson and many others, slavery is a complex of violence, legal nonrecognition, rituals, and symbols that transform human lives into so many animals and animate corpses.

As we have seen, the early penitentiaries used a similar set of practices and tropes to divest the convict of human rights and social identity, reducing him to "the condition of a slave." While many of the reformers who guided the prison movement were opposed to slavery in the South, the convict was regularly portrayed as a captive and a slave, as in Andrew M'Makin's poem about Eastern State Penitentiary:

> A doom'd and blighted race,
> Are toiling in thy cells,
> For whom the tear of grace,
> Or pity, seldom swells.[73]

Of course, there were also substantial differences between the plantation and the penitentiary, and between the imagined figures of the slave and the prisoner. The most obvious is the supposed justification for exclusion and mortification. Patterson identifies two "modes of representing" social death—the "intrusive" and the "extrusive." In the intrusive mode, the slave is seen as an alien, an enemy or a captive introduced into the community from the outside: "one of them" living and laboring among "us." In the extrusive mode, by contrast, the slave is "one of us" who has somehow "fallen," forfeiting his right to belong; he undergoes a "secular excommunication."[74] While the distinction is not absolute, we might roughly identify "intrusive" social death with the race-based slavery of the plantation, and "extrusive" social death with the mortifications of the penitentiary. According to the racist ideology of the slaveholders (and, indeed, of many abolitionists), African Americans were a foreign population, subdued and held captive by whites; they were inside the geographic bounds of the United States but alien to the body politic. The convict in prison, by contrast, does not begin life as an outcast or a slave; he begins as a rights-bearing subject. He is excommunicated as a consequence of a specific transgression against his fellow citizens, falling from the grace of humanity into the condition of a slave.

The connection to the social death of slavery illuminates the first use of civil death in the antebellum prison system: the legal divestment of rights explained how citizens convicted of crimes could justifiably be subjected to discretionary violence, exploited through brutal labor discipline, and alienated from family and society in a solitary cell. Civil death was a version of what legal scholars call the "forfeiture argument," according to which the criminal, in breaking the law, has given up his legal rights and protections, and may be put to whatever use his captors may devise.[75] Earlier punishments had been more openly violent but also, in a sense, more direct: the judge condemned a man to die by hanging, and he was hanged; the judge sentenced a woman to stripes, and she was whipped in the public square. Incarceration was a more complex kind of punishment, involving not only the explicit sentence—two or five or twenty years of confinement—but also a whole range of other, secondary afflictions. Prisoners who violated the strict regulations governing prison life were not tried for new crimes. They were punished at the discretion of prison officials. At Philadelphia's Eastern State Penitentiary, those who called out to each other through the walls of their solitary cells might be given the "iron gag," a metal bit fastened to straps that bound the inmate's wrists behind his back, tightening when he struggled.[76] At New York's Auburn Prison, convicts who disobeyed the guards might be beaten with a barbed whip known as the "cat's claw" or the "cat o' nine-tails" (figure 1). Other penitentiaries used other signature chastisements: the ball and chain in Maine, the "shower bath" in Connecticut and New Hampshire.[77] Such torments, which recalled the public punishments of older days and the implements of slavery, were not explicit parts of the

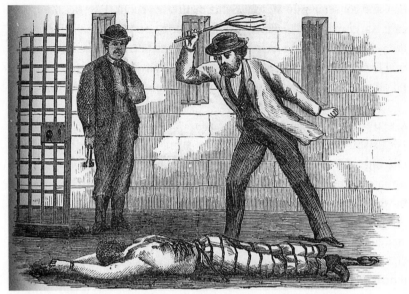

FIGURE 1. "The Cat o' Nine-Tails." The lash at New York's Auburn Prison. From Charles Sutton, *The New York Tombs: Its Secrets and Its Mysteries*, ed. James B. Mix and Samuel A. MacKeever (New York: United States Publishing Company, 1874), p. 591.

judicial condemnation, but they could be applied because, after civil death, convicts had no legal protections against them.

Elam Lynds, the legendary warden of Auburn who oversaw the building of Sing Sing in the 1820s, called his inmates "coarse beings, who have had no education, and who perceive with difficulty ideas, and often even sensations"—as if the men and women under his authority were somehow literally dulled to the world, and could be controlled only by violence and an atmosphere of terror.[78] "I consider it impossible," he said, "to govern a large prison without a whip."[79] Stephen Allen, an inspector at Auburn, similarly defined its inmates as creatures without any claim to humanity. New York, Allen noted in an 1826 pamphlet, had recently abolished the death penalty for most crimes. He reasoned that the state had yielded its claim over convicts' natural lives—but it had reserved its power to extinguish their civil being: "What are the natural and political rights of a criminal convicted of rape, highway robbery, burglary, sodomy, maiming, forging public securities, &c. the punishment of which is death by the laws of England; and in this state, imprisonment for life? Are they not *dead in law*, and consequently without rights, natural or political?"[80] Recalling Beccaria's argument for "penal servitude," Allen's point is clear: the inmates of the penitentiary are no longer protected, rights-bearing citizens. Their natural lives have been preserved, but the state's power over them recognizes no other limit. They are coarse beings, monsters in exile, dead in law.

A STUPID, LIMITED ANIMAL

For prison officials such as Lynds and Allen, civil death justified the brutalizing torment and servile labor to which the penitentiary subjected its inmates. This first, apparently cynical, use of the "fiction" of living death, however, was not entirely acceptable to the more sentimental factions of the penitentiary movement. When the British reformer William Roscoe visited Auburn in the 1820s, for instance, he protested that its harsh discipline violated the human rights of the incarcerated. In his view, a penitentiary system built for benevolent purposes had been misappropriated by petty tyrants. Roscoe compared the "immolat[ion]" of the solitary cell to the "antiquated" practices of live burial and human "sacrifice"; such a punishment was nothing more, he wrote, than a way of "tormenting . . . wretched beings, without any rational or beneficial effect."[81] Roscoe's protest was the "cry from the heart," arising from the feeling that the prisoner must be treated with humanity: "These," he insisted, "are still our fellow creatures."[82] In a sentimental idiom, he called for a kind of humanitarian intervention, intended to protect Auburn's wretched beings from torture by inspiring sympathy for their misery and a recognition of their human rights.

Yet the noble effort of Roscoe and his fellow reformers was hampered by contradictions of its own. They saw the misery of Auburn as an excess, a deviation from the otherwise benevolent principles of enlightened punishment. As much as they denounced the practice of "sacrifice," then, their goal was always to build a better penitentiary—or, as Roscoe put it, a "system of penal discipline, commensurate with the other improvements of the present day."[83] In a curious way, then, the critique of prison discipline in the name of "humanity" may actually have served to expand and refine the penitentiary system in general. "The prison," observes Foucault, "should not be seen as an inert institution, shaken at intervals by reform"; rather, it "has always formed part of an active field [of] projects, improvements, experiments, theoretical statements, personal evidence and investigations."[84] Again and again, critics pointed out that the penitentiary was a dungeon of dehumanization. Again and again, reformers promised a more "humane" institution. These were the dynamics of the movement that built the penitentiary: the "wretched" prisoner was displayed, then contained; a gothic vision of living death appeared, only to be drawn into a sentimental narrative of resurrection. Somehow, the revelation of dehumanizing violence inside the penitentiary system— what Roscoe called the prisoner's "sacrifice"—seems to have reinforced the very foundations of that system. Here we approach the second, perhaps more intractable, role of living death in the penitentiary.

Philadelphia's Benjamin Rush, one of the founders of the American "house of correction," dreamed about the institution in these terms: "Methinks I already hear the inhabitants of our villages and townships counting the years that shall complete the reformation of one of their citizens. I behold them running to meet him on the day of his deliverance. His friends and family bathe his cheeks with tears of joy; and the universal shout of the neighborhood is, 'This our brother was lost, and is found— was dead and is alive.' "[85] Rush was well versed in the language of reform. He used the familiar terms and tropes—the insistence that the convict was a citizen, one of us, not a stranger or an enemy; the sentimental tears that celebrate his restoration to family and community. But when Rush described the house of correction as a scene of death and rebirth, he touched the deepest problem of punishment in the modern age. The prison must not merely wound or contain the offender; it must lead him through a total reformation. Before the prisoner can receive the humanizing embrace of the community, he must be stripped down and dehumanized. Before he can be resurrected, he must be made to live out his death.

If the first use of civil death was a holdover from medieval punishment and a counterpart of plantation slavery, the second was peculiarly modern and a matter of free citizenship. Rush was part of a generation of reformers who, in the wake of the American Revolution, sought to build a new system of law and order based on the Enlightenment ideal of the social contract. And, as Thomas Dumm has shown, the penitentiary was "one of the crucial components in the reordering of the ideological universe" in the post-Revolutionary United States. Its disciplinary techniques, "by which the action of citizens might be assessed, managed, and controlled, became an integral part of the process of creating a constitutional republic."[86] In the furnace of the prison, the soul of the modern American citizen-subject would be forged.

Dumm argues that the penitentiary was designed to dominate the very souls of its inmates; through surveillance and strict disciplinary regimes, it trained them to govern themselves, becoming a factory for the production of individual "republican machines." Dumm is especially concerned with the ways in which apparently enlightened reforms, devoted to the reclamation of criminal souls, were at a deeper level tactics of social control. He therefore emphasizes the penitentiary's "techniques of pedagogy," seeking to expose the secret, ideological oppressions involved in penal rehabilitation.[87] And yet this analysis, drawing its concepts from Foucault and from the Marxist theorists Theodor Adorno and Max Horkheimer, also has its limits. Conceiving of the inmate in terms of subjectivity rather than abjection, accounts such as Dumm's can have little to say about civil death and mortification. They seem to accept the reformers' claims about nonviolence and respect for human rights, even if their ultimate goal is to show how such claims enabled certain subtle forms of coercion. However, another view is possible: a reading of one of the great theories of the social contract alongside the discourse of prison reform suggests that a kind of death or sacrifice—the very destruction of the embodied self that the reformers forswore—may actually have been fundamental to the reformers' conception of the prisoner as a reborn citizen-subject.

Rousseau, in *The Social Contract*, writes that the "passage from the state of nature to the civil state produces quite a remarkable change in man." The sacrifice of natural liberty that inaugurates political existence, he suggests, provides something more than a sustainable peace. The transition to the "civil state" is a kind of magical transformation through which "man," once little more than a beast, acquired in political society a transcendent spirit, the subjectivity of the citizen. "Although in [the civil] state he deprives himself of several of the advantages belonging to him in the state of nature, he regains such great ones. His faculties are exercised and developed, his ideas are broadened, his feelings are ennobled, his entire soul is elevated to such a height that . . . he ought constantly to bless the happy moment that pulled him away from it forever and which transformed him from a stupid, limited animal into an intelligent being and a man."[88] According to the mythology of the social contract, the sacrifice of the natural self is the virtual death that enables people to be reborn as higher beings. It replaces instinct with reason, appetite with enlightenment. It turns the "stupid, limited animal into an intelligent being and a man." Thus, in the political imagination of the societies that built the first great penitentiaries, the citizen was a double figure, an enlightened subjectivity rising from the remains of a sacrificed beast.

The original moment of sacrifice and transformation was fundamental to the modern political order, but where and when did it take place? "We often read," declared the American orator Thomas Dawes in 1781, "of the original Contract, and of mankind, in the early ages, passing from a state of Nature to immediate Civilization. But *what eye* could penetrate through the gothic night and barbarous fable to that remote period?"[89] According to social contract theorists, the founding act of submission had transpired in a mythic past. It was the origin of power and social existence, but it had disappeared irretrievably into the "gothic night" of "remote" times. What the penitentiary provided, in addition to its function in punishing crime and extracting labor, was an institutional scene for the incarnate *performance* of this fundamental political "fable."

Joseph Roach elaborates the meaning of "performance" by way of the term "surrogation," the embodied creation of substitutes for what has been lost to history. Performance, says Roach, "stands in for an elusive entity . . . that it must vainly aspire both to embody and to replace."[90] In Roach's terms, then, the penitentiary was a scene of performance: it conceived, conjured, and displayed the stupid, limited animal (the body deprived of rights and vulnerable to violence) who could be transformed into the citizen (the redeemed, self-governing soul). In its cells and workshops, the passage from the state of nature to the civil state—a modern myth of resurrection—was enacted. Civil death and mortification stood for the sacrifice; as we shall see in chapter 3, reflection and penitence in the solitary confinement cell were the methods of transformation, producing the spiritual, deracinated, and radically isolated "being" of the modern citizen. Perhaps, then, the problem was not merely that reformers such as Roscoe and Rush had failed to secure the inmate's humanity from cruelty and abuse; perhaps the very "humanity" offered in sympathy required, as a kind of precondition, the inmate's living doom. The violent dehumanization of convicts on the scaffold and in the crowded, filthy dungeons of unenlightened regimes was the crisis that reformers sought to address; but the reformers' solution, the modern institution built for the reclamation of lost souls, would incorporate its own, redefined practice of mortification.

Roach, like Goffman, theorizes the relations between the living and the dead in the language of performance. Colin Dayan, the most revealing and provocative scholar of civil death's new-world afterlives, uses the related term "ritual" to name the ways in which punishment enacts the political mythologies of the modern age. Civil death, writes Dayan, is one of the "rituals of exclusion" that have come to define legal personhood. Dayan's research suggests that Southern slavery and Northern incarceration were parallel sites for the enactment of such rituals: "The penitentiary . . . in the North, offered an unsettling counter to servitude: an invention of criminality and prescriptions for treatment that turned humans into the living dead."[91] For Dayan, the prisoner in solitary confinement is one of modernity's dark others, bound in body to serve as the negative image of the free mind and the transcendent spirit: "Like the furies buried beneath Athens so that the ideal city can be born, the idea of freedom became coterminous with the necessities of containment [in the penitentiary]."[92] Dayan's work exposes the "sorcery" of the law, the persistence of ancient superstitions into the codes and policies that govern the penitentiary: "The social, economic, and even spiritual practices of remote times persist in legal forms and pronouncements."

Carefully tracing the prison's connections to the plantation and other zones of terror in what she evocatively describes as a "transatlantic domain of penance, punishment, and possession," Dayan sees the solitary cell as a tomb; her critical idiom remains close to the language of Roscoe and Dickens. When she takes up the rhetoric of redemption used by many reformers, including Benjamin Rush—who, she writes, "wanted redemption on earth"—she does so in order to expose how the idea of rebirth was radically distorted by the architects of penitentiary discipline. In her analysis, the prison system redefined resurrection as the mere annihilation of the self: "What passed as an enlightenment endorsement of the 'human' . . . obliterated the claims of personhood." She goes on: "The point of indefinite solitude and sensory deprivation is to deprive of personality those who are incapacitated."[93] Emphasizing

the old-fashioned terrors of solitary confinement and other dehumanizing punishments, Dayan's work is a powerful counterweight to accounts
by Foucault, Dumm, and others who tend to present the prison as an institution for the rehabilitation and training of modern subjects. What
Dayan may overlook, however, are the uncanny similarities between the
solitary cell and the structures of modern social life at large. Unlike
slaves, prisoners were not always bound to languish indefinitely in the
shadow world of their captivity. Imprisonment was not only a ritual of
exclusion but also part of a cycle that would restore the fallen convict to
the grace of the commonwealth. As we shall see in detail in chapter 3,
the solitary cell, the tomb of living death, represented not just deprivation but an ideal of reflection and self-making—an image of humanity.
The prisoner, then, was not only a figure buried beneath the foundations
of the modern city or the modern self—his features, as Emily Dickinson
recognized, are also present to us as our own.

Civil death, as imagined and enacted in the penitentiaries of reform's
golden age, depended on a grotesque set of rituals and props. It involved
not only a changed legal status but also a drama of initiation into the
world of ghosts and, within that world, afflictions such as the solitary
cell, the iron gag, and the whip wielded by wardens who saw their inmates as coarse, inhuman creatures. Though they shocked some reformers, such mortifications and tortures were not, in the strict sense, abuses
of the prison's fundamental design. They were the implements and processes by which the institution reduced the prisoner to a figure of living
death, the first phase of his resurrection into a new, redeemed life. They
were not excesses but part of the perfect functioning of the institution as
a scene of death and reanimation. Nor was the prison itself an excess,
outside the commonwealth. It was a centerpiece, the stage on which a
new society of citizen-subjects played out the drama of its own mythic
origins. Thus the prisoner was neither an ideal self nor an abject other.
He was Janus-faced, a figure at the threshold, the sacrifice of life through
which the citizen-subject's transcendent humanity was born.

Having abolished the spectacle of the scaffold and erected the high,
imposing gates of the prison, however, the authorities who had reformed
punishment also needed to devise new ways to stage its rituals and communicate its meanings. The new system of penal death and rebirth was

private, but it was not supposed to remain a complete mystery, a performance without a public. It had to continue to teach its lessons and instill its disciplinary terror in the world. The reformers began to consider the uses of texts, especially narratives of prison life, that could circulate in print. As they did so, the imagination displaced the public square, becoming the scene for the ongoing performance of the resurrection myth at the heart of modern political life.

CHAPTER TWO

Cadaverous Triumphs

"ALL HARMS," wrote Cesare di Beccaria, reflecting on the difference between public punishments and secret ones, "are magnified in the imagination."[1] As the old spectacle of the scaffold decomposed, losing its effectiveness and its grounding in the prevailing political mythology, authorities confronted a problem: Without the theatrical terror of hangings and mutilations, how could crime be deterred? Without the scaffold and the pillory, the stocks and the whipping post, how could obedience to the law be secured in the hearts of citizens tempted to break it? After all, "one object of penal provisions," as the English reformer Charles James Blomfield put it in 1828, "is, to excite a salutary dread of the consequences of crime, in the minds of those who are not to be influenced by nobler and holier motives."[2] Punishment, as Foucault notes, does not only concern the individual offender; it "is directed above all at others, at all the potentially guilty."[3] In other words, it is not only a matter of force but also a set of signs and symbols presented to the public. If the allegory of transgression and vengeance that had played out on the stage of the scaffold was going to be withdrawn, some new kind of representation would be required. Abandoning spectacle, reformers began to explore the magnifying and terrifying power of the imagination.

The problem of punishment's disappearance was taken up by the leading lights of reform, around the Atlantic world. Beccaria hoped that the great "sum of unhappy moments" on display in perpetual penal servitude would be more terrifying than the "fleeting pains" of death or torture.[4] The English reformer Jeremy Bentham, inventor of the famous "panopticon" model for prisons, argued that their doors should be open to all, so that the interested public could witness the abjection of the condemned. In the United States, the question drew the attention of an influential circle of reformers who met for discussions in the house of Benjamin Franklin. There, in March of 1787, Benjamin Rush presented his thoughts on the crisis of public punishment. Like many of his American and European contemporaries, Rush noted that the spectacle of the scaffold was not accomplishing its intended mission; "public punishments," he wrote, "so far from preventing crimes by the terror they excite in the minds of spectators, are directly calculated to produce them."[5]

In particular, Rush was concerned that people invited to witness such violence, even to celebrate it, would suffer from a distortion in the faculty of *sympathy*. Forced to watch without commiseration the suffering of the condemned, the public would lose its ability to feel for anyone in need: "Misery of every kind will then be contemplated without emotion or sympathy," declared Rush. "The widow and the orphan—the naked—the sick, and the prisoner, will have no avenue to our services or our charity—and what is worse than all, when the centinel of our moral faculty is removed, there is nothing to guard the mind from the inroads of every positive vice."[6] The scaffold did not preserve order. It threatened to warp and sever crucial social bonds. In order to enforce the law while preserving the benevolent sympathy that held society together, the theater of punishment had to be recomposed.

TALES FROM THE ABODE OF MISERY

In place of the scaffold, Rush envisioned a secluded "house of correction" where experts would administer punishment as a complex of labor and bodily pain. Even in a free republic, Rush insisted, secrecy was necessary in the administration of justice, and courts would be serving the true "liberty" of the people by keeping them ignorant, and thus protected from the corrupting power of public punishments. Yet Rush was careful to assure his audience that such seclusion would not decrease the general fear of punishment; instead, the mystery of what happened behind the closed doors of the house of correction would paradoxically help to deter crime by "diffus[ing] terror through [the] community." Like Beccaria, Rush depended on the public's lively imagination. He suggested that people who knew nothing about the prison interior would invent the liveliest ghost tales and horror stories: "Children will press upon the evening fire in listening to the tales that will spread from this abode of misery. Superstition will add to its horrors: and romance will find in it ample materials for fiction, which cannot fail of increasing the terror of its punishments."[7] Rush and his followers wanted punishment out of sight, but not out of mind. Public torture was too grotesque, too difficult to manage, and an American polity conceived in enlightenment should extend its humanizing embrace even to the unfortunate criminal—but authorities could maintain control of crime by redirecting "terror" to the public "imagination." Mediated by the right kind of fiction, transmuted from spectacle to "superstition," the terror of punishment could be diffused without any damage to the community's human sympathy.[8]

A generation later, when Pennsylvania built the world-famous Eastern State Penitentiary, its architect, the previously unknown John Haviland, seems to have incorporated Rush's ideas. Haviland's design combined a concern for the prisoner's humanity with an effort to menace the public mind. The solitary cells, equipped with the most modern systems of plumbing and engineering anywhere in the world, were surrounded by a "gothic" façade meant to recall the notorious dungeons of the old world.[9] In reformist pamphlets, the result was praised as an architecture of a "grave, severe, and awful character" that "produces on the imagination of every passing spectator . . . [a] peculiarly impressive, solemn, and instructive" impression.[10] Haviland, having made his name at Eastern State, was soon hired to design more new prisons in New Jersey and New York. The massive edifice he built for Manhattan's Halls of Justice evoked ancient ruins; the place was soon nicknamed "The Tombs."[11] In the modernizing cityscape, The Tombs appeared ancient and bizarre, like something from another world (figure 2). "Built in a quaint Egyptian style of architecture," wrote one observer, "and fronted by massive columns of granite, it looms up vast, gloomy and terrible, producing in the breast of the spectator a sensation of profound awe."[12] Charles Dickens, who stopped by The Tombs while he was in New York, was not so impressed; he mocked the "famous prison" as a "dismal-fronted pile of bastard Egyptian, like an enchanter's palace in a melodrama."[13]

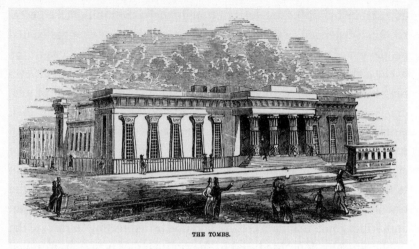

THE TOMBS.

FIGURE 2. "The Tombs." Façade of Manhattan's Halls of Justice, known as The Tombs. From Charles Sutton, *The New York Tombs: Its Secrets and Its Mysteries*, ed. James B. Mix and Samuel A. MacKeever (New York: United States Publishing Company, 1874), p. 78.

In any case, the gothic designs of Haviland's penitentiaries did not fail to stir the American imagination, and authors did find "ample material" for fiction in the "abode of misery." In popular novels such as George Wilkes's *Mysteries of the Tombs* and John McGinn's *Ten Days in the Tombs*, these marvels of modern engineering and reform were depicted as Dark Age dungeons, sites of grotesque suffering and cruelty. Karen Halttunen has identified a whole subgenre of fiction that emerged alongside penitentiaries and asylums, adapting a gothic literary mode to expose the abuses suffered by wretched inmates. And Colin Dayan has connected the architecture of Eastern State Penitentiary to the tales of a gothic master living in Philadelphia in the age of reform, Edgar Allan Poe.

Dayan writes that Poe's "decors of lavish, medieval ornament, gates of iron, crenellated towers and picturesque effects, premature burials, and the singular torments of narrators who experience unnatural solitude . . . owe their force to his knowledge of the excesses of the Pennsylvania System."[14] Living in the shadow of the "grave, severe, and awful" prison, Poe's tales depict dungeons of misery suited to Haviland's façade. And Poe's concern was not only with the impressions such architecture might impart to the passerby. He also envisioned the living doom of the incarcerated. In "The Cask of Amontillado," for instance, Poe's narrator, wishing to "punish with impunity," walls his rival up inside a catacomb, among abandoned bones. In "The Pit and the Pendulum," a prisoner is "unstrung" by his confinement, "becom[ing] in every respect a fitting subject for the species of torture which awaited [him]."[15] Watched by his unseen captors, subjected to a series of terrors, he comes to feel that a sudden death would be better than his captive fate, where the excruciatingly slow passage of time is measured by a descending blade. "The Premature Burial" and "The Fall of the House of Usher" also concern the nightmare of a living entombment. Poe's stories were often set in distant ages and foreign lands, but—like Hawthorne's novels and Dickinson's poems—they invoked the penal transformations of his own time and place, imagining imprisonment as a loss of subjectivity and a living death.

For Halttunen and Dayan, such representations of the penitentiary are, at least in part, a form of social critique. "Gothic exposés of asylum life," argues Halttunen, reveal the gap between enlightened theory and violent practice, between humane intentions and cruel realities.[16] Whatever may have been the political motives of those who wrote such tales of misery, however, there were complex problems involved in using the gothic as a language of protest. As we have seen, the penitentiary in the discourse of its makers was not only a humane asylum; in its legal premises, its initiation rituals, and its disciplinary methods, it was also a scene of mortification. Nor was the convict's living death merely an embarrassing abuse of the prison's otherwise benevolent designs, an "excess" to be hidden or excused. The key imagery of the reform movement was sentimental, extending its healing and redemptive embrace to the suffering criminal, but the authors of the penitentiary also knew how to work the gothic into their designs.[17]

The sentimental and the gothic were the two great popular genres of nineteenth-century fiction. Neglected for a long time by scholars who preferred the precision of lyric or the density of transcendentalist rhetoric, they have been recovered in recent years and reconnected to the social and intellectual contexts within which they once had such great power. The sentimental and the gothic were narrative patterns, but they were also structures of feeling embedded in nineteenth-century ideology and collective life. Each can be understood as a "complex" of tropes, styles, concepts, and affects shaping an encounter between self and other. In the sentimental mode, the free middle-class subject embraces a suffering other—typically an orphan, a "fallen woman," or a slave—and draws the victim into the community of the human, producing an affective charge of tearful sympathy. In the gothic, the subject experiences shock and a sense of his or her own unmaking through contact with a dehumanized other, giving rise to a delicious terror.[18]

While they are apparently opposed, the two complexes are also related.[19] The sentimental, according to several recent studies, provided polite audiences with a moral and aesthetic framework within which gothic thrills could be safely enjoyed. In the end, the threat of the other could be humanized and contained by a sentimental conclusion. The public story of the penitentiary provided just this kind of resolution—it brought ghosts and dungeons into view, but it used these gothic visions to reinforce its own designs, expanding its regime of humane, charitable correction. It displayed a dehumanizing misery, but it assured the public that a newer, better, and bigger prison would heal the body and redeem the soul of the afflicted. Writers who wished to use the gothic mode against the penitentiary, then, confronted a rhetorical double bind. On the one hand, if their fiction represented the prison interior as a site of torture and abjection, diffusing terror through the public mind, it might be doing just the kind of cultural work that Rush had assigned to the authors of fiction. On the other hand, if it displayed prisoners' abjection in order to call for sympathy and more penal reforms, then it reproduced the old "cry from the heart," similarly joining the company of the reformers who had built the penitentiary in the first place.

The dehumanization of civil death played two roles in the penitentiary: it justified mortifying violence and servitude, but it was also fundamental to the convict's rebirth as a citizen and a member of the human community. In antebellum literary works about prisoners, each of these two roles would be taken up and exposed to critique, producing two versions of the literary mode I call the "carceral gothic." In the first version, exemplified by Dickens's narrative of his visit to Eastern State Penitentiary, ghostly prisoners are displayed in the service of penal reform, helping to expand and refine the prison system. In the second, by contrast, the ghosts haunt their captors, disturbing rather than reinforcing the penitentiary's sentimental design. My key example is Melville's Bartleby, whose death in The Tombs leads his sentimental employer, in the final lines of his story, to a defeated double sigh: "Ah, Bartleby! Ah, humanity!"

With its mortifying violence and its promise of redemption, the antebellum American prison provoked Melville and a few other writers to search for a way of representing the inmate that would not reproduce the sentimentalism of the reformers. In the process, they devised some peculiar uses for gothic "othering," the counterpart of sentimental identification. At least since Leslie Fiedler's enormously influential *Love and Death in the American Novel*, critics have recognized a peculiar fascination with violence and the grotesque, an attraction to gothic fear and fantasy, in the literature of a body politic conceived in Enlightenment terms. For some decades, such visions appeared to be flights from the real world of power, politics, and commerce. Fiedler diagnosed a raw national psyche with no feeling for old-world courtship, turning to violence because it lacked a language of love.[20] Others interpret the gothic, and Romanticism more generally, as a kind of escapism from the rigid demands of the Age of Reason.[21]

More recently, scholars have shown that even ghosts might belong to a more specific history. We are beginning to perceive the gothic as an expression of, not a flight from, historical forces and struggles. Various contexts suggest themselves. Nineteenth-century medical technologies, for instance, had made the "boundaries which divide Life from Death," as Poe wrote in "The Premature Burial," "shadowy and vague."[22] Calvinist and other religious traditions, too, provided visions of a spiritual, perhaps even bodily, life beyond death. No history has been so illuminating of the gothic imagination in America, however, as that of slavery: the reality of repression and terror, whips and chains, social death and zombie life at play in the Atlantic world in the age of the American Renaissance.[23] Indeed, the carceral gothic mediates not only between the free self and the captive other but also between antebellum America's two great figures of captivity, the prisoner and the slave. In the end, however, the connection cannot be the sentimental bond of common "humanity"; at its most potent, the carceral gothic is a reckoning with the imprisoned other that disturbs the very foundations of humanity on which the self depends.

SUMMONED FROM THE GRAVE

When he visited the United States in the early 1840s, Charles Dickens said that he wished most of all to see two famous sights—the "Falls of

Niagara" and the Eastern State Penitentiary in Philadelphia.[24] His desire
to get inside the model prison was not as unusual as it may seem; Eastern State in those years was a wonder of the modern world and a popular destination, drawing tourists, groups of schoolchildren, and such
foreign dignitaries as Alexis de Tocqueville and Harriet Martineau.[25]
Like many others, Dickens received a cordial welcome. The authorities
knew that the prison was controversial, and they may have hoped that
the novelist, with his well-known sympathy for the suffering of inmates
in England's crowded, filthy gaols, would admire the order and cleanliness
of their experimental system. They gave Dickens a full tour, answered his
questions, and allowed him to spend some time with the inmates. "Nothing," he acknowledged in *American Notes*, "was concealed . . . , and every
piece of information that I sought was openly and frankly given."[26]

What Dickens saw at Eastern State, however, was no monument of reform; it was a terrifying scene of madness and living death. His narrative
records his passage through a dark dungeon inhabited by miserable, broken men and women whose appearance distresses his heart. Dickens believed that the reformers meant well, that their "motives" were "humane,"
but he was convinced that their experiment was not fulfilling their good
intentions. The system of prison discipline in Philadelphia, where each
prisoner passed his or her sentence in almost uninterrupted solitude, confined day and night to the same numbered cell, Dickens deemed "cruel
and wrong." His judgment was damning: "I hold this slow and daily tam-
pering with the mysteries of the brain," he wrote, "to be immeasurably
worse than any torture of the body." Isolation, the guiding principle of reform at Eastern State, led not to correction but to insanity and dehumanization (90–91). Like the prisoner-poet Harry Hawser, whom he almost
certainly encountered there, Dickens depicted Eastern State as "a living
tomb."[27]

The portraits of prisoners in Dickens's account of the penitentiary
all bore at least a touch of morbidity. One, imprisoned for "receiving stolen
goods," had built himself "a sort of Dutch clock" to measure the hours.
Like Poe's narrator beneath the glinting pendulum, he felt the painful
passage of every minute: "Time is very long, gentlemen," he cried, "within
these four walls!" (93). Dickens noted that the clockmaker composed
himself well under the eyes of his inspectors, but when he felt himself
unwatched "his lips trembled, and [Dickens] could have counted the

beating of his heart" (92–93). A sailor locked up for eleven years sat silently "star[ing] at his hands, and pick[ing] the flesh upon his fingers, and rais[ing] his eyes for an instant, now and then, to [the] bare walls." Dickens called him a "helpless, crushed, and broken man" (94–95). Another convict, he wrote, "look[ed] as wan and unearthly as if he had been summoned from the grave" (94). Dickens gave his most extravagant sentiments to an unnamed German thief who was serving a sentence of five years. With stolen "colours," the novelist noted, this unreformed convict had "painted every inch of the walls and ceiling [of his cell] quite beautifully." He had also turned his little exercise yard into a makeshift garden and, in its center, had "made a little bed . . . that looked, by-the-bye, like a grave" (93). The imprisoned genius was, to Dickens's eyes, a perfect "picture of forlorn affliction and distress of mind"; one of the world's preeminent artists of sympathy was moved to declare that he had never seen or heard of "any kind of misery that impressed [him] more than the wretchedness of this man" (93).

The law, by way of civil death, conceived of the felon as a kind of animate corpse. Dickens's narrative exposed how the discipline and rituals of the penitentiary were producing prisoners who seemed literally to incarnate that legal fiction: an assembly of cadaverous men and women buried alive, dead to the world. Using such imagery to protest the penitentiary, Dickens was making an important and controversial claim: that the warped, antisocial behavior of the prisoner is an effect, not a cause, of his punishment. Solitary confinement in the penitentiary, Dickens suggested, actually damages the minds it pretends to correct. This idea has been part of prison reform discourse for more than two centuries, and continues to have a place in the critique of captivity.[28] Erving Goffman, for instance, echoes Dickens when he describes a certain "prison psychosis" by which some inmates adapt to captivity, virtually disappearing into the depths of the self and "withdrawing apparent attention from everything except events immediately around [their bodies]," so that guards and other inmates observe passive, unmoving creatures, just barely animate.[29]

To an audience familiar with the debates surrounding the penitentiary, the meaning of Dickens's observations would have been clear. He had invoked a parade of ghostly figures to testify against the solitary system at Philadelphia and to support its rivals in New York and Boston. He signaled his agreement with his fellow traveler Harriet Martineau, who called Eastern State "a vast apparatus for the infliction of human misery"; and with William Roscoe, who in an open letter on the Philadelphia system had declared that the mind of the prisoner suffering in unrelieved solitude "rushes back on itself, and drives even reason from her seat."[30] Indeed, Dickens's sketch of life at the famous penitentiary belonged to an emergent consensus in prison reform: Philadelphia's system, although it endured at Eastern State, was rejected by most other states in favor of the Auburn model, which permitted congregate labor by day in factory-like workshops.[31] The congregate system, Dickens wrote, "has worked well, and is, in its whole design and practice, excellent" (100).

Dickens's account of Eastern State Penitentiary may be the most powerful nineteenth-century literary example of a carceral gothic whose aim is to inspire sympathy for the condemned and, in turn, promote penal reforms more respectful of prisoners' human rights. It develops the hints of gothic and sentimental language that appear throughout the writings of reformers (Beccaria, Rush, Roscoe, and the like) into a visionary nonfiction novella that has both a clear political motive and some devastating poetry. As an imaginative reckoning with the problem of the prison, however, Dickens's piece confronts a limit. Like the rhetoric of Roscoe, its ultimate aim is to develop a more "excellent" penitentiary. Containing the gothic horror of Eastern State within a sentimental call for greater humanity in punishment, Dickens became, in a sense, the greatest literary champion of the reform movement that was in the process of building the modern prison system.

In the end, what makes Dickens's account of Eastern State so rich and troubling is that, beneath its surface of sentimental protest, it seems to carry the secret knowledge that such discourse is inadequate to the larger problem of the prison. Dickens had talked with the reformers and read their pamphlets. He knew how well they spoke the language of sympathy; he recognized that Eastern State was, in a sense, a monument to the convict's redeemable humanity. The narrative tacitly acknowledges its own doom, as it becomes immanently commensurate with the designs of the penitentiary's authors. Such a fate was not inevitable, however, because sentimental feeling was not the only possible horizon of the carceral gothic—which, in the works of some of Dickens's contemporaries, was also used to imagine ghostly captives who could not so easily be enclosed in the embrace of a reformist humanity.

MATERIAL GHOSTS

A few chapters into Nathaniel Hawthorne's *House of the Seven Gables*, a mysterious "guest" arrives. Clifford, the reader will learn, has spent decades in a Boston penitentiary, probably the Massachusetts State Prison, a monument of the Auburn "system." Like the prisoners described by Poe and Dickens, Clifford has been mortified by incarceration: "Continually . . . he faded away out of his place; or, in other words, his mind and consciousness took their departure, leaving his wasted, gray, and melancholy figure—a substantial emptiness, a material ghost—to occupy his seat at the table. Again, after a blank moment, there would be a flickering tapergleam in his eyeballs. It betokened that his spiritual part had returned, and was doing its best to kindle the heart's household-fire, and light up intellectual lamps in the dark and ruinous mansion, where it was doomed to be a forlorn inhabitant."[32] The derangement Dickens encountered at Eastern State reappears here, in an "unnerved" character whose "spirit," as Hawthorne writes, "has been thoroughly crushed" by prison life (82). Hawthorne describes the ex-prisoner as a ruin, an empty house visited from time to time by a vagrant spirit. Released from his solitary cell, Clifford ambles through the world in an unredeemed "doom." He has endured more than the legal disenfranchisement of civil death; locked up and mortified, he has become an embodiment of the virtual death imposed by the penitentiary—"a material ghost."[33]

Like Dickens, Hawthorne may have wanted to use the figure of the ghostly captive against the power structure that had extinguished his humanity. Hawthorne, however, may also have been wary of Dickens's idiom of critique, the sentimental. Indeed, a long critical tradition has sought to distinguish Hawthorne's tales and romances from the sentimental fiction of what he called the "damned mob of scribbling women," female authors who turned out best sellers while he wrote his romances in what he considered to be a heroic, manly obscurity.[34] In *The House of the Seven Gables*, Hawthorne used the ex-prisoner to stage a moment when the feminized, tearful embrace of sympathy provides cold comfort. Preparing Clifford's breakfast and welcoming him back into the domestic sphere, his sister Hepzibah wraps him in the language of charity: "Poor, poor, Clifford!" she calls him (74). "There is nothing but love here, Clifford," she says, "nothing but love! You are home!" (77). She is attempting to humanize him, to domesticate the ghost he has become.

But Hepzibah's cries ring hollow. Clifford responds with a faint and false smile that, Hawthorne writes, "did not half light up his face" (77). The touch of family and humanity fails to soothe him, and he persists in a ghostly state, a "dark and ruinous mansion" without the "heart's household-fire" of domestic sentimentality. The version of the carceral gothic embodied by Clifford stands in contrast to that of Dickens's ruined inmates; rather than submitting to the sentimental designs of reformers, it holds its opaque alterity. A moment of disruption in *The House of the Seven Gables*, this antisentimental carceral gothic would be developed into a complex, haunting work of fiction by Hawthorne's neighbor and greatest admirer.

"Bartleby," says the lawyer who narrates the story of the ghostly scrivener, "was one of those beings of whom nothing is ascertainable, except from the original sources, and, in his case, those are very small."[35] Bartleby is among the most difficult ambiguities in Melville's fiction, as pale and inscrutable as the white whale. Who is he? The narrator passes through a series of speculations and, in the end, to a vision of Bartleby in a back room of the postal service, opening letters addressed to the dead (45–46). For decades, critics have been taking up the mystery, too, proposing resolutions—Bartleby as the narrator's double, Bartleby as a misunderstood artist like Melville, Bartleby as Jesus Christ, Bartleby as an allegory of alienated labor, and so on.[36] If the critic can guess the answer to the riddle of the title character, then the meaning of the story promises, at last, to be revealed.

Against the tradition of inventing identities for Bartleby, the French philosopher Gilles Deleuze makes a surprising counterproposal: "Bartleby," insists Deleuze, "is neither a metaphor for the writer nor the symbol of anything whatsoever."[37] Deleuze's surprising words echo Melville's own interpretation of another ghostly protagonist. When he received his copy of *The House of the Seven Gables* from Hawthorne, Melville read it with delight. A few days later he wrote to his neighbor praising the novel, especially his favorite character, the ex-prisoner: "Clifford," he declared, "is full of an awful truth throughout. He is conceived in the finest, truest spirit. He is no caricature. He is Clifford."[38] In Melville's view, Clifford was emphatically not a metaphor. The "material ghost" was simply and stubbornly himself, resisting absorption into any larger scheme. Indeed, it might not be too much to say that in Melville's view Clifford represented the possibility of a limit, a closed surface beyond which interpretation could not pass. In his opaqueness, he would become one of the models for Melville's Bartleby. What the "cadaverous" scrivener refuses, however, is nothing as general as narrative itself; Deleuze leaps over too much when he claims that the phrase "I prefer not to" somehow "hollows out a zone of indetermination that renders words indistinguishable, that creates a vacuum within language."[39] Bartleby's "cadaverous triumph" is achieved when he quietly undermines not language itself but the historically contingent set of labor relations, disciplinary codes, and narrative conventions that constituted the penitentiary system.

Bartleby, The Scrivener, A Story of Wall Street, is about work and about the spaces where work is done in the modernizing, industrializing North; it is also about *not* working, and about how such a society can account for and *correct* those who interfere with its smooth, prosperous operations. The novella, taking some of its conventions from Dickens, is narrated by a genial, easygoing lawyer who makes his living far from the criminal courts, in the back chambers of banks and offices, doing "a snug business among rich men's bonds, and mortgages, and title-deeds" (4). He stays clear of scandal and the public eye, though he is proud of his connections to the New York state government and to the millionaire John Jacob Astor, "a name which," he says, "I admit, I love to repeat" (4). He employs a twelve-year-old office boy called Ginger Nut and two copyists, Turkey and Nippers. As an employer, he considers himself generous, even indulgent; as a writer, he is familiar not only with legal codes but also with newspapers, moral philosophy, and popular stories that evoke tears from "sentimental souls" (3). When he is appointed Master in Chancery, an obsolescent but lucrative judgeship, he looks to hire a third scrivener. Enter Bartleby.

The new arrival stands in the doorway looking "pallidly neat, pitiably respectable, incurably forlorn" (11). Readers are given no history of Bartleby; we never learn what past has produced this ghostly presence. Carol Colatrella, in a detailed and provocative study, suggests that Bartleby is an ex-convict, a cadaverous victim of penitentiary discipline. In Colatrella's view, *Bartleby* is an encoded critique of the penitentiary, exposing how the institution failed to prepare its inmates to return to the labor force and "to deal with the entrepreneurial nature of life in America."[40] Colatrella points to the examples of Dickens's anonymous convicts and of Hawthorne's Clifford, and she notes Melville's long involvement with prisons and prisoners, including his family's participation in the reform movement and his visit to Auburn Prison in 1858.[41] Bartleby's cryptic words from within The Tombs—"I know where I am"—give some resonance to her hypothesis (43). Colatrella's analysis has a strong historical grounding, placing *Bartleby* firmly in the context of nineteenth-century prison reform.[42]

At the same time, however, Colatrella's reading, by providing an identity for Bartleby and thus a clear, reformist moral for the novella, too neatly resolves its mystery. In order to understand the full force of *Bartleby*'s challenge, we should accept the narrator's premise that "no material exists, for a full and satisfactory biography of this man" (3). Melville invokes the penitentiary not as an implied prehistory but as a complex of disciplinary and rhetorical structures used by the lawyer in his attempt to domesticate "the unaccountable Bartleby" (35). In the process, his narrator adopts at once a virtual penitentiary regime and a sentimental literary mode—related strategies available to an enlightened antebellum man of the law.

During the first days of his employment, Bartleby is an efficient but enigmatic worker. His boss reports that he is doing "an extraordinary quantity" of copying, staying at his desk for long hours. The lawyer is clearly getting good production from his new employee, but he is a little disturbed by Bartleby's ways. "I would have been quite delighted," he says, "had he been *cheerfully* industrious" (12, my emphasis). The nagging problem is that there is no spark of life in Bartleby's work, no affection for his boss, none of the comic humanity of Turkey and Nippers, with their big appetites and hot tempers. Bartleby writes on "silently, palely, mechanically" (12). The bare labor is being done, in other words, without the warmth, the little dramas of defiance and indulgence, that humanize the social relations of the office.

From Bartleby's arrival forward, the novella becomes the story of the narrator's effort to solve the problem of the scrivener's disturbing ghostliness. The first solution the lawyer devises is an architectural one. The office is divided into two sections, the lawyer on one side and the scriveners on the other. But when Bartleby arrives, the lawyer places him on his own side, behind a folding screen, "so as to have this quiet man within easy call" (11). Enclosed but available, Bartleby is given a desk facing a window that "commanded . . . no view at all, though it gave some light. Within three feet of the panes was a wall, and the light came down from far above . . . as from a very small opening in a dome" (11–12). As almost any reader will recognize, Melville in *Bartleby* pays careful attention to architecture, especially to the walls that surround the characters. In a classic study, Leo Marx calls the novella "Melville's parable of the walls," interpreting Bartleby's "hermitage" as an extreme form of the claustrophobic structures of modern consciousness and capitalism. But Melville may have something more specific in mind.[43] The key reference in his architectural description is to the great prisons of John Haviland, Pennsylvania's Eastern State Penitentiary and New York's Tombs. In the solitary cells of The Tombs, the only light came in "through a high chink in the wall."[44] At Eastern State, the vaulted ceiling of each cell was equipped with a small skylight, commonly called an "eye of God."[45] God's eye, watching over the labor and penitence of the captive, was arguably the most famous "small opening in a dome" in Melville's world, and the clearest sign that his lawyer is adopting for his scrivener the forms of labor discipline characteristic of Haviland's penitentiaries.

In their report on the American penitentiary, Beaumont and Tocqueville wrote that "absolute solitude, if nothing interrupts it, is beyond the strength of man; it destroys the criminal without intermission and without pity; it does not reform, it kills."[46] In many ways, such a representation of solitary confinement as a life-destroying torment seems to resonate with the protests of Dickens and Roscoe. Beaumont and Tocqueville, however, saw the power of Eastern State and made recommendations about using it as a model for new prisons in France. The important thing, for them, was that solitude should be mitigated by labor. Prisoners were tormented in their idleness by guilt and loneliness, but "labor, by comforting them, makes them *love* the only means, which when again free, will enable them to gain honestly their livelihood."[47] As evidence, Beaumont and Tocqueville published interviews with inmates who declared that "it would be impossible to live [at Eastern State] without labour" and that the work assigned to them was a "great consolation."[48] Analyzing Beaumont and Tocqueville, the Marxist historians Dario Melossi and Massimo Pavarini argue that the penitentiary was designed to turn the prisoner into "someone who [has] accepted the state of subordination" characteristic of the industrial economy and its "discipline of wages."[49] For nineteenth-century reformers, the affective element of labor relations was essential: the prisoner had not only to do his work; he had to embrace it as a life-saving gift of love from his keepers.

Part of the humanitarian reform built into the penitentiary, then, was a turn away from the "hard labor" of unenlightened punishment, toward a productive labor infused with a warm ethos of benevolence and gratitude. Such is the relationship the lawyer-narrator of *Bartleby* attempts to foster with his scriveners. He offers Turkey a hand-me-down coat, but his feelings are hurt when the "insolent" employee does not "appreciate the favor." "He was a man," the lawyer concludes, "whom prosperity harmed" (9). At first, like the prisoners at Eastern State, Bartleby appears to crave work; he "seem[s] to gorge himself" like someone "long famished for something to copy" (12). If all goes according to plan, Bartleby will be *corrected* by solitude, becoming grateful to his boss and accountable to his narrator. But labor, even at the beginning, does not move Bartleby to love. He is enclosed and illuminated but unreformed, becoming ever more mysteriously, elusively "cadaverous" (21, 32). Like the speaker of one of Dickinson's lyrics, he covers the abyss of his misery with a troubling, inscrutable trance. He baffles correction.

A few days after Bartleby's arrival, the lawyer asks him to proofread some copies. Bartleby, from behind his screen, delivers for the first time his demurral: "I would prefer not to" (13). Twice the narrator repeats his request, and twice more Bartleby replies that he would prefer not to. His quiet resistance, the motivating problem of the novella, has emerged. "I looked at him steadfastly," says the narrator. "His face was leanly composed; his gray eye dimly calm. Not a wrinkle of agitation rippled him." Bartleby's resistance is not defiance; it is something quieter and more unnerving. "Had there been the least uneasiness, anger, impatience or impertinence in [Bartleby's] manner," the lawyer explains, "in other words, had there been any thing ordinarily *human* about him, doubtless I should have violently dismissed him from the premises" (13, my emphasis). "Nothing so baffles an earnest person," he confesses later, "as a passive resistance" (17). Bartleby baffles because he prefers to make no claim on "humanity." As Michael Rogin observes, he "has the power of negativity. He drains his surroundings of the humanity in which the lawyer would like to believe."[50] In Melville's terms, Bartleby inhabits a ghostliness—a "cadaverously gentlemanly *nonchalance*"—outside the whole economy of the human (21).

As the story progresses, Bartleby prefers to do less and less. First he declines to correct the copies made by Turkey and Nippers, then to correct his own; finally, he does "nothing but stand at his window in his dead-wall revery" (28). He merely persists in his cell, apparently "harmless in his passivity" but more and more disturbing to the lawyer and his business (17). Commanded to take his earnings and get out, he remains, unmoving, solitary and idle behind his green partition. The lawyer, trying to break Bartleby's resistance—to repair the ethical relation of master and worker and, along the way, to discover a narrative pattern fit to hold Bartleby— comically rehearses the history of punishment in miniature. He begins with the threat of "some terrible retribution," fantasizing about ways to provoke Bartleby into open defiance, "to elicit some angry spark from him answerable to my own" (19, 20). Briefly, he contemplates killing Bartleby— but a spirit of mercy stays his hand. It is essential to Melville's design that the narrator never commit any open cruelty against the scrivener. Bartleby must be dehumanized, but not by violence, or else the novella would become yet another reformist exposé of abusive conditions. Melville's target is something more subtle but also, perhaps, more insidious: the mortification inflicted by the most humane and sympathetic of keepers.

Declining to harm Bartleby or to throw him out into the lonely streets, the narrator seeks "to drown [his] exasperated feelings by benevolently construing [Bartleby's] conduct" (34). He considers the possibility that Bartleby is "demented" and ought to be committed "to some convenient retreat" (27, 29). He is willing to accept even Bartleby's idleness, if only Bartleby will accept his own place in the sentimental narrative of humanizing charity:

> "Will you tell me, Bartleby, where you were born?"
> "I would prefer not to."
> "Will you tell me *anything* about yourself?"
> "I would prefer not to."
> "But what reasonable objection can you have to speak to me? I
>   feel friendly towards you." (25)

Bartleby's eyes, "dull and glazed" by cataracts, are screens blocking every attempt to expose his character. As the conflict becomes more absurd, Bartleby becomes not more human but more "cadaverous," a haunting presence inspiring a growing terror. The lawyer is visited by "sad fancyings—chimeras . . . of a sick and silly brain" (23). Cold and unresponsive as "a very ghost" (19), Bartleby provokes this crisis by exposing the inadequacy of the whole cultural system on which the lawyer's snug "tranquility" depends (4). In his walled-in section of the Wall Street world, the law does its work without violence; the demands of labor are mitigated by a benevolent relation between the boss and his workers; and, when any sign of suffering arises, it can be absorbed into the patterns of sentimental narrative. Bartleby's "I prefer not to" dismantles these enlightened ideals. It is more than a refusal to work—it withdraws the scrivener from the recognizable humanity that is the foundation for the lawyer's only means of understanding and correcting his recalcitrance.

Bartleby stands at the limit of reformatory discipline and sentimental narrative, and his ghostliness is, to the eyes of the lawyer, the apparition of a life stubbornly outside those structures: "My first emotions had been those of pure melancholy and sincerest pity; but in just proportion as the forlornness of Bartleby grew and grew to my imagination, did that same melancholy merge into fear, that pity into repulsion. So true it is, and so terrible, too, that up to a certain point the thought or sight of misery enlists our best affections; but in certain special cases, beyond that point it does not" (24). Bartleby's inhumanity, the lawyer concludes, is an "innate and incurable disorder" (25). No asylum can correct him, and no sentimental narrative can account for him. As Sianne Ngai suggests, Bartleby is "a character so emotionally illegible as to foreclose the possibility of sympathetic identification altogether."[51] Thus the sentimental story, baffled by a life that eludes work, discipline, and charity, encounters its opposite and counterpart, the gothic. Ghostliness becomes the sign of a life that quietly but unbreakably refuses the humanity liberally offered by the reformer's cell and sympathy. The "pale form" of Bartleby unhinges the lawyer from security, and he "tremble[s] to think that [his] contact with the scrivener ha[s] . . . seriously affected [him] in a mental way" (27). Jittery and insecure, he keeps the door locked, frightened by "every footfall in the passages" (38).

Frustrated in his efforts to reconcile Bartleby to labor or to account for his resistance, embarrassed in front of his employees and clients—

"A whisper of wonder was running round," he says, "having reference to the strange creature I kept at my office" (16)—the lawyer finally rents a new office, leaving the old one to Bartleby. When the landlord threatens to have the cadaverous loiterer arrested for vagrancy, however, the lawyer makes one more charitable proposition: he invites Bartleby into his home. Part humanitarian intervention, part pickup line, the lawyer's gesture is an odd turn in an odd story. It can be understood as the lawyer's last attempt to domesticate Bartleby, this time through the relation of force that Richard Brodhead calls "disciplinary intimacy."[52] The lawyer's invitation does not depart from his efforts to get control of Bartleby: rather, it completes a sequence of related attempts to draw this unmoving vagrant into the disciplinary structures that regulate social life in the cities of the antebellum American Northeast—bureaucratized office, corrective prison, domestic fireside. The rhythms and regulations of the workplace have failed, even with the promise of extra pay. The enclosures and silence of a virtual prison cell have done no better. Finally the lawyer offers a room in his house, a place at his own table; it is his last, desperate attempt to humanize and discipline his recalcitrant hireling. When it, too, fails, he abandons Bartleby to the landlord and the police, who haul him off to The Tombs.

Visiting Bartleby there, the lawyer records that the "Egyptian character of the masonry weighed upon me with its gloom" (45). The gothic façade makes its grave and solemn impression on his imagination. In a small, grassy courtyard—perhaps the "narrow, grave-like place" where Dickens witnessed a hanging[53]—the lawyer finds Bartleby "huddled" against a wall, his body "wasted" and cold (45). Bartleby's death in The Tombs, unaccountable to the lawyer-narrator, is in a sense the only fitting conclusion for his story. In his ghostly passivity, the scrivener has eluded the matrix of mechanical labor, penitentiary discipline, and sentimental narrative—but he has achieved that escape only by holding fast to the living death that is that cultural system's negative image.

In their "Theory of Ghosts," Theodor Adorno and Max Horkheimer write that the living are "placed in the proper relationship to the dead" only "when the horror of [our own] annihilation is raised fully into consciousness."[54] As he stands over the body of "the wasted Bartleby," Melville's narrator approaches this self-annihilating horror. He recognizes, as if for the first time, that the scrivener is beyond correction and beyond recovery. He speculates about a possible past in the Dead Letter Office and, in conclusion, delivers the famous lines that make up his answer to Bartleby's "I prefer not to"—"Ah, Bartleby! Ah, humanity!" (46). Rogin reads this double sigh as the narrator's "last effort to circumscribe the meaning of his scrivener's fate," to bury Bartleby in sentiment.[55] Yet the phrases might also be read as a loss of faith, as if Bartleby's death had finally given a bitter taste to the "delicious" language of "conscience." Saying farewell to the scrivener, the lawyer may also be dispensing with an old, familiar way of negotiating with the social world. Like so much about *Bartleby*, the final turn is ambiguous. What remains is no resolution but, perhaps, the sense of a lack. Melville has presented a problem for sentimentalism, conceiving a ghostly figure who lurks beyond the limit of "humanity," refusing its lure. But Melville himself goes only as far as the lawyer-narrator can, to the gothic border of sentimentality. He imagines an encounter with a ghostly, imprisoned other that provokes not a charitable humanization but, instead, the disturbance of the very humanity on which the sentimentalizing self depends—a humanity that, as we have seen, involved a myth of sacrifice and a practice of carceral mortification. Bartleby's death decomposes this self and leaves it searching for an alternative foundation. The hollow ringing at the end of the story, then, may be the sound of an absence, the missing subjectivity of Bartleby calling for a counterpart in a reader who can encounter this cadaverous captive, with all the force of his negativity, without sympathy.

NO WAY BUT THROUGH THE GRAVE

In "The American in Charity: 'Benito Cereno' and Gothic Anti-Sentimentality," Peter Coviello makes an argument similar to the one I have made about *Bartleby*. Coviello notes that Melville's *Benito Cereno* features a narrator, the New England ship captain Amasa Delano, whose sentimental tropes and racist presumptions blind him to the gothic reality of the slave revolt aboard the *San Dominick*. The novella is not only about the violence of slavery and resistance but also about how sentimentalism misreads that violence: "Sentimentality is, for Melville, a way of . . . subsisting in a state of often grossly self-satisfied ignorance of [slavery's] most dire aspects and consequences." Coviello suggests that Melville uses the gothic, with its ambiguities and terrors, as an alternative language better suited to the "explosive, inhumane, and unsustainable" scene of racist domination in the Atlantic world.[56] Read this way, *Benito Cereno* manifestly responds to and opposes a text published a few years earlier, the most famous document of the abolitionist movement and the best-selling novel of the nineteenth century, Harriet Beecher Stowe's *Uncle Tom's Cabin*. Parodying Stowe's "self-satisfied and pointedly sentimental" work, Melville's novella attacked at once an inadequate literary reckoning with race and a literary marketplace that trafficked in platitudes instead of difficulties.[57]

As Coviello recognizes, however, Melville may have been guilty of his own misreading. *Uncle Tom's Cabin* is obviously a sentimental fiction written for a mass audience, with hopes of opening hearts and changing minds about the miseries of slavery. Yet despite its "authorial promises of transparency," the novel does not resolve all the problems it raises— it is haunted in its own way by a "terrifying uncontainable excess."[58] In the suffering figure of Tom, it invites the reader to feelings of humanizing sympathy; in the rebellion of George, it makes its enlightened declaration of the God-given humanity of the slave. Both of these paradigms invite the slave to pass from the darkness of abjection into the light of humanity—either through the sympathetic embrace of the feminized Christian conscience allegorized in Little Eva, or through the masculine, revolutionary self-assertion dramatized in George's conflict with the slave catcher Tom Loker. But *Uncle Tom's Cabin* also presents a third possibility, a figure who appeals not to humanity, whether in the idiom of sentiment or of inalienable rights, but to a ghostly inhumanity.

Cassy appears late in Stowe's novel, on the plantation of the villainous master Simon Legree. The reader learns that she has been Legree's mistress for some years, though he has recently turned his attention to younger slaves. Like many of Stowe's more articulate and resourceful victims, Cassy is light-skinned, "a woman delicately bred," but Legree, her "tyrant and tormentor," has "crushed her . . . beneath the foot of his brutality." A history of violence and degradation has given Cassy a cadaverous, inhuman affect. Like Melville's Bartleby, she is an ambiguous, obscure text. Stowe describes the "strange, weird, unsettled cast to all her words," and her "unearthly expression" of "partial insanity."[59] The social death of slavery is much more than a legal condition for this captive; her whole life is intimacy with death. When Legree begins pursuing the young Emmeline, the girl seeks protection from Cassy—"Do tell me," she asks, "couldn't we get away from this place? I don't care where,—into the swamp among the snakes,—anywhere!" Cassy's reply is unwelcome: "Nowhere, but into our graves" (325). When Tom, anticipating his own death under Legree's fists, encourages Cassy to make her escape, she gives him the same answer: "I know no way but through the grave" (345).

Unable to conceive of freedom except in terms of death, Cassy is caught in the conceptual trap that Russ Castronovo calls "political necrophilia." Remarking how persistently antislavery literature embraced death as the only way out of bondage, Castronovo explores why liberal antebellum reformers could often see no escape "but through the grave." "Because abolitionists, both black and white, advanced a definition of freedom that grasped for absolutes and turned away from accidents of the flesh," explains Castronovo, "their texts reproduced a nationalized vocabulary that made the agitation for freedom at times uncannily consistent with proslavery defenses."[60] To those who thought of freedom in abstract, disembodied terms, locating it outside the living and dying world in an idealized realm of concepts, freedom for African Americans could only be imagined as freedom from their racially marked and historically burdened bodies. This deathly escapism expresses itself in the many suicides, infanticides, and other sacrifices of antislavery literature.

Castronovo's critique is directed against a bloodless intellectual tradition that protects the privileges of white men by binding freedom to disembodiment, thereby aligning unfreedom with the conspicuous embodiments of women and people of color. In its examination of the contradictions in abolitionist arguments for freedom, his analysis anticipates some of the problems that haunt any universalizing discourse of human rights in a heterogeneous social world. Along the way, however, Castronovo notes an "unlikely convergence between social death and freedom" in certain stories of liberation that curiously reproduce the loss of self associated with enslavement. Fugitives like Frederick Douglass and James Pennington, he observes, imagined themselves not so much born again into freedom as dead again into alienation and solitude. But there is another way to read such passages.[61] The intimate relations between captivity and death generate not only despair but also some unlikely kinds of creativity in political and aesthetic culture. The secrecy and isolation of the fugitive slave are, after all, not metaphors; they are strategies for preserving his natural life in a time when the law encouraged citizens to hunt him as an outlaw or a beast on the prowl.[62] In the context of a dehumanizing violence, the condition of inhumanity—invisibility, the absence of identity and the dissolution of social connections—opens the possibility that the slave might vanish like a ghost, without a trace. Rather than evading the worldly struggle for freedom, then, fugitives like Douglass reclaimed the conditions of captivity for the purposes of survival, resistance, and escape. Castronovo is right to perceive that the tropes strategically invoked in pursuit of freedom sometimes reproduce those invoked on the side of coercion, but the repetition is not always the effect of a flight from history. The issue is not only that Americans have been unable to imagine freedom together with embodiment but also that we are unable to imagine liberty without captivity.

In the end, Stowe's Cassy does devise a way to escape through the grave. In the deteriorating plantation house is a garret where Legree once confined "a negro woman, who had incurred [his] displeasure" (346). After "several weeks" of torment, her body was removed and buried, and since then the garret has been regarded as a "weird and ghostly place" by all on the plantation: "It was said that oaths and cursings and the sound of violent blows, used to ring through that old garret, and mingled with wailings and groans of despair" (346). Using this structure of captivity "for the purpose of her liberation," Cassy begins to prey on Legree's guilt and superstitions (346). She fixes an old bottleneck in a "knot-hole," so that it catches the wind and makes "doleful and lugubrious wailing sounds" (347). Having exploited the haunting associations of the garret, Cassy hides herself and Emmeline there, secure in the thought that any sounds they make will strike Legree as the racket of ghosts. At night, she wraps herself in sheets and sneaks into the old tyrant's bedroom, haunting his fitful sleep.

Legree is finally broken by Cassy's gothic strategies. Like Melville's lawyer, he grows nervous and confused in the company of the living dead. The secure boundaries of his sovereign realm have been overrun. By day he drinks "imprudently and restlessly." By night, lying awake and miserable in his room beneath the "fatal garret," he fears the white ghost. Soon, word travels around the plantation that he is "sick and dying," in the grip of "that frightful disease that seems to throw the lurid shadows of a coming retribution back into the present life." He shakes and raves about the "horrors" that torment him in his final days (367). As their master loses his health and his mind, Cassy and Emmeline slip away to freedom, still wrapped in white. The fugitives have made their escape not by any reformer's sympathetic recognition of their humanity, and not by any direct overthrow of their inhumane master, but by discovering a line of flight in the condition of "social death" itself. Hidden away in a garret made notorious as a site of captivity, Cassy has turned all that once made captivity a ghostly half-life—social death, ritualized mortification, brutal violence, even madness—to the purposes of vengeance and escape. In this brief, haunting passage, Stowe gives her narrative up to excess, to power dynamics and affects outside the usual ordering patterns of sentimentality. The gothic is not contained; as in *Bartleby*, it is a way of escaping through the borders of humanity, into the swamps and shadows.

Unlike Melville's grim vision in *Bartleby*, a novella whose inscrutable antagonist dismantles it from within, Stowe's story of Cassy has a happy ending. Cassy gets away to freedom and is reunited with her long-lost family. The history of her origins and trials comes to light, and she is recaptured, in a sense, within a sentimental frame. What desolates Melville's design is in Stowe's novel only a temporary disturbance, a moment of excess. The difference between these two stories of cadaverous triumph might be explained in terms of the two authors' different relationships to the sentimental mode and its reformist promises. Melville's attack on his society's practices of captivity, unlike Stowe's, does not comfort itself with the hope that benevolent reforms might lead to a brighter, more humane future. But this more cynical position is not only an effect of Melville's gloomier temperament, or of his grudge against sentimentality. It also arises from the different kinds of captivity in question in the two works.

Stowe's antislavery novel seeks to extend the embrace of sentimental and juridical humanity to slaves who, according to antebellum codes, were socially dead, thus inhuman or even monstrous figures. Melville's subject, the convict in the penitentiary, is not so neatly excluded from sentimental or legal humanity. He is held in the name of a law that applies to all citizens, enduring a punishment that claims precisely to restore his humanity. In such circumstances, no call for a wider inclusion

can suffice. Such a reform would only expand the reach of the prison itself. The circle of humanity must be resisted, as it were, from within. In
Bartleby, therefore, the monster engendered by captivity is not domesticated; it returns to torment its maker. The death of sentimental humanity is the occasion of cadaverous triumph.

PART TWO BORN AGAIN

A Prison gets to be a friend—
Between its Ponderous face
And Ours—a Kinsmanship express—

—EMILY DICKINSON, "A Prison gets to be a friend" (652)

I study the art of solitude.

—RALPH WALDO EMERSON, in his journal, 4 July 1835 (141)

CHAPTER THREE

The Meaning of Solitude

"I KNOW WHERE I AM," says Bartleby in the gloomy corridors of The Tombs. Despite its gothic nickname, the New York criminal justice complex that became the scene of Bartleby's death—and of Melville's radical interrogation of "humanity"—was not some ancient, decaying catacomb. It was one of the monuments of the reform movement, designed in the 1830s by the most famous penitentiary architect in America, John Haviland, and a model of modern penitentiary discipline. Before the building of The Tombs, the great Manhattan prison had been Newgate, an institution that shared in the notorious troubles of its London namesake—the offensive intermingling of prisoners of all classes, epidemics of "gaol fever," conspiracies and riots. By 1816, the reform movement had ascended to authority in New York, and the state built a new penitentiary at Auburn. Eventually, this would become one of the most celebrated prisons in the world, the birthplace of the "Auburn system" of penitentiary discipline adopted in almost all of the United States. The first steps toward that achievement, however, were blind experiments, undertaken on faith, in the powers and the limits of human suffering.

The original plan at Auburn had called for a set of moderate reforms. It segregated inmates into classes, depending upon the type and severity of their crimes. The idea was to keep the most intransigent convicts away from younger and petty criminals who might be more amenable to correction. But when it opened in 1817, the prison was shaken by riots and a general "disorder." In response, administrators and reformers turned to a more extreme segregation. Using convict labor, they built a new wing on the north side of the building, with cells for solitary confinement. Between 1821 and 1824, New York courts sentenced their most "hardened offenders" to uninterrupted isolation in Auburn's north wing.[1] Following the British reformer John Howard's maxim that "prisoners indicted for felony should not be compelled to work,"[2] Auburn left the inmates alone and idle for long stretches of time. The cells were oblong boxes about the size of three stacked caskets: seven and a half feet long, three feet eight inches wide, seven feet tall. A small vent permitted air to circulate, and guards could inspect the prisoners through slits in the walls. The doors were oak, fitted with an iron grating to admit some little light.

Inside the narrow, dismal chambers of Auburn's north wing, the prisoners began to lose their minds and their vitality. Many died, some of disease, some by suicide. Eventually, the governor would pardon the survivors. The trial of solitude had become a notorious massacre. It was denounced by William Roscoe as a human "sacrifice." George Washington Smith, a defender of Philadelphia's Eastern State Penitentiary, called Auburn a "horrid" institution run by "cruel experimenters on the capabilities of human nature to endure excruciating, lingering suffering."[3] Recording Auburn's awful early history in their *Report*, Beaumont and Tocqueville concluded that "absolute solitude, if nothing interrupts it, is beyond the strength of man; it destroys the criminal without intermission and without pity; it does not reform, it kills."[4] Auburn had exposed the full power of solitary confinement, its devastating effects on the minds and bodies of the condemned. Perhaps no other scandal so forcefully supported critics of the penitentiary who saw it as a dungeon of torture and other horrors.

Yet the scandal of Auburn did not bring down the penitentiary movement, and reformers' faith in the corrective power of solitary confinement was, somehow, unshaken. Even the most severe critics of what had happened in the north wing could not bring themselves to abandon the idea that isolation, properly administered, must lead the prisoner to reflection, penitence, and improvement—a "philosophical and true conception" in the appraisal of Beaumont and Tocqueville (39). Smith recognized that isolation would "inevitably produce" feelings of "anguish and remorse," but, like virtually all of his fellow reformers, he saw such suffering as the first step toward a spiritual renovation.[5] The unbroken consensus of the movement was that, as Jeremy Bentham wrote, "solitude is in its nature subservient to the purpose of reformation."[6]

The historian Michael Meranze observes how deeply the idea had penetrated the common sense of the culture that built the first penitentiaries: "Neither the prison's critics nor its defenders questioned the value of solitude."[7] The long and passionate debate about penitentiary discipline, then, would not touch the fundamental "first principle" of solitary confinement, the "key to all" other elements of reform.[8] More than surveillance or religious instruction or even labor discipline, it was isolation that defined the modern prison. The two great rival systems that would take shape in New York and Pennsylvania were "opposed to each other," Beaumont and Tocqueville explained, but they shared "a common basis, without which no penitentiary system is possible; this basis is the *isolation* of the prisoners" (55). A radical concept just a few decades earlier, solitary confinement had come so fully into alignment with the culture's common sense about the character of the human soul that it appeared self-evident: "It seemed to have no alternative," observes Foucault, "as if carried along by the very movement of history."[9]

What made solitary confinement seem so inescapable, so fundamental to the penitentiary and to the modern American order? The obvious answers are tactical: isolation allowed authorities to disperse and manage the prison population, an assembly of rebels, wretches, and miscreants that they saw as a "black cloud" roiling with disease and conspiracy; and it broke the spirit of the malefactor, rendering him docile and submissive. It was a method of oppression, reinforced when necessary by the violence of the whip or the iron gag. It made organized riots almost unthinkable, and it left inmates hopeless in the hands of their keepers. It isolated them from the familiar world of society and family, and it ensured that they could form no new social bonds inside the prison. Solitary confinement showed the offender that, as the New York prison official Ransom Cook wrote, "he is degraded as a felon, cut off from society, and stripped of his rights of citizenship."[10] The solitary cell was the concrete sign of civil death.

Across the reform movement, however, from Britain and Western Europe to New York and Philadelphia, solitary confinement was imagined as much more than a strategy for managing unruly prison populations. Drawing from centuries of Christian monastic practices and Romantic dreams, adapting them to a proto-industrial economy and a political order based on the individual citizen-subject, reformers were convinced that isolation would carry the prisoner from the darkness of living death to the light of rebirth. In a sermon called "The Christian's Duty Towards Criminals" (1828), the Reverend Charles James Blomfield preached that the true hope of reform was "to *quicken those who are dead in trespasses and sins*, by the efficacy of Gospel faith and love; to make those, who were *sometimes darkness*, to be *light in the Lord*; and to send them forth into the world, emancipated from its evil influence, *transformed by the renewing of their mind*."[11] Solitude would lead, at first, to a painful alienation, but reflection and remorse would finally convert the offender into a subject worthy of freedom and grace.

Thus, according to the narrative of prison reform, the prisoner would be separated from the world as he knew it, condemned to a tomblike box where his only constant companion would be the stinging memory of his crime—a presence that confronted him like a cruel face in the mirror—but he could free himself from that torment through a righteous discipline of penitence. Enclosed within the cell, he experienced the even more difficult confinement of a radical enclosure within the self—but the self was also the agent of relief and the only true space of freedom. The prison was a tomb of darkness, abjection, and soul-destroying loneliness, but from this tomb an enlightened and renewed soul was supposed to rise.

What is the character of the humanity—the religious conscience, citizenship, and subjectivity—toward which the fallen and mortified prisoner must aspire? Prisons, according to the Philadelphia reformer Richard Vaux, "are to be managed on principles which philosophy, science, experience, and common sense make authoritative."[12] In other words, the prison draws from a wide range of discourses and ideologies associated with the progressive improvement of humanity. The reformist imagination touched on ecclesiastical, academic, literary, and popular ideals, cobbling them together into a representation of the perfect subject. As the movement rose to power, ancient Christian visions of the soul's transformation through solitude were joined to other, more modern concepts—sentimental dreams about the recovery of lost and wayward lives; radical Protestant notions of divine communion through silence and forbearance; scientific theses about racial character and the relations between body and mind; proto-industrial ideas about the laboring self; Enlightenment political theories of the radically individuated citizen-subject. The prisoner in solitude would stand for all of these and more.

Reduced through civil death and mortification to an empty life, the inmate's captive body became the blank screen onto which the world could project its fantasies. Indeed, warden Elam Lynds of Auburn—a celebrity of the penitentiary movement and a no-nonsense materialist who was known for his ruthlessness with the lash—saw something important about the poetics of punishment when he described the idealistic reformers as men "who know human nature from books only."[13] What actually happened to the living and dying inmate in the cell, from the disaster of Auburn Prison in 1824 to many other histories of wretchedness and struggle, all but disappeared behind the screen. In writings about prisoners in solitude, then, eighteenth- and nineteenth-century society articulated much more than a program of penal reform. It expressed certain deeply held principles of the modern social imaginary as it conceived and represented its most cherished image, the private soul.[14] The figure of the prisoner was not only the monstrous other but also the ideal self.

A HORRID, LOATHSOME COMMUNION

Historians have traced the genealogy of the modern penitentiary through the great variety of dungeons, hulks, closets, and pits that held convicts in the eighteenth century.[15] Some prisons were the converted remnants of older structures—confiscated monasteries, parts of castles, fortresses outmoded by new military technologies. Others, built in the seventeenth or early eighteenth century for the purpose of housing prisoners, nonetheless seemed no more enlightened than medieval ruins to the reformers of the 1780s and beyond. The old institutions were *oubliettes*, places where offending bodies were hidden and forgotten. Notorious, for instance, was the pit at Warwick Gaol in England, an octagon buried nineteen feet deep in the ground, where as many as forty-five prisoners, chained together at their ankles, slept on the floor "in a ring round an open cess pit . . . with only a small grating let through the top for ventilation. In the winter months human steams would billow out . . . like smoke from a chimney." Other pits at Bristol, Nantwich, and Worcester, dug in the early or middle eighteenth century, "were made to appear the cruel remnants of a perverse medievalism" by reformers around the turn of the nineteenth.[16] By all accounts, the oubliettes were filthy, dank, and dismal places, dungeons of corruption and contamination. All kinds of disease and misery spread within their walls, and "[n]o writer on early prisons," according to the British historian Robin Evans, "neglected to mention the ubiquity of fevers, sores and infections in them."[17] Such scenes shocked and offended the sensibility of the rising reform movement, whose sentimental designs meant to expose and eliminate the gothic dungeon.

The most famous physical ailment infecting the prisoners of the eighteenth century was the so-called gaol fever—this was typhus, a common epidemic spread by lice, but the magistrates and physicians of the time diagnosed it as an affliction peculiar to carceral institutions, traveling through the stagnant air and infecting prisoners as they breathed. One trouble with this pestilence, aside from the unsightly suffering it produced, was that it killed convicts at random: epidemics "made the penalties of the law into a lottery" and spoiled official efforts to achieve "concordance between offence and penalty."[18] John Howard, an English sheriff who became the great hero of the eighteenth-century reform movement on both sides of the Atlantic, complained that "many more prisoners were destroyed by [gaol fever] than were put to death by all the public executions in the kingdom."[19] And gaol fever's threat to the ministers of justice was not only a threat to the logic of their sentencing schemes. It was a palpable, deadly menace.

Often, the epidemic spread beyond the walls of the oubliette. When it did, the most vulnerable outsiders were the ministers of justice themselves, who in the course of their business came into close contact with prisoners. Evans recounts one of several widely publicized examples: "In April 1750 attendants at the Old Bailey sessions remembered being struck by a 'noisome smell' in the court. A week later a number were taken with a highly malignant fever. Most died. The death toll included the Lord Mayor of London, two judges, an alderman, a lawyer, an under-sheriff and several of the jury, [and] 40 others."[20] In such cases, authorities saw the suffering they had dealt to accused criminals literally come back to smite them. Bentham wrote that reform must address "the danger of *infection*—a circumstance which carries death, in one of its most tremendous forms, from the seat of guilt to the seat of justice, involving in one common catastrophe the violator and the upholder of the laws."[21] The "upholders of the laws" may have wished to cast offenders into a separate and forgotten world, but they had not devised a proper quarantine. Containing the contagion, then, was not only about caring for the condemned; it was a matter of vital self-interest: "Even if no mercy were due to prisoners," Howard admitted, "the gaol-distemper is a national concern of no small importance."[22]

In the discourse of the reformers, the contagion of gaol fever was related to a second kind of contagion, one whose potential violence against authority was still more disturbing—the spread of viciousness and bad intentions from convict to convict in the dungeon. Reformers discerned "a quite close similarity between the way that fever spread itself and the way that vice spread itself."[23] Mutual corruption became one of the most common themes of prison reform writing. Jacob Ilive, a visitor to the Clerkenwell House of Corrections in 1757, complained that he had seen "a great number of dirty young wenches intermixed with some men . . . sunning and lousing themselves; others lying sound asleep; some sleeping with their faces in men's laps, and some men doing the same by the women."[24] In the unreformed oubliettes of France, Beaumont and Tocqueville similarly observed "the contagion of mutual communications, which in our prisons corrupts the inmates" (113–114). Again and again, reformers expressed their horror at the filth and idleness of prisoners, and especially at their grotesque intermingling. The carceral institutions seemed to house a sick and malign intimacy.[25]

In the depths of reformers' repulsion was the fear that a revolutionary conspiracy might be brewing in the oubliette. Robert Denne, reporting to the London aldermen in 1771, drew upon the highest literary authority: if his audience would "only recollect some parts of *Paradise Lost*," wrote Denne, they would "perceive" how the "close recess of the Pandemonium, where the chiefs of them sat in council to work the destruction of mankind, answers but too well to the principal ward in the prison."[26] The conspiracy of the damned was not just a poet's fantasy; it was an urgent problem for government and society. The wicked were preparing a rebellion—and their wickedness was spreading even to the pettiest and most innocent citizens of the oubliette. "In some gaols," wrote Howard, "you can see (and who can see it without sorrow) boys of twelve or fourteen eagerly listening to the stories told by practised and experienced criminals, of their adventures, successes, stratagems, and escapes."[27] Bentham agreed, lamenting the "thronging" and "jostling," the "confederatings" and "plottings" that plagued British gaols.[28] And in the United States, George Washington Smith presented the unreformed prison as a "den of abomination, [where] were mingled in one revolting mass of festering corruption, all the collected elements of contagion; all ages, colours, and sexes, were forced into one horrid, loathsome communion of depravity."[29]

Disease and disobedience seemed to be in the air of the oubliette, breathed in common by prisoners in a menacing conspiracy.[30] The grave problem for reformers of the late eighteenth century, then, was the "loathsome communion" of prisoners' bodies and souls, the conspiratorial mingling that threatened to spread from the jail to the public at large, and there to inspire open rebellion. In search of a solution to the intertwined problems of epidemic disease and riotous disorder, English and American reformers in the eighteenth century looked to a few European experiments in the isolation of offenders. There they discovered the practical benefits of solitary confinement: disease quarantined, riots prevented, viciousness contained. In time, they would also discover other, more elevated promises, drawing from more ancient practices of solitude. The solitary cell would become the most concrete, most intractable piece of the discursive and material architecture that condemned the prisoner to civil death, and it would also become the scene—miraculously, impossibly—of rebirth. But the first calls for reform were more administrative than missionary, concerned mainly with the orderly management of offending populations.

For the Anglo-American reform movement, the most important precedents were the House of Correction of San Michele in Rome (1704) and the Maison de Force in Ghent (1772–1775).[31] The Rome House of Corrections, designed by the architect Carlo Fontana and endorsed by Pope Clement XI, was a reformatory for delinquent boys. Each slept in his own cell, worked under supervision during the day, and observed religious rituals at the appropriate time. The architecture of the institution represented a righteous Roman Catholic matrix of solitude, labor, and prayer:

"At the east end was an altar, at the west end a whipping post and a sign demanding silence. Between were lines of benches to which certain children were chained and set to work spinning wool. Others were kept in their cells all the time. Each cell had . . . a barred window . . . from which the altar could always be seen, so that Mass could be celebrated without necessarily letting the children out."[32] Above the entrance gate, the purpose of this enlightened institution was inscribed: "For the correction and instruction of profligate youth: that they, who when idle, were injurious, when instructed might be useful to the State."[33] The House of Corrections combined under one roof a carceral institution, a protofactory, and an altar of worship. The institution had clearly incorporated some aspects of monastic discipline, but its inmates were not expected to renounce the world of civil and economic life; their correction would prepare them to be better workers and more useful citizens.

Some of the major designs of reform, then, had already been realized in Rome in 1704—the House of Corrections provided a single cell for each offender, silence and supervision, labor and the production of a subject "useful to the State." This arrangement was strongly endorsed by Howard in *The State of the Prisons*, and in 1839 the French reformer Bernard-Benoît Remacle called it "the most perfect model that could be chosen for a penitentiary."[34] On the other side of the Atlantic, George Washington Smith cited it as a predecessor of Pennsylvania's model penitentiaries.[35] But the House of Corrections was open only to male offenders under twenty years old, and only to the most promising of these; a special tribunal selected the "spiritually innocent" offenders and consigned the rest to the ordinary gaol.[36] The Rome House of Corrections was a promising model, but a limited one. The effects of such a model on a larger and more diverse population of convicts, including the most thoroughly hardened and unregenerate offenders, remained to be tested.

The Ghent Maison de Force, built under the direction of Count Jean Philippe Vilain, went some distance toward testing them. The institution was founded on some of the principles that would become dear to the reformers of the ensuing century, including solitary confinement, segregation of the sexes, and the classification of inmates according to the severity of their crimes. Each of its eight self-contained units housed a specific class of offender, and each offender was assigned a private cell with a window onto a courtyard.[37] Like the boys in the Rome House of Corrections, the prisoners at Ghent spent their days working cloth. Smith strongly praised the institution for its power to quarantine disease and prevent conspiracy.[38] Howard, who visited the Maison de Force several times in the 1770s, called it a "well-regulated manufactory" where "there are excellent rules for preventing all quarrelling; mending [prisoners'] morals; preserving their health; and making them for the future useful in society."[39]

In Howard's view, English legislators and prison administrators had much to learn from the example of Ghent. "Most of our gaols," he wrote, "are riotous alehouses and brothels."[40] Howard wanted to stop the spread of disease and malevolence that the old oubliette had promoted. He argued that prisoners with gaol fever and other infections should be quarantined, so that the sentences passed by judges would remain meaningful, corresponding to the severity of the crime, and so that the ministers of justice would not become the victims of the misery they handed down. The more innocent classes of offenders—juveniles, debtors, and the like—should be kept away from the corrupting influence of hardened felons, so that an army of rebels would not take shape. With his aim of *prevention* (as opposed to *correction*, a remaking of the captive's subjectivity), Howard was asking for "moderate" reforms.[41] His plan let prisoners out of their cells for congregate meals, work, and religious services during the day, but he did wish "to have so many small rooms or cabins that each criminal may sleep alone" (21). Night separation would suffice to prevent escapes, protect the vulnerable, and discourage the kinds of vice most likely to spread in the dark. Howard insisted that he wanted no extravagance, and "[pleaded] only for necessaries, in such a moderate quantity, as may support health and strength for labor" (33). He also suggested that "solitude and silence are favourable to reflection, and may possibly lead [prisoners] to repentance" (21). But, in Howard's work, the promise of correction had not yet risen to dominance, and the "crucial role" of the architecture of solitude "was only dimly perceived."[42]

In some special cases, however, Howard did recommend a more rigorous and prolonged solitude: "closer confinement," he suggested, might be imposed as a punishment against inmates who resisted their keepers or disturbed the orderly operation of the institution (34). Philadelphia's

Benjamin Rush agreed, calling for the solitary confinement of inmates who seemed otherwise incorrigible. Already the solitary prison cell—developed at Rome and Ghent as a remedy for disease and conspiracy—seemed, in the view of its Anglo-American admirers, to have another value in the control of prison populations. It did not only prevent contact among the mass of offenders; it also broke the spirit of each. It was a humane way, in the view of Jonas Hanway, to "subdue the ferocious."[43] A generation later, Beaumont and Tocqueville elaborated the idea, which they had seen in practice in Philadelphia: "When, in his solitary cell, in the midst of the pains of a stinging conscience, and the agitations of his soul, [the prisoner] has fallen into a dejection of mind, and has sought in labor a relief from his griefs; from that moment he is tamed, and forever submissive" (72). The inmate's civil death, his loss of self and his entry into the half-life of the carceral tomb, had been written into law, enacted in the rituals of prison initiation and discipline, and made manifest in the concrete architectural space of the solitary cell; there, subdued and "fallen into a dejection of mind," the moribund prisoner lay divested of rights and subjectivity, finally transformed into a deathly, passive object—and thereby prepared for his resurrection.

THE TRUE RESEMBLANCE OF HIS MIND

To reformers who wished to dispel disease and prevent riots, and to wardens who wished to break prisoners' unruly wills, the solitary confinement cell was an elegant solution to administrative problems. But the project of prison reform was much more than a search for practical solutions. The penitentiary was bound up with the far-reaching revolutions of its age, radical transformations in how societies around the Atlantic conceived of power, knowledge, and the character of humanity. For the authors who championed the emergent modern prison system in the public sphere, the solitary cell expressed the truths and values of an enlightened modernity. It was not just a zone of quarantine, and not just an instrument for the domestication of the wicked; it was a means to the recovery of damaged souls, an institution from whose iron gates model citizen-subjects would emerge.

Reformers took their ideas about the captive soul from a wide variety of discourses and material contexts—a long history of religious asceticism; medicoscientific concepts of healing and racial difference; the demands of a proto-industrial division of labor; and liberal-democratic views of the radically individuated citizen-subject. Each of these languages helped the authors of the penitentiary to represent the prisoner in solitude as an ideal subject. The prisoner's body was mortified and passed through a ritualized sacrifice. A dismal confinement taught him to despise idleness, to perform any assigned labor with pleasure and gratitude. His connections to a social circle of rebels and miscreants were severed, creating a radical individuation. Condemned to civil death, a discipline of labor, and an absolute isolation from the social world in a small, spare chamber, his subjectivity seemed to take the shape of its miniature world; in the imagination of reformers, the prisoner would come to appear as a *cellular soul.*

Like the legal codes and carceral rituals of civil death, the modern dream of penitential resurrection had a very long history. "The earliest cases of solitary confinement as an *intended means of reform,*" George Washington Smith recalled in his *Defence of the System of Solitary Confinement* (1833), "may be discovered in the records of ecclesiastical history," in "monastic and other religious institutions."[44] The search for the perfect architecture of confinement led reformers not only into the literary, political, and scientific knowledge of their own times but also into ancient accounts of the relationship between solitude and the shape of the soul. The first Christian disciplines of isolation were hermetic—radical versions of asceticism through which believers withdrew from worldly matters to achieve personal sanctity and communion with God. "Seek ye first the kingdom of God, and his righteousness," Christ commanded in the Sermon on the Mount—"Take no thought for your life, what ye shall eat, or what ye shall drink; nor yet for your body."[45] To the early ascetics, the lines were a call to abandon the comforts and pleasures of the social world, even to sacrifice their bodies to the purification of the spirit. The mortification of the flesh, they believed, would bring them closer to redemption. By the third or fourth century in Egypt, groups of ascetics and virgins had begun to withdraw from ordinary congregations, establishing small communities of their own. In part, their movement was a reaction against an increasingly "established" church, which was growing in size and worldly power, losing the ardency and "distinctiveness" of its original days. The early Christian ascetics and virgins had none of the elaborate rules that would come to characterize the monasteries and convents of the European Middle Ages, and no hierarchy of authority governed them. Members prayed and labored together; they sometimes ministered to the nearby villages, caring for widows and the sick, distributing alms to the very poor.[46]

Not long after the ascetics had withdrawn into miniature societies of their own, a few began to undertake a further withdrawal, going into the desert to live alone. For them, the mortification of the body was joined to a discipline of solitude. The renunciation of society promised intimacy with God. The adventures and teachings of the first Egyptian hermits are recorded in such texts as *The Sayings of the Fathers*, Paphnutius's *Histories of the Monks of Upper Egypt*, and the *Conferences* of Cassian. In Paphnutius's *Life of Onnophrius*, the spiritual biography of an ascetic who claims to have spent sixty years alone in the desert, the hero achieves sustained communion with God and his angels, becoming from time to time a welcomed visitor to paradise: "To everyone in the desert who lives there on account of God and sees no other human being, the angel comes and gives the eucharist and comforts them. What's more, if they desire to see anyone, they are taken up into the heavenly places where they see all the saints and greet them, and their hearts are filled with light; they rejoice and are glad with God in these good things. Now when they are seen they are comforted and completely forget they have suffered."[47] The early hermits of the Egyptian desert renounced human company and earthly comforts for a mystical contact with the divine; their wish to "see anyone" was granted in the form of "heavenly visions" and fellowship with the angels. Passing lives of isolation and hunger in caves, tombs, and abandoned towns, they sacrificed the worldly self to the sanctification of the spirit.

News of the Egyptian ascetics traveled to Europe, and by the fifth century Christians in France and Britain had undertaken lives in monasteries or in hermetic solitude.[48] Often, the believer took shelter in an anchorage or *reclusoire*, built into the walls of a church and fitted with slats through which the "anchorite" could view the altar and receive Communion. Civilly dead and buried in a version of the funeral ceremony, anchorites spent the rest of their lives in their cells, often without heat, bed, or blankets, sometimes even without light.[49] Some were rumored to have oracular visions; some distributed potions and worked spells. Anchorites were mysteriously powerful figures, connected to the church but with an uncertain relationship to its hierarchy. The anchorite's mission was never to return to any kind of social life, certainly not to emerge a more useful servant of worldly authority, but to come closer and closer to God until the body gave way in the final communion.

Soon, however, the leaders of an increasingly powerful church became suspicious. Hermits and anchorites began to seem less like the most devout adherents to the faith, and more like renegades, freakish and perhaps dangerous: "The loneliness of the solitary's life increased the chance of abnormality, eccentricity, even madness."[50] To regulate ascetic practice, the church began to establish codes for the organization and governance of monastic institutions. The most influential of the codes was the *Rule* of St. Benedict, published in Italy in the sixth century A.D.; over the next three hundred years, most European monasteries would adopt it.[51] Benedict's *Rule* promoted the organization and collective life of monks under the direction of an abbot, and served as the foundation for a larger organization of monasteries under a common, hierarchical system of authority. The *Rule* distinguished the monks known as Cenobites, with their organized communal practice, from the various solitary ascetics, of whom it disapproved: "If we keep close to our school and the doctrine we learn in it," the text declared, "and persevere in the monastery till death, we shall here share by patience in the passion of Christ and hereafter deserve to be united with him in his kingdom."[52] The Cenobites, obedient to their abbot who, in turn, would answer to a centralizing authority, were recognized as the true servants of the church, most worthy of redemption.

Benedict's *Rule* prescribed daily and annual routines: when the monks must be silent and when they must sing, what they must eat and drink and wear on their feet, how they must work, and how they must sleep. It also prescribed several degrees of discipline for disobedience—the *Rule* was, in part, a penal code. "The brother who is convicted" of serious offenses, the text indicates, should be sentenced to solitude: "None of the community shall keep company or converse with him. He shall pursue alone the work enjoined to him, in tears of penance."[53] These lines represent a change in the meaning of solitude. Dismissed earlier in the text of the *Rule* as a flawed and dangerous version of ascetic practice, it reappears here in a different form—as a punishment. The isolation of the ascetic is absorbed and domesticated by the institutional church, becoming a discipline that makes dangerous monks submissive and penitent.

The eighteenth- and nineteenth-century reformers who built the penitentiary system may or may not have read such ancient texts as the *Life of Onnophrius* or Benedict's *Rule*, but a Christian mission was clearly central to their program. Howard was only one of many who took it for granted that "a chapel is necessary in a gaol."[54] As reformers in England and the United States moved beyond the tactical values of order and obedience, beginning to imagine the prisoner's spiritual transformation through solitary confinement, they adapted ancient Christian ideas to the demands of their modernity: "The cell, that technique of Christian monachism . . . becomes in this protestant society the instrument by which one may reconstitute both *homo oeconomicus* and the religious conscience. Between the crime and the return to right and virtue, the prison would constitute the 'space between two worlds,' the place for the individual transformation that would restore to the state the subject it had lost."[55]

The shift from prevention to correction, and the place of the ancient monastic soul in modern prison architecture, can be seen in the writings of the late eighteenth-century English reformer Jonas Hanway. In a series of letters published as *Distributive Justice and Mercy* (1781), Hanway complained that the moderate reform promoted by Howard and written into law in the Hard Labour Bill (1779) "requires prisoners to be separated in a partial and inconsistent manner; whereas experience teaches, that *intercourse in prisons* has been prostituted, not less to the disgrace of human nature, than of all civil and religious economy."[56] Prisoners who slept alone but worked and ate and prayed together still had too many occasions for contact. Only total, round the clock solitude, Hanway concluded, would "break up the communities of thieves, and purify the source whence such foul streams of immorality flow" (xii). Hanway prescribed a radical and pure method of correction, in which the solitary cell became the convict's entire world: a chaplain would visit each prisoner in his cell for Christian education; labor would also be performed in the cell, in solitude; even the prisoner's daily exercise would consist in nothing but walking around inside the cell. For Hanway, the allure of solitude was more than prophylactic. "Our object," he wrote, "is nothing less than the souls and bodies of the most miserable part of our fellow-creatures, our fellow-Christians" (45). His system would "*correct* our fellow-subjects, instead of *destroying* them," as the gaols of the day were likely to do (ii). It would "curb and soften [the inmate] into a religious, humane, and obedient temper"; it would "bend and incline the *perverse*, and teach the *unprincipled*" (45, 96). Isolation would transform the malefactor into a humble servant of God and of the state, redeeming the corrupted soul.

Christian teaching was part of Hanway's program, and in phrases echoing the testimonials of the ancient Egyptian hermits he exhorted the prisoner to "receive the visits of thy spiritual teacher, as an angel sent from heaven" (67). Labor was another element, designed to cultivate in the prisoner "a desire of being employed profitably" upon his release (v). But in Hanway's system, the major work of correction would be accomplished by solitude itself: the convict's soul would be transformed by the very architecture of his confinement. The key to this transformation was the idea of *reflection*. For Hanway and the reformers who followed him, the term was more than a metaphor for memory or deep thought; it was the image that defined the relation between prison architecture and the architecture of mind. Hanway imagined that the prisoner, alone in his cell, facing its blank walls, would "discover the true resemblance of [his] mind, as it were in a mirror" (65). Somehow the walls of the solitary cell, as Hanway's poetics of punishment represented them, would confront the prisoner with an undistorted picture of his guilt. Revealed to himself, no longer distracted by vice and bad company, he would struggle to redeem himself from his crime—precisely because the crime, apparent all around him, made his confinement a torment. Indeed, in a kind of magical sublimation, the living body and the stone cell were recast in the conflict of a soul divided against itself, and the suffering of prisoners was imagined as a spiritual affliction.

Solitude, reflection, penitence—the prison in the discourse of reform was a relation between cell and spirit, architecture and soul. Beaumont and Tocqueville saw it this way: "Thrown into solitude [the prisoner] reflects. Placed alone, in view of his crime, he learns to hate it . . . in solitude, where remorse will come to assail him" (55). Thus the defenders of the solitary confinement cell conceived an image of the criminal soul fitted to its design. They described a subject split into two opposed parts, one surrounding the other, the confined and righteous self laboring to reform the criminal self that binds it, to overcome division and achieve a redeemed integrity. The sublimation of architecture and confined bodies into a spiritual fiction is completed with the figure of the convict's cellular soul.

As the prison reform movement took power, the cellular soul—self-binding and self-correcting—would become its dominant image. It was the centerpiece of the great model penitentiaries of the Pennsylvania and Auburn systems, and it shaped the terms according to which many in the world at large imagined the great institution of modern punishment. Emily Dickinson's "A Prison gets to be a friend" captures the combination of dread and hope inspired by the cell, as the poet reflects on

> this Phantasm Steel—
> Whose features—Day and Night—
> Are present to us—as Our Own—
> And as escapeless—quite— (652)

In the poetics of punishment, the solitary cell is not so much a chamber for the body as an architecture of mind, enforcing, through reflection, the prisoner's consciousness of the inescapable walls of the self.

One famous model prison may seem to depart from the orthodoxy of solitude, depending not on private reflection but on a hierarchical social relationship between the prisoner and those who watch over him. Jeremy Bentham's panopticon has received a great deal of attention for its techniques of surveillance. But even this famous carceral design was concerned less, in the end, with actually observing the inmate than with the invisible structures it might produce within his mind. Bentham set out to create an architecture within which "at every instant, seeing reason to believe as much, and not being able to satisfy himself to the contrary, [the prisoner] should *conceive* himself to be [under inspection]."[57] At the center of the panopticon stands the inspector, who holds the authority to punish disobedience whenever it appears—but when the panopticon is at its best, when everything is operating perfectly, the actual presence of the inspector becomes redundant. The true aim of surveillance is the creation of a certain mental state in the prisoner: "The greater chance there is of a given person's being at a given time actually under inspection," writes Bentham, "the more strong will be the persuasion—the more *intense . . . the feeling*, he has of his being so."[58] Again, the language emphasizes subjectivity; each prisoner, knowing he is visible, becomes his own inspector, his own master, and the subject of his own correction.

Bentham's model was admired by many reformers in the United States, notably Thomas Jefferson, whose sketches for a penitentiary in Virginia made use of principles from Bentham's design. But in the discourse of the American penitentiary system—soon to become the most advanced and most controversial in the world—the dominant theme was not surveillance but solitude. The central figure was not the watched body but the penitent, cellular soul.

The first capital of reform in the United States was Philadelphia, where the ideal of humane punishment had a history going back to early colonial days. From 1682 until William Penn's death in 1718, Pennsylvania had lived under Quaker criminal codes, mainly written by Penn himself. Based on Quaker tenets of pacifism and a rigid morality, these codes combined an "aversion . . . to unusual cruelty, suffering and the shedding of blood"—extremely "progressive" for its time—with an "almost puritanical asceticism and austerity," involving detailed provisions against sexual deviance, profanity, gambling, drunkenness, and various "public amusements." With their turn from the scaffold to the prison, from the torture of the body to the remaking of the soul, Penn's codes represented an "epoch-making departure in criminal procedure," unknown anywhere else in these years, "the first instance in which imprisonment at hard labor was prescribed as a punishment for a majority of [crimes]."[59] The advancement in the art of punishment did not arise from a society willing to tolerate sin and crime—it signified that no soul should be abandoned, that even the corrupt and wayward could be reclaimed to godliness through severe spiritual discipline.

After Penn's death, the Anglican faction overcame the Quakers in the government of Pennsylvania, abandoning Penn's progressive experiment in criminal justice. Torture returned, and the scaffold was put to use more often, for lesser offenses. Through the middle of the eighteenth century, the prison in Pennsylvania followed the course of its British counterpart: it turned into an oubliette, a "moral pest-house," to the eyes of nineteenth-century reformers.[60] After the American Revolution, then, reformers were able to advance their cause by associating the spectacular violence of the scaffold and the pestilent misery of the oubliette with European despotism. "Independence," the historian David Rothman records, "made the time and place right for reform. The rhetoric of the Revolution had prepared Americans to fulfill a grand mission, and now they would demonstrate how to uplift one part of mankind, the criminal class."[61] "Happy citizens of the United States," Benjamin Rush exclaimed, "whose governments permit them to adopt every discovery in the moral or intellectual world, that leads to benevolent purposes!"[62] Reformers argued that tyrants favored the lash, and that dungeons belonged to decadent aristocracies; the new Republic, dedicated to Enlightenment and the citizen-subject, should build its modern values even into its system of punishment.

By 1786—thanks to the efforts of Benjamin Franklin, Benjamin Rush, and their friends in the Society to Alleviate the Miseries of Public Prisons—the cause of reform was again ascendant in Philadelphia. New criminal codes, as Beaumont and Tocqueville noted, banished the spectacles of "death, mutilation and the whip . . . in almost all cases" and reestablished imprisonment as the standard in punishment (37). In 1790, a block of solitary cells was added to the Walnut Street Jail in Philadelphia, which was converted into a state penitentiary. The idea at Walnut Street was total isolation, day and night, for the worst offenders. But in reality the cells were used by prison authorities to punish disobedient inmates, who were held in solitude for brief periods, then returned to the general population. The Walnut Street Jail never put isolation into practice as a specialized corrective discipline.[63]

In 1818, a new penitentiary, also designed for solitary confinement, opened in Pittsburgh. Again, however, the physical structure proved inadequate to its purpose, as inmates were able to communicate with each other through its walls: "The construction of this penitentiary is so defective," wrote Beaumont and Tocqueville, "that it is very easy to hear in one cell what is going on in another; so that each prisoner found in the communication with his neighbor a daily recreation, i.e. an opportunity of inevitable corruption" (44). In a system founded on solitary reflection, communication was always understood to mean corruption. Not until the opening of Philadelphia's Eastern State Penitentiary, popularly known as Cherry Hill, would Pennsylvania perfect its "system."

Eastern State was designed by John Haviland in the early 1820s. It received its first inmates in 1829 and was completed in 1836. Built on a radial plan, the prison was composed of 450 solitary cells, each lighted by a small skylight (figure 3). Ground floor cells were attached to private, enclosed exercise yards; second-floor cells were attached to private workrooms. Food and work materials were passed to the prisoner through an opening of about a foot square which, when not in use, was closed with a wooden hatch. A small peephole allowed officers to inspect the prisoner from the corridor, into which the prisoner could not see. A bed hung by chains from the ceiling. There was a vent, a water tap, and a flush toilet. Prisoners had human contact only with prison officials. For the most part, they ate, exercised, worked, and slept in complete isolation.[64]

Solitary confinement, according to Roberts Vaux and the other advocates of the Pennsylvania system, "is intended to furnish the criminal with every opportunity which christian [sic] duty enjoins, for promoting his restoration to the path of virtue, because seclusion is believed to be an essential ingredient in moral treatment."[65] The cell, in the words of Eastern State's first Board of Directors, would serve "to turn the thoughts of the convict inwards upon himself, and to teach him how to think."[66] At Cherry Hill, the ideal of reflection was manifest in one of the most sophisticated architectural achievements in nineteenth-century America. The prisoner's universe, for the duration of his confinement, was bound by four walls, and the effect was that the walls became mirrors. Facing the stone structure of the cell, wrote George Washington Smith, the prisoner at Eastern State "will be compelled to reflect on the error of his ways."[67] Throughout their many histories, pamphlets, and open letters on the Pennsylvania system, reformers invoked this image, of a prisoner's consciousness divided against itself, the "penitent" mind struggling against the "criminal" one that binds it.

The convict at Eastern State is removed from friends and family, locked into a cell, subjected to surveillance, enjoined to silence, and exposed to physical violence, but none of these, according to the authors of the penitentiary system, is the true source of the inmate's anguish. What stings him most is his guilty conscience—and the "genius of solitude," according to the reformers, is that the conscience, the force of torment, is also the force of penitence, redemption, and a kind of liberation: "Moral and religious reflection," wrote the Philadelphia inspectors, "divest [the convict's] solitary cell of all its horrors, and his punishment of much of its severity."[68] Thus solitude, as Foucault explains, "makes possible a spontaneous individualization of the punishment: the more a convict is capable of reflecting, the more capable he was of committing his crime; but, also, the more lively his remorse, the more painful his

Interior View of Cell, taken from the Corridor.

These two Views constitute One Cell.

Interior View of Cell, taken from the Yard of the Cell.

FIGURE 3. "Interior View of Cell." A prisoner working in his cell at Eastern State Penitentiary in Philadelphia. From Richard Vaux, *Brief Sketch of the Origin and History of the State Penitentiary for the Eastern District of Pennsylvania, at Philadelphia* (Philadelphia: McLaughlin Brothers, 1872), n.p.

solitude; on the other hand, when he has profoundly repented and made amends without the least dissimulation, solitude will no longer weigh upon him."[69] Solitude is suffering, in other words, but it is also redemption. Dickenson's "A Prison gets to be a friend" explores precisely this transformation, in which the inmate passes from suffering to a kind of passive contentment. The sound of the speaker's lonely footsteps on the floor of the cell is "miserable . . . at first" but, after a period of accommodation, it becomes "so sweet" (652).

"The ultimate benefit conferred, even on the criminal himself," wrote Smith, adds to the "severity" of solitary confinement "a measure of real humanity."[70] The Pennsylvania reformers eagerly published testimonials by ex-convicts who claimed to have found redemption in their solitary cells. In an interview with Beaumont and Tocqueville, for example, an unnamed Philadelphia inmate rehearsed the central tenets of reform: "It is better to live in absolute solitude than to be thrown together with wretches of all kinds. For all, isolation favours reflection, and is conducive to reformation."[71] Even Harry Hawser, the ex-sailor and convict who had depicted Eastern State as a "living tomb" in a poem called "The Captive," finally declared that his confinement there had been "the happiest event of his life": "It has dissolved improper connections, remodeled his tastes, improved his mind, and, he trusts, made better his heart. He is neither morose, imbecile, dispirited, or deranged, and whatever reformation his imprisonment may have produced, he can attribute it to the separate seclusion [of the Pennsylvania System]."[72] According to the published testimony of inmates, supported and circulated by the reformers who ran Eastern State, the Pennsylvania system had "carried the doctrine of isolation to a logical and appropriate conclusion."[73] The correspondence between the prison's design and the fantasy of spiritual reformation was practically complete: the "tomb" of the solitary cell was a scene of "reformation."

THE SOLITUDE OF HIS OWN HEART

A prison reform movement that had been evolving for decades found its ideals enshrined in the monumental architecture of Cherry Hill. The authors of the Pennsylvania system had invoked ancient ascetic ideas about the redemptive power of solitude and mortification; they had adapted them to the pacifism and strict morality of a Quaker community, with its faith in the "inner light" of the individual believer; and, as they defended their solitary system in reports and pamphlets, they had developed an architectural image of the soul in the act of redemption. As authorities such as Smith, Roberts Vaux, and Beaumont and Tocqueville described the achievement of the Pennsylvania system, their poetics of punishment worked a kind of alchemy. In place of confining walls, they saw the moral burden of guilt. In place of captive bodies struggling to resist and escape, they saw the moral force of repentance yearning toward redemption. They transmuted the stone cell and the imprisoned body into a spiritual figure, the cellular soul.

Religious traditions and modern architecture had combined to conceive the soul at the center of the American carceral imagination, but religion was by no means the only cultural source of this soul. It was also the offspring of emergent scientific knowledge, of a proto-industrial economy, and of a revolutionary conception of the citizen-subject. Franklin and Rush, Smith and Vaux, and their collaborators were no parochial Quakers; they were people of the Enlightenment world, travelers and scholars for whom, in Rush's phrase, "humanity, philosophy, and Christianity, shall unite."[74] Rush, a physician who had studied at Edinburgh, was especially concerned to apply the truths of modern science to the problems of social and political reform: "The great art of surgery has been said to consist in saving . . . the diseased parts of the human body," he wrote. "Let governments learn to imitate, in this respect, the skill and humanity of the healing art."[75] Rush, the European-trained man of science for whom the penitentiary belonged to a larger and grander program of social improvement, virtually embodies the advent of a Foucauldian modernity. In his writings, the spectacular violence of the scaffold gives way to the mediated power dynamics of the human sciences; the condemned body becomes an object of knowledge and a subject of self-discipline. Along the same lines, Rush might be considered the model for Hawthorne's Roger Chillingworth, the European-trained physician who pretends to care for the body of his patient, but whose secret intention is to expose and manipulate Dimmesdale's vulnerable heart.

In at least one major respect, however, the medicoscientific discourse of the prison reform movement does not support the periodized account developed in Foucault's *Discipline and Punish*. For the discourse of reform was not a universalizing humanism: it divided humanity into racial categories, distinguishing prisoners capable of salvation from those who would remain bound to their unredeemable bodies. The *segregation* of discipline was a part of the U.S. prison system from its earliest days. In the antebellum South, of course, penitentiary discipline would be virtually unthinkable as a punishment for slaves. As Thomas Cobb's *Inquiry into the Law of Negro Slavery* indicated, "The condition of the slave renders it impossible to inflict upon him the ordinary punishments, by pecuniary fine, by imprisonment, or by banishment. He can be reached only through his body."[76] For people who had no claim to self-possession, in other words, the deprivation of liberty would be a meaningless punishment. Worse, it would confiscate the property of slaveholders, the proper authorities to "reach" the unruly slave "through his body."

The law made it "impossible" for a slave to be deprived of liberty or restored to citizenship. The emergent racial concepts of the human sciences added further reasons for excluding African Americans from the penitentiary. A notorious passage from Jefferson's *Notes on Virginia*, in which the author emphasizes the differences between the white and black races—differences that Jefferson saw as "fixed in nature"—sets out to draw its distinction by demonstrating that each race suffers in its own peculiar way. The white man, explains Jefferson, is a creature of "memory, reason, and imagination"; by contrast, the black appears as an "animal . . . who does not reflect." The "griefs [of Africans and their descendants] are transient," writes Jefferson: "afflictions . . . are less felt, and sooner forgotten with them. In general, their existence appears to participate more of sensation than reflection." Jefferson's racial distinctions are familiar to any student of early American culture: they divide the thinking mind from the feeling flesh, the "tender delicate . . . sentiment" of the white heart from the "eager desire" of black skin, the reasoning white subject from the black object with its "strong and disagreeable odor." They map the opposition between white subjectivity and black abjection that would come to be the organizing principle of Toni Morrison's *Playing in the Dark* and many other cultural studies of race and the American imagination. But these divisions would have certain peculiar applications in the discourse of penal reform. According to Jefferson's categories, blacks were not endowed with the essential capacity necessary for penitentiary discipline, the power of *reflection*. They could be made to feel "numberless afflictions," but their grief would not lead to the renewing of their minds.[77]

Many of the enlightened humanitarians who built the penitentiary system—Benjamin Rush, Roberts Vaux, Francis Lieber—were also abolitionists who protested the violence and dehumanization of slavery; Vaux, for instance, explicitly defined the penitentiary's enlightened "moral incentives" against the plantation's barbarous "inflictions of the lash."[78] Yet the segregation of discipline was not a uniquely Southern practice. In the Northern capitals of reform, authorities who took great pride in their advanced knowledge and humanity also drew lines between black and white. In his 1843 investigation into the frequent deaths of black prisoners at Philadelphia's Eastern State Penitentiary, for example, the physician Benjamin Coates concluded that "individuals of the African variety" were racially unfit for the rigors of solitary discipline: "Cheerful, merry, lounging and careless, the Ethiopian American deeply enjoys the sun and light; delights in the open air; and is, as a general rule, constitutionally free from that deep, thoughtful anxiety . . . so conspicuous in his paler neighbor. The face of heaven seems to him necessary to his existence; and though long confinement is, in his case, less productive of gloomy remorse, it is far more depressing to his vitality."[79] In Coates's report, the sickly, embodied "Ethiopian American," withering toward death, was defined against the self-corrective and spiritual subjectivity of the white convict. In the poetics of the penitentiary, "individuals of the African variety" could be weakened and killed by solitude, but never redeemed.

Thus an emergent medicoscientific discourse about race and embodied consciousness was joined to ancient Catholic and newer Quaker images of the soul in the representation of the ideal subjectivity to be produced in the solitary cells of Eastern State. The combination was compelling to many reformers, and the great printing presses of Philadelphia helped to promote the "Pennsylvania system" around the world. In the end, however, this monumental experiment would be displaced by an alternative model, forged at New York's Auburn Prison in the aftermath of the 1821 scandal. Rather than abandoning the practice of solitary confinement that had debilitated and killed so many of the inmates in their first experiment, the Auburn authorities set out to expand and perfect it. In many ways, they agreed with their rivals at Eastern State— they shared a common commitment to solitude and the making of the cellular soul. The Auburn system, as Thomas Dumm notes, "won its 'victory' only by conceding that the fundamental form of punishment on which it was built was developed and first implemented in Philadelphia."[80] What allowed New York to triumph in the rivalry was that it brought its system in line not only with the religious and scientific discourses of the antebellum United States but also with the demands of an industrializing economy. Charles Sutton, a warden at The Tombs, would recall in 1874 that "under [the Auburn system] the man was a machine, wound up in the morning to work so many hours, and at night laid away to remain silent and motionless until the morning came again."[81]

The Pennsylvania system as practiced at Eastern State was expensive. It required large individual cells, even private exercise yards for each prisoner. Worse still, the form of labor it accommodated was becoming outdated in the American North of the middle nineteenth century. Confined to their cells day and night, without machines, the Pennsylvania prisoners could only practice artisanal labor or process raw materials. They could only do the work of the proto-industrial economy which, at the turn of the century, had first imagined this system; Eastern State Penitentiary could not serve as a factory. As Richard Vaux lamented, this great monument of correction was viewed with "continued antagonism" by legislators and the public because "it costs too much."[82] In the Pennsylvania system, then, a contradiction had arisen between the spiritual ambitions of reform and the realities of the antebellum economy.

Auburn's celebrated "silent system" evolved to remove that contradiction. William Roscoe, one of the fiercest critics of the Pennsylvania system and a defender of the alternative conceived in New York, insisted that "the discipline of the prison must be assimilated as far as possible to that of a great workshop or manufactory, where, by the stimulus of proper and judicious motives, the labour is rendered voluntary, and where past offences are to be forgotten, as long as the individual conducts himself in a dutiful, submissive, and industrious manner."[83] As Melossi and Pavarini argue, "The originality of this new [Auburn] system lay essentially in the introduction of work structured in the same way as the dominant system of factory work."[84] At Auburn, and later at Sing Sing and hundreds of other American prisons built on the same plan, inmates slept alone but assembled for labor during the day. They moved back and forth between the seclusion of the cell and the congregate labor of the factory.

Beaumont and Tocqueville praised this "ingenious combination of two elements, which seem at first glance incompatible, isolation and reunion" (42). Thus the Auburn system advertised "the best of both worlds, economy and reform."[85]

The problem, of course, was to bring prisoners together without enabling conspiracy, to put them to work side by side without compromising the great achievement of solitary confinement, the cellular soul. The solution was silence. Auburn's regulations prohibited any communication among inmates, from talking down to the exchange of glances and hand signals. Any violation, any attempt at conversation or conspiracy, was punishable by the whip or worse. Thus Auburn took the solitary prisoner, Pennsylvania's divided and self-binding soul, out of his cell and put him to work beside other prisoners in a carefully managed assembly. It congregated bodies but preserved the isolation required for penitent reflection. "Though united," wrote Beaumont and Tocqueville, "they are yet in fact isolated." No "moral connection," no "sympathy" can unite them (58). The Auburn system thus conceived of its prisoners as laborers who, despite the congregate work they perform, remain in a spiritual isolation: "Their union is strictly material, or, to speak more exactly, their bodies are together, but their souls are separated; and it is not the solitude of the body which is important, but that of the mind" (58). Assembly without communion, congregate labor without collaborative resistance, industrial production without riot. This is the design of the Auburn system: a "model and small-scale society"[86] of laboring and self-governing subjects, each of whom preserves the hermetic architecture of the cellular soul.

In 1825, just a year after the adoption of the congregate, silent system in Auburn's north wing, authorities in New York decided to expand by building an enormous new penitentiary on the banks of the Hudson River. The Auburn warden Elam Lynds took about a hundred prisoners in leg shackles to the site, where they went to work in the building of what would soon become another world-famous monument of reform, Sing Sing Prison. The cells at Sing Sing, for night isolation, were three and a half feet wide and just under seven feet long, with a six and a half foot ceiling. The main block, called the "east house," included a thousand of these "extremely damp, dark, and poorly ventilated" cells, which contained no toilet other than a bucket. In the decades that followed, Sing Sing would become the "prototype for most American prison construction."[87]

Eventually almost all of the states, not including Pennsylvania, adopted its system of night solitude and congregate labor. The American prison was entering its golden age.

As impressive to reformers as the physical institution at Sing Sing was the way Lynds had managed to build it. Beaumont and Tocqueville celebrated the warden's achievement: "There, encamped on the bank of the Hudson . . . without walls to lock up his dangerous companions; he sets [the prisoners] to work, making of every one a mason or a carpenter, and having no other means to keep them in obedience, than the firmness of his character and the energy of his will" (43). Instrumental to this process, however, was not just the character of the overseer but also the character of his workers, criminals reformed by solitude and congregate labor at Auburn; Lynds had personally selected the Auburn prisoners most "accustomed to obey" (43). When reformers praised the construction of Sing Sing, then, they were advertising the power of the Auburn system itself—a society of laborers, each looking inward, even as he toils in the company of others, toward the care of his own soul.

Citizens divested of human rights, exposed to the violence of the lash and the unfettered authority of a violent warden, condemned to work in a profound alienation—the Auburn ideal is a dismal world, similar in many ways to Jacksonian America's other dark zones of servitude, especially the plantation. Again, it is tempting to conclude, as some scholars have, that the rhetoric of "correction" was little more than a ruse deployed by authorities whose true aim was the creation of broken and submissive laborers, cast out from the free, enlightened body politic; the penitentiary is commonly depicted as "a realm of unfreedom in an otherwise free world."[88] Such a view, however, does not quite do justice to the American carceral imagination. For while convicts were sentenced, for a time, to the "condition of a slave," they were not always locked into that condition forever. Just as white prisoners were distinguished from African Americans by their "capacity" for reflection, convicts were distinguished from slaves by their legal potential for a restoration to citizenship. Indeed, civil death and the alienation of solitude were the very foundations of that rebirth.

In addition to the languages of religion, science, and economics, therefore, the authors of the penitentiary would describe their ideal subject in the language of modern, liberal-democratic citizenship. The penitentiary was a zone of exclusion and exploitation, but it also symbolized a model of political organization. It might even be seen as a kind of democratic *polis* in miniature, where the governing ideals of the new age were manifest in concrete. The links between the prisoner in solitude and the democratic citizen at large were observed by several commentators on the rising penitentiary systems, among them the great theorist of Jacksonian culture, Alexis de Tocqueville.[89] In fact, it was during his tour of the new penitentiaries, in the company of Gustave de Beaumont, that Tocqueville made the notes and sketches that would eventually become *Democracy in America*.

In this larger work, incarceration and criminal law seem to receive relatively little attention—but, as a few critics have observed, Tocqueville's theory of democracy seems haunted, at times, by the penitentiary.[90] In particular, Tocqueville was impressed by the radical isolation of the citizen-subject in the liberal-democratic political order. The familial and class relations of the old world's regimes had created a great social chain, binding their members together and situating the identity of each in a pattern of meaningful relationships. One effect of a stable aristocratic hierarchy, in Tocqueville's account, is a sense of mutual interdependence and strong "bonds of human affection." In the modern liberal-democratic society of the United States, by contrast, the chain was broken, the pattern decomposed, and the individual was left in a stark isolation. "Each man" in a democracy, writes Tocqueville, "is forever thrown back on himself alone, and there is danger that he may be shut up in the solitude of his own heart."[91] The lines, clearly informed by Tocqueville's tours of the prisons, resonate with the claustrophobic nightmares of Edgar Allan Poe. They present a world in which every private heart is an inescapable tomb. Tocqueville's most fearful vision was one of the Auburn system expanded to contain all of American society, a vast national assembly of cellular souls.

Reading *Democracy in America* alongside the history of prison reform that Tocqueville knew so well, Thomas Dumm provides an account of the difference between the Pennsylvania and Auburn systems based not on economics but on models of political order. The Philadelphia system, writes Dumm, had taught prisoners "one fundamental lesson, that they were alone in the world"; the Auburn system had then developed to teach them a second lesson, "that loneliness was to be a shared condition."

Pennsylvania, in short, enforced the radical individuation of liberalism, while Auburn achieved the paradoxical triumph of democracy: a society of isolated individuals. The common truth of the penitentiary system and the post-Revolutionary political order in the United States, according to Dumm, was "that solitude was the condition of all members of society."[92] The disembodied spirituality and profound isolation of the prisoner were conditions shared by the citizens of the United States at large.

What was the character of the soul conceived by the authors of the penitentiary system? Having examined the sources of their tropes in religious tradition, the sciences of their age, an industrializing division of labor, and political philosophy, we can return to the question and grasp the figure at the center of reform's imaginative world. It was perhaps less a character than an *image*, architectural and arrested in time. Through an ascetic regime, its living body was sacrificed to its spiritual salvation. The transmutation of body into spirit was aided by a modern science that distinguished the penitent consciousness of the white convict from the dying body of the "African." Isolated from the contagions of disease and conspiracy, taking on the structure of its solitary cell, the soul was then reintroduced into a kind of collectivity—but this collective, laboring in the silent workshop, was prevented from recognizing any bonds of sympathy or solidarity; it was a mechanistic assembly of radically individuated components. Such a system, moreover, was not only a model of labor discipline. It was also an ideal of liberal-democratic political organization for a society that had broken the chains of monarchy and devoted itself to the individual citizen-subject. Disembodied, colored white, isolated, and inward looking: this was the soul born from the sacrifice of prison discipline, the innocent self rising after the abjection and death of the guilty other. This was the purified subject worthy of freedom—the prison's perfect humanity.

For critics such as Dumm and Meranze, the penitentiary's promise of redemption masks the secret oppression of the modern liberal-democratic order. The new regime of power is less spectacular in its violence than the old scaffold, but, with its designs on the soul, it may be even more insidious. Reformers might announce their charitable wish to "quicken those who are dead in trespasses and sins" and "send them forth into the world, emancipated . . . by the renewing of their mind"— but the penitentiary is after all less concerned with emancipation than

with punishment and social control.[93] Following Adorno and Horkheimer
as well as Foucault, Dumm describes how the prison serves "the regu-
latory capacity of modern societies" by "constitut[ing] the modern self
as a disciplined body."[94] Similarly, Meranze emphasizes how Philadelphia elites, afraid that the fire of rebellion kindled by the American Revolution might blaze toward anarchy, developed institutions such as the
penitentiary to reestablish order. Designing pedagogic regimes for the
making of the self-governing subjects that Rush called "republican machines," they secured the rule of law and protected their own authority
from the otherwise unruly masses.

Such arguments, central to the critique of power since the 1970s,
were anticipated by a number of nineteenth-century literary figures—by
Poe, who depicted solitude as the worst of all possible tortures; by Douglass, who articulated some of the connections between the prison and
the plantation; by Melville, who narrated Bartleby's resistance to sentimental "humanity"; by Hawthorne, who presented the modern man of
science as a malignant experimenter on the penitent soul; and, as we
shall see in the following chapter, by many others, including such literary lights as Dickinson, Thoreau, and Emerson. In search not only of the
historical and ideological conditions that motivated the reformers but
also of the language that made the prison a subject of terror and an object of critique, then, we might turn to the imaginative literature of the
age. Beyond prison walls and reform debates, the prisoner in solitude
was becoming a figure of great symbolic power. As both a wretched, abject victim of oppression and a metaphor for modern subjectivity at large,
he seems to lurk around every corner in the literature of an antebellum
American society preoccupied with the problem of freedom.

Indeed, the imagery of liberty seems almost always deeply bound to
the history of captivity. The prison informed not only Poe's tales of men
buried alive but also the whole American Romantic discourse of solitude
and the self. In Thoreau's "Civil Disobedience," the cell becomes a scene
of personal transformation, where the prisoner discovers a core of being
that separates him from his fellow citizens and liberates him from the
tyranny of the majority. In Emerson's essays, the image of "man . . .
clapped into jail by his consciousness" is invoked to call for a radical nonconformity, an inward-looking self-reliance. Thoreau and Emerson se-
verely criticized the powers that built and managed prisons for offenders,

but they shared, in a sense, the reformers' faith in the redemption of the private self through a discipline of solitude. Taken seriously as a regimen for the conduct of the contemplative life, Emersonian self-reliance takes the soul out of the body and out of the social world. The American Romantic ideal of the free and transcendent self—disciplined, disembodied, solitary—is in some ways a version of the prisoner conceived by reformers, reinvented for the world at large.

But Emerson's transcendent soul was not the only vision of free subjectivity conceived by antebellum writers who confronted the penitentiary. A few would imagine the prisoner in ways that did not reinforce the penitentiary's fantasy of redemption. Like Melville in *Bartleby*, they recoiled from its mortifications, and especially from the isolation it imposed. In Dickinson's multiple and dialogic lyric subjectivities, and sometimes in Whitman's expansive acts of identification, the stony walls of the self were opened to vibrant intimacies, and the promise of liberty was an escape from solitude. Their project was an imaginative dismantling from within; they sought to unmake and recompose the very ideal of humanity enshrined in the penitentiary.

CHAPTER FOUR

Captivity and Consciousness

BY THE LATE 1820S, the movement that built the world's first great penitentiary system had entered its triumphant phase. The experimental ideas of eighteenth-century pioneers such as Cesare di Beccaria, John Howard, and Benjamin Rush had become the next generation's doctrine, written into law and enshrined in the monumental architecture of the famous model prisons of New York and Philadelphia. The violence and degradation of plantation slavery and Indian Removal were still shaping the American social landscape, but reform had extended its humanizing embrace to citizens convicted of crimes. The gallows, the whipping post, the pillory, and other implements of torture were being removed from the public square. Behind the high, imposing gates of the penitentiary, authorities administered a discipline aimed not at the destruction of the body but at the salvation of the soul. In this new world, solitude and silence reigned.

The building of the penitentiary system was generally acclaimed as a sign of progress for humanity, but it also raised some troubling new contradictions and questions. Among them was the problem of the relationship between the prison interior and the world at large. To some, the relation was one of stark opposition. They saw the prison as a separate and secret zone, within the geographic bounds of the United States but symbolically outside American society—a place of exile from which, in time, the transgressor might step forth as a remade citizen. Rush had argued that the realities of prison life should be hidden from the public, so that a lively "imagination," enflamed by terrifying fictions, would fear the worst. Secrecy, for Rush, was "of the utmost importance": "There is no alternative."[1] The Board of Directors of the Massachusetts State Prison adopted the same approach in its plan for penitentiary management, declaring that "the prison should be considered as a world by itself," with an absolute minimum of communication between prisoners and the free public.[2] Gustave de Beaumont and Alexis de Tocqueville, too, drew a clear boundary between the penitentiary and the rest of the American social world: "While society in the United States gives the example of the most extended liberty, the prisons of the same country offer the spectacle of the most complete despotism."[3] Here, the prison appears as the negative image of a modern U.S. body politic whose great pride is its liberty.

Others who confronted the problem of the prison, however, took a different view. They saw the institution not as a despotic "world by itself" but as the most complete, and most concrete, manifestation of power structures fundamental to all of American social life. They saw its architecture and disciplinary regimes reproduced in a whole range of other institutions—asylums and military barracks, factories and schools, even the sacred space of the private home. Herman Melville, in *Bartleby*, used the imagery of prison cells to characterize a Wall Street office. Emily Dickinson regularly linked the enclosures of the domestic sphere with the prison interior. In the same period, in the essays of Henry David Thoreau and Ralph Waldo Emerson, the vision of an entire society modeled on the prison became the background against which new conceptions of individual freedom would emerge.

Each of the two imagined relationships between the prison interior and society at large can become the foundation of a specific kind of protest. Criticism of the prison will have different implications, depending on where the critic places the institution in the larger social framework. For those who see it as a "world by itself," a zone of dark terrors where the enlightened codes of free society do not apply, prison critique tends to call for progressive measures that would suppress bodily violence and respect the civil rights of the incarcerated. Like the original reformers who confronted the barbarous oubliette, these critics often describe the prison as an institution left behind by history, stuck in an obsolescent age of cruel tyranny. Their protests emphasize the convict's humanity and the need for a more sympathetic penal regime. According to Francis Lieber, who translated Beaumont and Tocqueville for an American readership, inmates should be treated as "redeemable beings, who are subject to the same principles of action with the rest of mankind."[4] For William Roscoe, the challenge of reform was to perfect a "system of penal discipline, commensurate with the other improvements of the present day."[5] The prison should be less like a medieval dungeon, more like a modern asylum or a school. Reform remains an incomplete project, and the prison is one of its darkest frontiers.

To those who take the second view of the prison's place in the social order, who see it as an exemplary institution of modern coercion, the conventional project of reform can never suffice. For Tocqueville, Dickinson, and a few of their contemporaries—as for Michel Foucault and his followers a century later—the prison is no remnant of brutality, left over from the age of sovereignty; it already belongs to the matrix of modern governmental and social structures that, as Tocqueville suggests, constitute citizen-subjects by remaking the soul. The prison, Foucault writes, "merely reproduces, with a little more emphasis, all the mechanisms that are to be found in the social body."[6] Its discipline, in the haunting language of Theodor Adorno and Max Horkheimer, is "the specter" of the ordered, self-governing world at large: "Absolute solitude, the violent turning inward on the self, whose whole being consists in the mastery of material and in the monotonous rhythm of work, is the specter which outlines the existence of man in the modern world. Radical isolation and radical reduction to the same hopeless nothingness are identical. Man in prison is the virtual image of the bourgeois type which he still has to become in reality."[7] Such an understanding of the prison leads critics beyond reform, to interrogate the very forms of subjectivity available to modern citizens. The sentimental reformers had said, "Prisoners are just like us, our fellow creatures; we must treat them with humanity and sympathy." The radical critics, by contrast, said, "We are just like prisoners, oppressed and degraded; we must liberate ourselves from the tyranny of our modernity." In order to grasp the prisoner's oppression, they turn a critical eye inward, upon the ideological and disciplinary conditions of the modern soul.

This self-critique, however, can create a bind of its own. Many authors who confronted the penitentiary during its golden age perceived the potential oppressiveness of the "correction" it offered. They saw how surveillance, the threat of alienation, and the demands of penitence could work to ensnare the soul in a chain of submission. But, in some of their most famous and influential texts, they also sought to break that chain through a discipline of solitude and "self-reliance." Such a program of liberation comes dangerously close to reproducing the regime of the reformers, imagining redemption through the inward-looking self-discipline of a cellular soul. The Romantic call for self-liberation, so important to American dreams of freedom over the past two centuries, presumes that, beneath the false consciousness formed by the tyranny of the majority, a true self awaits its opportunity for redemption.

STRAIGHT FOR THE SOUL

Beaumont and Tocqueville's *Report* neatly divided the "complete despotism" of the penitentiary from the "extended liberty" of society at large. As Tocqueville turned his attention from local debates about prison management to the larger question of power in the United States, however, he did not see such a simple opposition. Indeed, he seems to have drawn his narrative of modernization and democratization directly from the history of penal reform. Considering the difference between the sovereign use of force in the old regime and the "tyranny of the majority" in modern democracies, Tocqueville writes: "Princes made violence a physical thing, but our contemporary democratic republics have turned it into something as intellectual as the human will it is intended to constrain. Under the absolute government of a single man, despotism, to reach the soul, clumsily struck at the body, and the soul, escaping from such blows, rose gloriously above it; but in democratic republics that is not at all how tyranny behaves; it leaves the body alone and goes straight for the soul."[8] Here, the epochal shift in the history of punishment—the transition from the scaffold to the prison cell—plays out, in miniature, the history of power at large.

According to the heroic narrative of U.S. independence, the Revolution had thrown off the shackles of tyranny and turned the ex-colonists into free citizen-subjects. Tocqueville, with his aristocratic heritage and his experience of revolutionary turmoil in France, was unconvinced by that story of heroic liberation. Surveying U.S. politics and culture, contrasting them to the old regimes of Europe, he did not see a simple passage from bondage to freedom. Tyranny, for Tocqueville, could take a variety of forms. It shaped all political societies, ancient and modern. In the shift from monarchy to democracy, then, tyranny had not been vanquished. It had reinvented itself in a new guise. As Tocqueville imagined it, the new form of tyranny was certainly as powerful as the old one—there is even a sense in his writing that democracy involves more refined, and more effective, strategies of domination. Tocqueville presents the bygone despot as a clumsy, incompetent giant who attempts to control people through brute force while their souls "gloriously" escape his grasp. Modern tyranny, meanwhile, is more nuanced and insidious, recognizing that true domination must bind the private soul.

The difference between ancient tyrannies directed at the body and modern ones directed at the soul was taken up by Dickinson in a poem about torture and consciousness, "No Rack can torture me." The lyric develops Tocqueville's imagery of a soul rising gloriously above the ruins of the violated body:

> No Rack can torture me—
> My Soul—at Liberty—
> Behind this mortal Bone
> There knits a bolder One—
>
> You cannot prick with saw—
> Nor pierce with Scimitar—
> Two Bodies—therefore be—
> Bind One—The Other fly— (384)

The rack, the saw, and the scimitar, emblems of despotic violence, are all wielded in vain. Leaving the "mortal Bone" of the afflicted body in the hands of the torturer, the soul ascends, untouched, into the open skies. Like Nathaniel Hawthorne's Hester Prynne, Dickinson's speaker has the victory over her captors; their clumsy methods cannot touch her sovereign soul. In another stanza, Dickinson invokes the "Eagle," the symbol of the free Republic, perhaps suggesting that the struggle between tyrant and spirit here stands for the Revolutionary struggle between England and the United States. In any case, the key idea is that true "Captivity"—

and true "Liberty"—are not conditions of the body but states of a private "Consciousness."

The notion that the inner world of the soul is the true territory of freedom was a Romantic commonplace. However, Dickinson's poem indicates a suggestive exception:

> Except Thyself may be
> Thine Enemy—
> Captivity is Consciousess—
> So's Liberty. (384)

In the first half of this final stanza, just before the fascinating and memorable closing couplet, Dickinson suggests that not all souls enjoy the condition of private liberty. There is also the possibility of a conflicted soul, directing a kind of torment against itself. Such a soul is its own "Enemy," held captive more profoundly than the victim of any external torturer. The body endures, but consciousness is doomed. Dickinson's language here, especially her use of the term "Enemy," suggests that the soul's self-affliction is an effect of social or political, rather than personal, trauma. It seems to be suffering a version of the alienated, stigmatized condition that Tocqueville describes as "a life worse than death."

In this passage, Tocqueville extends his reflections on the new guise of tyranny by imagining a "master's" address to his subjects: "The master no longer says: 'Think like me or you die.' He does say: 'You are free not to think as I do; you can keep your life and property and all; but from this day you are a stranger among us. . . . You will remain among men, but you will lose your rights to count as one. When you approach your fellows, they will shun you as an impure being. . . . Go in peace. I have given you your life, but it is a life worse than death.'"[9] In Tocqueville's allegory of how power works in the modern democracy, the offending body is not harmed; instead, the transgressor enters into an abject state of internal exile. Like the civilly dead convict in the penitentiary, the nonconformist in society at large retains his natural life, but he has been transformed into something less than human. He becomes "an impure being," a kind of monster lingering in "a life worse than death."

The "master" in this narrative is no longer any single figure, no prince or despot. Rather, it is a symbol of what Tocqueville calls "the tyranny of the majority," the power that pervades American society in the democratic age, subjecting each citizen to the surveillance and judgment of all. The tyranny of the majority should not be misunderstood as a term for how the interests of larger groups prevail over those of smaller groups in democratic institutions. It is a relation not among interest groups but between the mass public and the individual. It works at the intersection of the social world and the private consciousness. The tyranny of the majority is the way modern power leaves the body alone and goes straight for the soul.

Again, Dickinson seems to be in conversation with Tocqueville. She explores the soul-constraining power of the majority with special attention to the social construction of the categories of insanity and reason:

> Much Madness is divinest Sense—
> To a discerning Eye—
> Much sense—the starkest Madness. (435)

The difference between madness and sense, Dickinson suggests, depends on the observer's point of view. What appears crazy to some might appear sensible to others. And yet the difference is much more than a matter of two contrasting opinions. It is a matter of power structures that govern social life and enforce a rigid conformity. It is the tyranny of the majority:

> 'Tis the Majority
> In this, as All, prevail—
> Assent—and you are sane—
> Demur—you're straightway dangerous—
> And handled with a Chain. (435)

Watched over by an all-powerful majority, the mind that transgresses the norms of reason comes under suspicion and a dehumanizing discipline—like a beast, a slave, or a prisoner, it is "handled with a Chain."[10] For Dickinson, as for Tocqueville, modern American society at large cannot be placed in simple contrast against the penitentiary's regime. The ordinary social world seems instead to reproduce the prison, with its structures for remaking the offender's consciousness. In acts of imaginative identification with prisoners, both writers protest the carceral tendencies of modern American society in general.

For a contemporary of Tocqueville and Dickinson, meanwhile, identification with the incarcerated would be something more than an act of
the imagination. In 1846, Henry David Thoreau, of Concord, Massachusetts, was arrested for refusing to pay his taxes and clapped into the local
jail. He spent just one night behind bars—friends covered his debts and
secured his release—but Thoreau would remember his confinement as a
"wholly new" and transformative experience. It provoked the reflections
that would become one of his most celebrated works, the essay known as
"Civil Disobedience." The night in jail opened Thoreau's mind to previously obscure truths about the character of his familiar city: "It was a
closer view of my native town," he recalled. "I was fairly inside it. I had
never seen its institutions before." From the peculiar vantage point of the
cell, he "began to comprehend" the secret truths of the social order.[11]

"As I stood considering the walls of solid stone," Thoreau wrote of
his cell, "and the iron grating which strained the light, I could not help
being struck with the foolishness of that institution which treated me as
if I were mere flesh and blood and bones, to be locked up." Like Dickinson's soul rising above the rack, Thoreau in jail experiences a renewed
sense of his freedom. The local officials, he writes, "had resolved to punish my body," but "they could not reach me"; "I did not for a moment feel
confined" (126). Thoreau in jail experienced a new kind of freedom. Just
as forcefully, too, he was impressed by the unfreedom of the world at
large.

What Thoreau discovered was that the free citizens of Concord, his
friends and neighbors, were in some ways more deeply oppressed than
the criminals they incarcerated: "I saw that, if there was a wall of stone
between me and my townsmen, there was a still more difficult one to
climb or break through before they could get to be as free as I was" (126).
His own confinement was a blunt matter of stone and iron. But they, be-
lieving that they belonged to the greatest society of free citizens in the
modern world, went about their lives in "ignorance" of the tyranny that
really governed them: "The mass of men serve the state thus, not as men
mainly, but as machines, with their bodies. They are the standing army,
and the militia, jailers, constables, *posse comitatus*, etc. In most cases there
is no free exercise whatever of the judgment or of the moral sense. . . .
Such command no more respect than men of straw or a lump of dirt.
They have the same sort of worth only as horses and dogs. Yet such as

these are commonly esteemed good citizens" (112). What has turned these "good citizens" into the instruments of power? One answer is the tyranny of the majority, or as Thoreau puts it, "an undue regard for the opinions of men" (131). Ordinary townspeople do not fall under the lash or into the cell, but they have surrendered the "free exercise" of their consciences.

Thoreau used the occasion of his confinement to rail against the passivity and conformity of his fellow citizens, the invisible prisons that captured them by depriving them of meaningful possibilities of moral and political action. He also began to consider how they might liberate themselves from their spiritual captivity. Thoreau recommended an inward-looking search for the individual's true "moral sense" or conscience: "You must live within yourself," he wrote, "and depend upon yourself always" (124). "Let [each man] see that he does only what belongs to himself and to the hour" (131). "What force has a multitude?" he asks. "I was not born to be forced. I will breathe after my own fashion" (127). All the while, Thoreau insists that he has discovered his own true freedom in the jail cell, after his keepers have "locked the door on my meditations" (126). "Civil Disobedience" thus tells the story of a man who is placed into a cell and there, in captivity, throws off the wicked social influences that had once oppressed him. His confinement is "like traveling into a far country, such as I had never expected to behold," a journey into another world from which the traveler returns with new eyes and a new conscience (126). The captivity of his body liberates his soul.

In a curious way, then, Thoreau's story, which begins with an inmate laughing at the "foolishness" of his confinement, has much in common with the narratives scripted by the great prison builders of his time. It rejects the notion that bodily punishments can ever fully govern their victims. It recoils from the soul-corrupting influences of modern collective life. And its hero seeks redemption in the solitude of his own heart. As Jason Haslam has recognized, the author of "Civil Disobedience" arrives at a paradoxical position: Thoreau wished to liberate the private self from tyranny, but his idealization of the individual self, the inner conscience, risks reproducing the ideological assumptions—about solitary reflection and the relation between body and soul—that were becoming the foundations of the modern prison system. "By tying together his political rebellion and his transcendental subjectivity," argues Haslam,

Thoreau is in danger of "reproduc[ing] the ontological foundations of the carceral matrix (both the actual jail and the society that surrounds it) that he is attempting to critique."[12] Thoreau, however, seems unaware of these connections. Perhaps because he was confined for only one night, and that in a jail, rather than a reformed penitentiary, he presents incarceration as just another affliction of the body; he does not see how much the "rulers and reformers" of his day shared his ideas about the discipline of solitude and the remaking of the soul.

Thoreau was not content with a merely personal salvation. The purification of conscience was, for him, the foundation of a kind of "action" that would return the body to the realm of power, using it to create what he called "friction" in the "machine" of government. This project of self-purification in preparation for dissident action makes Thoreau's brief incarceration one of the defining myths of American Romanticism, and of modern radicalism in general, sometimes compared to the nonviolent resistance practiced in twentieth-century anticolonial and civil rights movements. Thoreau also belongs to a long tradition of offenders who, in prison, have learned a discipline of principled opposition, rather than conformity. *The Autobiography of Malcolm X* and the prison letters of George Jackson, for example, tell the stories of modern convicts hardened into militant radicals. As for Thoreau's friends and collaborators in the antebellum period, they did not tend toward the same militancy, but many of them did explore, as he did, the relations between incarceration and the more highly mediated oppressions of the modern world at large. The little-known story of Emerson's decades-long engagement with the penitentiary is a revelatory example.

CLAPPED INTO JAIL BY HIS CONSCIOUSNESS

Unlike Thoreau, Emerson has not often been understood as a writer concerned with prison cells. F. O. Matthiessen's classic study of the literary movement he called the American Renaissance, which helped to establish the canon of antebellum letters for critics during the cold war, defines Emerson's "cheerful temperament" against the morbid sensibilities of his contemporaries: "The turning of the individual upon his own inner life," writes Matthiessen, "was [for Emerson] a matter not for resignation but for exuberance. The possible tragic consequences of the soul locked into its prison, though not envisaged by his optimism, were the burdens of Hawthorne and Poe."[13] Matthiessen confines the prison, and even the metaphor of "tragic" solitude, to the gothic imaginations of the times, and Emerson's critics since Matthiessen have tended to follow him in excluding the penitentiary from consideration.[14] They seem not to hear the prison's reverberations, the Melvillian echoes of Auburn's silence, when Emerson ponders, in a letter to his aunt, "What stone walls of incommunicability do exist between mind and mind."[15]

Emerson, with Hawthorne and Poe—and with Melville and Thoreau and Dickinson and Douglass and their whole generation—knew the penitentiary movement and the enormous reforms it had recently undertaken. Emerson's close friend Margaret Fuller was among the public figures who praised Auburn's "righteous" program of correction and called for continued reforms of prisons and jails according to its principles.[16] And Emerson himself sometimes lent his voice to the progressive cause: "We make, by distrust, the thief, and burglar, and incendiary, and by our court and jail we keep him so," he wrote in "Man the Reformer." "An acceptance of the sentiment of love throughout Christendom for a season would bring the felon and the outcast to our side in tears."[17] Thus Emerson adopted the sentimental mode and promoted the social ideals of reform. Even when he was addressing other subjects, he often took up the themes that defined the penitentiary. With its vision of a soul working toward a solitary transcendence, with its radical Protestantism, and with its faith in the redemptive power of labor, prison reform is a discourse whose traces can be discerned throughout Emerson's philosophy and poetics. Precisely because the prison appears somewhat obliquely in his works, and because those works have so profoundly informed how generations of Americans have thought and written about freedom, they serve as an illuminating case study in the powerful, sometimes secret bonds between the history of captivity and the imagery of liberty.

For Emerson, the meaning of solitude took shape in the first week of January 1828. On New Year's Day, in a letter, he imagined "a protestant monastery, a place of elegant seclusion where melancholy gentlemen and ladies may go to spend the advanced season of single life in drinking milk, walking in the woods & reading the Bible & the poets."[18] Whimsical, with a touch of irony, Emerson pictured a mock utopia where solitude and simplicity would free the mind, bringing it into contact with great thoughts and divine currents. In the Protestant monastery, melancholy gentlemen

and ladies of the privileged classes would adopt the habits of rustic laborers, tasting the spiritual delights of transcendence. Milk and meditation
would remedy their melancholy of body and soul. These Protestant
monks would find themselves improved and uplifted—*corrected*, but *gen-
tly*—by the paradoxical, impossible institution of Emerson's fancy.

Seven days after imagining the Protestant monastery, Emerson entered its negative image, the nightmarish inversion of his earlier day-
dream, in a real institution: "In Concord, N.H. I visited the prison &
went into the cells. At this season, they shut up the convicts in these little granite chambers at about 4 o'clock PM & let them out, about 7
o'clock AM—15 dreadful hours."[19] "This season" was the dead of winter
in New England, and the New Hampshire State Prison chilled Emerson's tone, tempering his irony and playfulness. He measured the prisoners' suffering in hours and recorded his dread at the prospect of their lives.
The encounter with condemned bodies in granite cells seems to petrify
Emerson's prose, engaging his fantasies with a melancholy reality, the
modern penitentiary. The meaning of solitude solidifies for Emerson
when the fantastic protestant monastery meets the material prison,
when "elegant seclusion" meets the hard time of incarceration.

From independence, New Hampshire had been, with other Northern states, a leader in prison reform and "humane" punishment. "A
multitude of sanguinary punishments is impolite and unjust," declared
the state constitution, "the true design of all punishments being to reform, and not to exterminate, mankind."[20] In post-Revolutionary New
Hampshire, as in Pennsylvania and New York and Massachusetts, imprisonment had become the standard punishment. The rationalized correspondence between crime and punishment was achieved by adjusting
the length of the prison sentence, and prison labor helped to offset the
cost of the new institutions, even to make them profitable. But the aim
of penitentiary discipline was not just rational organization and efficient
management; as we have seen, the reformers imagined that they could
renovate the very soul of the convict through a regimen of solitary reflection and repentance. In their poetics of punishment, the prisoner
was a flawed spirit in need of correction. The inmate's captivity, properly
administered to produce the cellular soul, should promise him a kind of
freedom—freedom from the vice and guilt that were his true tormenters.
Redemption was the highest aspiration of a movement that hoped, at

least in its early, utopian phase, to improve materially the daily lives of prisoners: "To reform, and not to exterminate, mankind."

Under the direction of Warden Moses Pilsbury (1818–1826), the New Hampshire State Prison had adopted an early version of the Auburn system, achieving two crucial aims of reformed discipline—correction through solitary confinement at night, and economic productivity through congregate labor by day. Pilsbury turned the prison into a stone-cutting workshop, where convict labor processed rough granite to be used in construction. From 1822 forward, his operation earned the state between $1,000 and $5,000 per annum.[21] The inmates' proto-industrial labor was performed in silence, and at night each returned to his cell, to be quarantined from the malignant influence of his fellow convicts. An early twentieth-century historian records that "the satisfactory discipline of the prison was achieved by warden Pilsbury through constant vigilance. He was an ardent believer in separate confinement. Plots, he said, were hatched in night-rooms, and he had frequently overheard whole histories of villainy in listening to the conversations of convicts at night."[22] Pilsbury, detecting and disrupting prisoners' secret exchanges, was a minor champion of reform.

Following Pilsbury's departure in 1826, however, the New Hampshire State Prison deteriorated. A new warden, Abner Stinson, drove it into debt. Stinson was publicly accused of covering his corrupt uses of public goods by destroying documents and falsifying his reports.[23] At the same time, a rising inmate population made solitary confinement impossible in the small prison. The fundamental principle of penitentiary discipline was abandoned. By June 1830, inspectors reported to the state legislature that conditions were "extremely defective. There are only thirty six cells, and between fifty and sixty convicts, and hence two or more are confined all night in the same cell."[24] By 1831, eighty-two men would be held in cells designed to isolate thirty-six.[25] To the eye of reform, this arrangement was dreadful. Thrown together, obscenely intermingling as in the old oubliettes, prisoners were conspiring with—and corrupting—each other. The inspectors feared the spread of disease and disobedience. Overcrowding, they wrote, "gives the old and experienced criminal complete opportunity to instruct the young and inexperienced in the great mysteries of his art, and . . . they seldom fail to be expert and active in this employment."[26] Such contact was disastrous to the aims of correction, disturbing the clear contours of the inmate's individuality, the bound and bordered shape ensured by the solitary cell. A collective, conspiratorial menace was gathering "like a black cloud kept back by the wind which is ready to burst with redoubled fury on the objects in its way."[27] This was the nightmare of a reform discourse that prized the purifying effects of solitude—an image of riot and contamination.

To break up and contain the "black cloud," New Hampshire reformers recommended an expansion of the State Prison and a return to strict enforcement of the Auburn system. More cells and more solitude were called for to break the collectivity; inspectors recommended to the state legislature that prisoners "ought to be debarred the privileges of society, and in silence and solitude to reflect on their evil ways."[28] New Hampshire lawmakers, moved by this argument and attempting to keep pace with the modernization under way in other states, funded the addition of a new cell building, a "north wing." Built in 1832, a few years after Emerson's visit, it contained 120 solitary cells, six feet ten inches by three feet four inches, with six and a half foot ceilings. The Auburn system of night solitude and silent, congregate work by day governed its discipline.[29]

When Emerson saw it in January 1828, the prison was in the decline that would lead to its reform. His "dread," as it turns out, was shared by the warden and the chaplain, by the New Hampshire inspectors, and by the Boston Prison Discipline Society, the major defender of the Auburn system in the United States.[30] The New Hampshire prisoners passed their "fifteen dreadful hours" locked up in their "little granite cells," as Emerson said, away from the woods where his protestant monks went walking, but most did not pass them in solitude. The New Hampshire State Prison was an institution in transition, caught up in controversy—it had once been a jewel of the reform movement, but it was slipping back into the darkness of overcrowding and poor stewardship. By all accounts, the prison was a miserable place, entering a crisis.

Having recovered its history and the language in which that history was being recorded, we can begin to analyze the dread Emerson expressed in January 1828. There are two inviting interpretations. On the one hand, we might think of the prison as the concrete realization of the Protestant monastery, a cold architecture that could have revealed the soul-destroying misery of solitude and led Emerson to abandon his earlier fantasy. Certainly his horror at the "15 dreadful hours" passed each night by the inmates in their cells has none of the romance of "elegant seclusion." On the other hand, however, we might see how Emerson agreed with the prison authorities of the time—his "dread" may have been a fear of intimacy and contagion, rather than of solitude. Emerson's language is so petrified, so bare of elaboration, that the question remains open. Over the next few decades, Emerson's writings would be shaped by a similar tension. He would become a great critic of the tyranny of the majority, unrelenting in his attacks on social structures that coerced consciousness. And yet he would also become a great rhapsodist of the transcendent and solitary self. His essays at once attack oppressive institutions and announce the penitentiary's dream of a cellular soul to the world at large.[31]

Emerson's most intense engagement with the tyranny of the majority—and his most fervent calls for the liberation of the private soul—followed his public fall from grace in the aftermath of the controversial address to the Harvard Divinity School (1838). In his speech to the graduating class, Emerson had attacked the institutions of "Historical Christianity": the oppressive authority of the church, the Bible as the testament of a distant age of miracles, and the worship of Christ as a God on earth, rather than as a common human individual capable of access to the divine. This lecture, initially delivered to an audience of six students and their families, soon became Emerson's most notorious work. The controversy began when the well-known minister Andrews Norton indicted Emerson in print, accusing him of "a great offense" against religion. Norton condemned Emerson and insisted that the truths of Christianity could never be perceived directly, without the mediation of institutions and traditions. The debate soon filled newspapers and journals, and severed Emerson from an increasingly conservative Unitarian establishment. His biographer, Robert D. Richardson, writes that Emerson in this period "was impressed with how society could whip an individual for not conforming."[32] Tried and punished in the public sphere, Emerson came to see himself as a kind of abused convict.[33]

In a key passage written during his conflict with the Unitarians and later included in the seminal essay "Self-Reliance," Emerson imagines the tyranny of the majority as a force that imprisons the individual mind. The young boy not yet initiated into society, Emerson writes, is like a judge who "gives an independent, genuine verdict." In time, however, this independence is lost, and the self is incarcerated: "But the man is as it were clapped into jail by his consciousness. As soon as he has once spoken with *éclat* he is a committed person, watched by the sympathy or the hatred of hundreds, whose affections must now enter into his account."[34] This passage presents Emerson's analysis of the insidious social pressures that coerce the mind in an ostensibly free society. It is comparable to Tocqueville's critique of the tyranny of the majority and to Thoreau's attack on the social cowardice that turned "men" into "machines" and "dogs." The jail cell of Emerson's metaphor, the structure that binds consciousness, is wrought by a panoptic social world, which the individual in his weakness allows to "watch," judge, and sentence him. As Emerson most intensely feels the pressure—as he comes under the disapproving gaze of a society which "is everywhere in conspiracy against the manhood of every one of its members" (178)—the solitary cell becomes a symbol of the isolation and surveillance through which power shackles the private soul.

Publicly censured for his controversial ideas, Emerson devoted himself to liberating "consciousness" from its "jail." His proposed escape was a discipline of solitude. "I am ashamed to think," he admitted, "how easily we capitulate to badges and names, to large societies and dead institutions" (179). The desire for success and fame, for the approval of authorities such as Norton, would only lead to a humiliating submission. Emerson felt that "Solitude is fearsome & heavy hearted," but he clung to the faith that this hardship was the only true way to self-discovery and freedom. In his journal, he called it his "destiny."[35] Indeed, his faith in solitude led him to reject not only the criticism of enemies like Norton but even the company and collaboration of his friends. A few months before the publication of "Self-Reliance," Emerson was invited to join George Ripley's experimental commune at Brook Farm. After a long deliberation, he declined the invitation. According to Richardson, Emerson had decided that he "could join no association that was not based on the recognition that each person is the center of his or her own world."[36] He wrote to Ripley that he had deliberated "very slowly & I may almost say *penitentially*," but had decided that "all I shall solidly do, I must do alone."[37]

Emerson, convinced that the way to liberty was self-reliance, turned his studio into a lonely chamber; he studied the art of solitude. Nor did the "destiny" of solitude belong to Emerson alone. In his public lectures and essays, Emerson promoted a discipline of self-reliance for all. He preached that his listeners had to forgo the temptations of flattery and the comforts of society, devoting themselves instead to the care of their own souls. If they would escape the tyranny of the majority, they had to discover what Emerson called the "aboriginal Self," the primary core of being, undomesticated by society (187). Emerson's model subject declares, "I must be myself. I cannot break myself any longer for you" (193). Above all, "We must go alone" (192).

Only through the rigors of solitary reflection could Emerson's followers prepare themselves for any intervention in the social world. In "Man the Reformer," published in the same year as "Self-Reliance," 1841, Emerson agreed with many of his contemporaries that the "money we spend for courts and prisons is very ill laid out" (144). And he hoped "that each person whom I address has felt his own call to cast aside all evil customs, timidities, and limitations, and to be in his place a free and helpful man, a reformer" (130). But reform, for Emerson, began with the self. The transformation of institutions such as the prison was a necessary and useful undertaking—but the reformer must be concerned above all with the correction of his own soul. "I think we must clear ourselves each one," writes Emerson, "by the interrogation, whether we have earned our bread to-day . . . and we must not cease to *tend* to the correction of flagrant wrongs, by laying one stone aright every day" (142, emphasis original). In a surprising reversal, it is the reformers, not the prisoners, who are charged with the task of self-correction.

Using the language of criminal justice and the imagery of architecture, Emerson's call for self-discipline has much in common with the vocabulary of prison reform. Indeed, it seems to invoke the key image of the penitentiary, the cellular soul. For Emerson, of course, the discipline of solitude is by no means designed to produce obedient workers or submissive believers. It is designed to free the soul from the prison-house of the social world. What Emerson imagines, then, is a subversion of reform's cellular soul. In Emerson's figure, the cell is not the private guilt of the soul, projected outward, but an intrusive social pressure. The bound, central self is not remorse struggling to repair guilt but the "nonconformist" agent freeing itself from and expressing itself against the falsity of "customs." To achieve a genuine redemption, in Emerson's vision, the prisoner would have to push his deviant individuality through the walls of social pressure in a liberating jailbreak. The drama of self-redemption is recast: the soul saves itself not by coming into unison with social standards but by discovering and adhering to those aspects of itself that are the most deviant, the most peculiar and therefore, paradoxically, the most universal and divine. "Nothing is at last sacred but the integrity of your own mind" (178). Deviancy, the contemptuous disregard of social strictures, is the method and the sign of self-reliance.

"No law can be sacred to me," Emerson insists, "but that of my nature" (179). With his poetics of self-liberation, Emerson might be understood as a subversive who turns the oppressive designs of the modern prison inside out. Insisting that the "consciousness" produced by modern society is an effect of coercion, Emerson protests the institutions of social control. The penitentiary seeks, through isolation and surveillance, to render inmates docile and submissive. Emerson despises docility and submission; his discipline seeks to cultivate a radical individualism. The penitentiary goes straight for the soul, but Emerson's soul rises gloriously above the cage of conformity.

Emerson's subversion of the cellular soul, however, is an ambivalent triumph. He calls for a program of personal exploration and development, but what are the consequences of self-reliance in the social world? In order to understand them, it is necessary to see how Emerson's imagination moves across the boundary between the material and the abstract. Russ Castronovo has criticized Emerson's tendency toward a kind of abstraction that abandons the problem of how freedom might actually be realized in a heterogeneously embodied social world: for Emerson, "the poet's consciousness must be purified, ascending from mountains to stellar climes to heaven itself. Stripped of earthly trappings, he enters a generalized citizenship."[38] Emerson's engagement with structures of coercion such as the prison actually depends on two levels of abstraction. First, prison reformers introduce the image of the cellular soul, using a poetics of punishment that obscures the realities of stone cells and confined bodies. Second, Emerson uses the prisoner, the figure "clapped into jail," as a metaphor for modern consciousness *in general*: everybody is, in a sense, an inmate, suffering a universal kind of mental captivity. This double abstraction, in the end, is what enables Emerson's protest of coercive institutions. The discourse of prison reform provides him with the metaphor of the cellular soul, and he imagines opposition by subverting it. Abstraction allows him to turn the poetics of the penitentiary against itself.

Ascending into the ether of abstraction—transcending the world— enables Emerson to tinker with prison reform's conceptual figure, to master and redeploy it in new directions, but abstraction also limits his protest. If the coercion of the cell is mainly a state of mind, if everybody in the social world is really a prisoner, then the particular violence of life inside real prisons can be forgotten. Emerson's call for a universal liberation ignores the most physically urgent, most torturous kinds of unfreedom at work in his time and place. The walls of the New Hampshire State Prison, for instance, all but disappear. Now you see the criminal soul correcting itself, now you don't see muscle against stone. Now you see the prisoner as a metaphor, now you don't see the Auburn system and its silent laborers. In Emerson's view, a common redemptive "light dawns welcome alike into the closet of the philosopher, into the garret of toil, and into prison-cells" (126). Like Tocqueville in his own century and Foucault in the next, Emerson saw a coercive penitentiary reproduced throughout modern society, locking subjectivity into a "jail" of docility and conformity—and he called for all subjects, both bound and ostensibly free, to liberate their minds. But the very scope of the insight leads away from the prison, away from all institutions, into the self. Locating the struggle for liberty within "consciousness," Emerson imagines a free society that in many ways re-creates the disembodiment and alienation of the penitentiary system.

As early as 1815, the Board of Directors of the Massachusetts State Prison had drafted a code of discipline for reformed prisons, a model that would eventually shape the practice of the Auburn system: "The diet of a convict ought, though wholesome and sufficient to support the calls of nature, to be of the coarsest kind; his clothes, while calculated to keep him warm, ought to be so arranged as to be considered as a means of punishment; his mind ought to be reduced to a state of humiliation and discipline; all intercourse with each other, and more especially with the world, ought to be suppressed . . . if the convict wishes to commune with the world, let him do it by reading moral books . . . the prison should be considered as a world by itself, and its inhabitants know nothing of what is passing without its orbit."[39] By 1841, thirteen years after his conception of the Protestant monastery and his visit to the New Hampshire State

Prison, Emerson had composed his own disciplinary code, one that sub-stantially echoed the premises of prison reform. These were his charges not to convicts but to melancholy gentlemen like himself—especially to the free person who felt "any strong bias to poetry, to art, to the contem-plative life": "That man ought to reckon early with himself, and, respect-ing the compensations of the Universe, ought to ransom himself . . . by a certain rigor and privation in his habits. For privileges so rare and grand, let him not stint to pay a great tax. Let him be a caenobite, a pauper, and if need be, celibate also. Let him learn to eat his meals standing, and to relish the taste of fair water and black bread. . . . He must live in a chamber, and postpone his self-indulgence, forewarned and forearmed against that frequent misfortune of men of genius—the taste for luxury" (139). In its subjunctive commandments, its invocation of the solitary cham-ber, its denigration of human collectivities for the communion of books and the "compensations of the Universe," even in its sexual prohibitions, Emerson's program re-creates the isolation and asceticism of the Auburn program. Like the reformers who built the "congregate" system around the cellular soul, Emerson dreamed of a redeemed "man . . . who in the midst of the crowd keeps with perfect sweetness the independence of solitude" (181). The discipline of his Protestant monasticism, now recon-ceived as a transcendentalist practice, promises a redemption, but it re-quires the mortification of the body and the isolation of the soul.

In Jeremy Bentham's panoptic system, a chaplain positioned at the center of the prison would allow the inmates "to receive the benefits of attendance on Divine service . . . without stirring from their [solitary] cells."[40] In Emerson's "Self-Reliance," this Protestant monastery reap-pears: "I like the silent church . . . better than any preaching. How far off, how cool, how chaste the persons look, begirt each one with a precinct or a sanctuary! So let us always sit" (192). Perhaps inspired by the si-lence of Quaker religious services, this frigid and lonesome arrange-ment of selves also repeats the penitentiary's atomized social pattern. Emerson reconfigures meanings and reassigns value, but he accepts the cellular soul, a disembodied and isolated self. He finally takes a view quite similar to that of the New Hampshire reformers, recoiling from collectivity as from a contagion. He assembles a congregation only in or-der to sever any connection among its members, sentencing each to an inescapable solitude.

BAFFLING KEY

Emerson had set out to free the self from a society that watched and judged it, from the subtle but insidious tyranny of the majority. He had seen the prison's disciplinary techniques at work everywhere in the modern world, and he had searched for an escape. He called on his listeners to look within themselves, to see what cages they had built through undue obedience to "badges" and "institutions," and to liberate the "aboriginal Self" from the false binds of "consciousness." His social critique had led him inward, to the structures of subjectivity, and to a vision of self-reliance that subverted the penitentiary's cellular soul. Yet this clever escape had perhaps depended too much on the architecture of captivity. It led back, after all, to a discipline of ascetic forbearance and "fearsome" solitude—back to the prison of the self. The liberated society Emerson envisioned appeared ominously similar to the penitentiary's silent and inward-looking congregation.

Emerson's "Self-Reliance" presents the most extreme version of contradictions that shaped much of his generation's struggle to imagine a free selfhood that could oppose the institutions of unfreedom. The Romantics, with their deep commitment to the "integrity" of the private soul, often retreated from the real world of contingent, interdependent politics, into a disembodied and radically isolated subjectivity. Even in the modern age of a tyranny that went "straight for the soul," they held onto the fantasy of a soul rising gloriously above the violent grasp of power. Their poetics of personal escape have proved to have great force and endurance in the American imagination. For hundreds of years, people confronting various tyrannies have drawn from this resource. Indeed, the image of an inviolable core of being—a selfhood deeper than skin and bone, eluding the assaults and degradations of punishment—is among the most common tropes in the writings of those living and dying inside prison walls. Judee Norton, an inmate at the State Prison Complex in Goodyear, Arizona, writing in 1990, is one of many who have invoked such a self:

> I am captured
> But not subdued
> THEY
> Think they have me

> but
>
>   my mind
>   wheels and soars and spins and shouts
> no prisoner
> I am free[41]

No saw can pierce this soul, and no prison can hold it; it rises above power, soaring and spinning into a private heaven of freedom. Like Dickinson on the rack or Thoreau in his Concord jail cell, Norton's speaker is bound in body but liberated in the private, infinite space of the "mind."

The tradition of writing about the modern penitentiary also presents another view of the imprisoned self, one that seeks a different liberation. Here and there in the literature of the antebellum period is a subject that yields its own "integrity," the self-containing structure of the cellular soul, and sees itself composed of many voices, myriad possibilities. It imagines freedom not in a redeemed solitude but in contact and concert with others. It turns its attention not inward but out, through the stone walls and iron gates, in search of company. The solitude and "rigours of prison," as Jean Genet writes in *The Miracle of the Rose*, "drive us toward each other in bursts of love without which we could not live."[42]

The early penitentiaries in Philadelphia and Pittsburg, even Auburn's notorious "north wing," were plagued by what Beaumont and Tocqueville called "the contagion of mutual communications," as prisoners discovered ways to mitigate the rigors of isolation (113–114). When the walls of the cells were built of the thickest and densest stone, inmates sometimes used the plumbing systems or the ventilation ducts to whisper in the night. To the architects of the penitentiary system, communication signified pestilence and corruption. To the inmates, it meant at least some consolation from loneliness, at most the possibility of a concerted resistance. Without romanticizing such desperate practices, we can see how the sounds of other voices may have promised an escape from the penitentiary's designs that would not return the self to solitude. Instead, it would yield the boundaries of the self to multiplicity:

> Alone, I cannot be—
> For Hosts—do visit me—
> Recordless Company—
> Who baffle Key— (298)

In this poem, Dickinson imagines a self that, even though it has been withdrawn from the world, into solitude, receives mysterious and nameless visitors. Unlike the lyric about "madness" and "sense," which considers the psychic consequences of the tyranny of the majority, these verses present an isolated self that is in contact with a company of vagrant, elusive entities. Dickinson reverses the ordinary meaning of "host"—her speaker is visited not by *guests* but by a multitude of *hosts*; the two correlative terms slide into one another. At the same time, Dickinson invokes a range of other connotations, including military and religious ones and, perhaps most faintly but also most hauntingly, the archaic use of "host" to mean "a victim of sacrifice." Indeed, since the prison cell was imagined as a scene of penitence and salvation, the language of punishment in the age of the penitentiary often echoes the language of religious ritual. Even in the isolation of her chamber, Dickinson feels herself to be in the company of "Recordless" others, remnants of exclusion and sacrifice to whom she must play the host.

The "Company" that visits Dickinson is able to "baffle Key"—another phrase with several meanings. To baffle key is, in one sense, to pick a lock and pass through a fastened door. But there may also be a reference here to the "keys" of music; the "Company" is a chorus of voices without order or harmony—a dissonant multitude. By the end of the poem, with the discovery that the voices are "never gone," Dickinson suggests that they are more than visitors—they may actually constitute the self, a multiplicity that never quite resolves into integrity. Thus Dickinson's speaker, though withdrawn from the social world, experiences the collapse of the two pillars of the penitentiary system: Philadelphia's absolute solitude and Auburn's inviolable silence.

Dickinson's myriad self has a counterpart in the poetry of Walt Whitman, where the "callous shell" of the ego yields to the electric intimacies of a self that "contain[s] multitudes."[43] Like Dickinson, Whitman imagines a subjectivity constituted by the several voices that pass through it: "Through me many long dumb voices, / Voices of the interminable generations of prisoners and slaves."[44] To some recent critics, Whitman's acts of identification seem to mask a project of exclusion—his containment of multitudes becomes an allegory of an expanding American empire, or of a false sympathy that speaks for "prisoners and slaves" but does not invite them to speak for themselves. For other readers and writers in the twentieth century, however, particularly those who have explicitly engaged the long history of the American prison, the myriad selves of Dickinson and Whitman would provide a more promising legacy.

The golden age of the penitentiary lasted only about a generation, from the 1820s, when the great model institutions opened their doors in Pennsylvania and New York, to the Civil War. The upheavals of the 1860s transformed the political, economic, and legal order of the United States, altering the foundations of the prison system. The rupture was perhaps most profoundly felt in the South, where the antebellum disciplinary structure had depended on a near-perfect segregation between the penitentiary and the plantation. As we have seen, the penitentiary's promise of rebirth involved various forms of mortification that had much in common with the practices of slavery, but the reformers had made every effort to deny the connection, defining their humanitarian project against the brutal plantation. In the aftermath of Reconstruction and the Civil War amendments, Southern states dismantled the old structure and recomposed its elements into a kind of hybrid, the "prison farm," at sites like Angola, Cummins, and Parchman. Profound changes in the character of incarceration were under way outside the South, too, particularly in the West, where the "Indian Wars" of the 1860s deployed a combination of military force and mass captivity that had little to do with "correction."

The Civil War represents a turning point in the history of the United States, but for those who have seen how deeply violence, exclusion, and captivity inform the meanings of belonging and freedom on the American scene, the story is one of both transition and continuity. Like the classic penitentiary, postwar carceral spaces were taken up in twentieth-century expression—in the post-Reconstruction South, the prison blues of Parchman Farm and the fiction of William Faulkner, among others; in the frontier West, the verses of the Native American poets such as Jimmy Santiago Baca and Simon Ortiz. In the prison blues and in Faulkner's novels, mobile and "myriad" and modes of being would replace the static architecture of the cellular soul. In the poetry of Ortiz and Baca, composed in captivity in Colorado and Arizona, Whitman's aesthetics would be invoked in an effort to imagine forms of contact between captives and captors, victims and victors. Thus as the penitentiary evolved and merged with its counterparts, the plantation and the reservation, its Romantic poetics, too, began their long and various afterlives. In each case, the isolated and disembodied version of human identity enshrined in the solitary confinement cell is rejected: in Faulkner and the blues, each self is composed of many voices, and may therefore enter into a transindividual chorus; in the poems of the Native American inmates, the harrowing of the self leads not to redemption but to an elemental, inhuman condition of being.

Reckoning with twentieth-century spaces of captivity, these verbal artists would call on an ancestry that includes not only Romantic poets such as Dickinson and Whitman but also what Whitman called the "voices of interminable generations of prisoners and slaves": plantation work songs, memoirs of incarceration, narratives of captivity from dark, mysterious frontiers. Together, these various works make up the beginnings of an imaginative tradition that illuminates the afterlife of the penitentiary and, at the same time, provides an alternative to the rigid forms of identity politics that define much contemporary critique of the American prison. In the archive explored here, human identity is not only formed by the blood and cultural community it inherits; it is made, unmade, and remade by the violence and captivity it endures. Passing through these phases, the self discovers in language the possibility of a mediation between the prison and the world at large, between the living and the dead.

PART THREE AFTERLIVES

In this central and centralized humanity, the effect and instrument of complex power relations, bodies and forces subjected by multiple mechanisms of "incarceration" . . . we must hear the distant roar of battle.

—MICHEL FOUCAULT, *Discipline and Punish (308)*

they didn't know
that walls
would be constructed,
that wars were to make
these men possible.

—SIMON J. ORTIZ, *from Sand Creek (87)*

CHAPTER FIVE

Mississippi Voices

IN THE CHORUS OF CHARACTERS making up William Faulkner's *Absalom, Absalom!* (1936) is the minor figure of Goodhue Coldfield, "that queer silent man whose only companion and friend seems to have been his conscience."[1] When the Civil War erupts, Coldfield closes his dry-goods store in protest and withdraws from the world: "He mounted to the attic with his hammer and his handful of nails," writes Faulkner, "and nailed the door behind him and threw the hammer out the window." His daughter, Rosa, passes food to him in a basket "by means of a well pulley and rope attached to the attic window." Coldfield spends three years in his "voluntary incarceration," a kind of self-imposed solitary confinement, while Rosa, pressed into service as his attendant, begins to hate him. Her hatred nourishes her faith in the honor and romance of the Confederate cause, and in her own solitude she writes the first of her thousand "odes to Southern soldiers" (65).[2]

Then Coldfield dies, and something striking happens in Faulkner's prose. The passage begins in clipped sentences that seem to belong to a different novel: "Then he died. One morning the hand did not come out to draw up the basket." With this death, however, the narrating voice changes: "The old nails were still in the door and neighbors helped her break it in with axes and they found him, who had seen his sole means of support looted by the defenders of his cause, even if he had repudiated it

141

and them, with three days' uneaten food beside his pallet bed as if he had spent the three days in a mental balancing of his terrestrial accounts, found the result and proved it and then turned upon his contemporary scene of folly and outrage and injustice the dead and consistent impassivity of a cold and inflexible disapproval" (65–66). When the solitary, self-incarcerated objector dies, when his cell is torn open by an assembly of unnamed "neighbors," Faulkner's rhythm shifts away from short, static sentences, away from a "cold and inflexible" style; it moves to the undulant voice of *Absalom, Absalom!* itself, which is not so much any character-narrator's voice as what Peter Brooks calls the "transindividual voice that speaks through all of Faulkner's characters."[3] As Coldfield passes away, two images of subjectivity are starkly opposed: the minister is immured both in his stern "conscience" and in his makeshift cell, walled up in a fortified self; the group of neighbors strikes like a wave at the walls, finally entering the citadel of Coldfield's solitude and reclaiming his remains for its "cause." The encounter between these two subjectivities is enacted not only in Faulkner's plot but also on the textual surface, in the shapes and rhythms of the prose. Each model of selfhood, the solitary and the communal, has its own distinctive voice. "Cold and inflexible" sentences yield, at the instant of Coldfield's passing, to the fluid, dynamic speech of an undifferentiated collective.

The little story of Goodhue Coldfield's "voluntary incarceration" and solitary death is easily overlooked, but it has the illuminating power of a parable. Like the speaker of Dickinson's "Alone, I cannot be," Coldfield builds an imperfect chamber for his seclusion and reflections—a host of other voices enters, baffling key. For Dickinson, the intrusion of "numberless company" is a matter of the soul's character; the speaker discovers, in solitude, that the self is composed of many, sometimes dissonant voices. For Faulkner, by contrast, the decomposition of the cellular soul seems instead to be a historical event, transpiring during the Civil War, the traumatic historical rupture that terminates the plantation order and inaugurates a confused modernity. An important and understudied part of that transformation, as we shall see, was the dismantling and reconstruction of the Old South's penal structure: when Coldfield enters solitary confinement, he is practicing a form of discipline that, in the wider world of the wartime South, is being destroyed. In this and other surprising ways, *Absalom, Absalom!*, one of the monumental achievements of American modernist prose, takes up the problem of the penitentiary's afterlife in the late nineteenth and twentieth centuries.

Just before the Civil War, as the plantation economy reached its fullest development, Mississippi built a segregated disciplinary system that included a reformed penitentiary for white convicts and notorious bodily punishments such as the lash and the branding iron for unruly slaves. When Emancipation forced the South to reconstruct its penal system, new systems emerged: first the convict-lease system, then the great carceral plantation known as Parchman Farm. The racist, dehumanizing violence of slavery clearly persisted in these postwar disciplines, which degraded the convict and extracted his labor without mercy. It may be more difficult to discern what role, if any, the penitentiary—with its goals of rehabilitation and human redemption—played in the making of twentieth-century Southern prisons.

The question raises a critical controversy. On one side are those who see twentieth-century prisons, in the South and elsewhere, as little more than the new plantations, spaces of dehumanization and servile labor justified by the Thirteenth Amendment's provision that there must be "neither slavery nor involuntary servitude, *except as punishment for crime* whereof the party shall have been duly convicted."[4] On the other side are those who, following Foucault, see the twentieth-century prison as a more or less continuous elaboration of Enlightenment reforms, a progressively refined institution for the disciplining of modern subjects. Does the contemporary prison descend from the plantation, or from the penitentiary? Again, the institution seems to represent an irreconcilable opposition between, on the one hand, an institution beyond the pale of the body politic and, on the other hand, an exemplary scene of subject-making. In critical studies of Southern prisons, the opposition involves a deep disagreement about the role of race, which, depending on the critic's position, may appear either fundamental or virtually irrelevant to the design of the American prison system in the twentieth century and beyond.

The expressive voices rising from Mississippi in the 1920s and 1930s provide a different way of imagining the post-Reconstruction prison and its relations to the social world at large. For Faulkner, the end of the plantation order meant, among many other things, the emergence of a fluid, dynamic, and miscegenated collectivity that was both an object of new disciplinary structures and, potentially, a subject of liberation from the old cell of the self. The voice of this collective can be heard not only in Faulkner's experimental prose forms but also, perhaps even more vitally, in the blues music of his Southern contemporaries, including rambling legends like Robert Johnson and the often anonymous singers of the prison blues in Parchman, Angola, and other prison farms—music that records the violence of prison life but also certain promising strategies of endurance and hopes of liberation.

MISSISSIPPI DISCIPLINE

From 1795, when the United States acquired the territory from Spain, until about 1820, discipline in Mississippi was a disorganized affair. Faulkner would describe the territory in this frontier period as "a region where for no more than the boots on his feet, men would murder a traveler and gut him like a bear or deer or fish and fill the cavity with rocks and sink the evidence in the nearest water."[5] No unified legal code governed criminal justice, and convicts, depending on their class and reputation, the drunkenness or sobriety of the judge, and other contingencies, might receive the lightest or the most severe of sentences.[6] Discipline was often carried out at the fringes of government structures. The bowie knives and lynching ropes of vigilantes became notorious. Slaves, meanwhile, were generally consigned to the control of their overseers and masters, whose discretion in the matter of punishment was virtually unlimited.

In 1821, Governor George Poindexter drew up a uniform code of crimes and punishments. Poindexter, however, was no reformer; he sought only to describe and organize the system of punishment, such as it was, that he had inherited. For most serious offenses, the penalty was hanging, in public, before an assembly of spectators. Other punishments included branding—thieves, for instance, received a *T* on the palm and face—whipping of up to thirty-nine lashes, and terms in the state's squalid county jails, often dirt-floor shacks where fugitive slaves slept beside white convicts. Faulkner writes of "local brawlers and drunkards and runaway slaves" held alike in Jefferson's one-room "log-and-mudchinking jail."[7] Mississippi's criminal law under Poindexter, in the analysis of one historian, remained a "bloody one based upon the principles of *retributive rather than corrective* justice."[8]

The confused and often cruel conditions of frontier justice in Mississippi persisted into the 1830s, when major social transformations broke them apart. By 1831 a booming cotton economy, together with an increasingly oppressive slave code throughout the South, had given rise to the full-scale plantation order. Mississippi's population boomed. Immigrants came from Virginia and Kentucky, Louisiana and Ohio—some, like Faulkner's Thomas Sutpen, the antihero of *Absalom, Absalom!*, to make their fortunes in cotton, some to build the new infrastructure, and many thousands more to work the fields. With these rapid changes came an anxious sense that the old criminal code would no longer suffice. An observer described the river towns churning with "villains of every description, outlaws from other States, [and] refugees from justice."[9] At the same time, the humanitarian rhetoric of reform began to appear in newspapers and pamphlets. The criminal justice system was not only ineffective; it was a cruel and shameful relic of barbarism in a civilized age. The old laws were failing, obsolete.

When the Jacksonian Democrats took control of the state government in 1831, they began revising the codes of crime and punishment. For guidance, they looked toward the international reform movement that had already redefined punishment in Philadelphia and New York. No longer a decentralized affair depending on violent spectacles—whipping, branding, and the lash—discipline in the North now sought to rehabilitate criminals into moral citizens and productive laborers. The age of the penitentiary was under way. By the 1830s, a number of Southern states had experimented with Northern disciplinary models. Mississippi lawmakers, hoping that industrialized prison labor would earn money for the state, decided to adopt the New York system of solitary confinement by night and congregate labor by day. In early 1836, the legislature appointed an architect, William Nichols, to design a penitentiary at Jackson, and set aside $75,000 for its construction. Like its Northern models, the institution surrounded its modern cellblocks with an imposing façade; the state penitentiary was popularly known as "The Walls."

In Mississippi as in other states, the prison was intended to organize and regulate discipline, and especially to break up the conspiracies and contagions that appeared to fester in the local jails. With these strategic aims came the familiar poetics of punishment, the discourse of solitary

confinement as a corrective discipline, leading the prisoner through reflection and repentance to redemption. Nichols promised that his design
would combine "salutary discipline and profitable labor, with moral instruction."[10] The penitentiary chaplain declared that the convict under
his instruction "should be viewed with an eye of compassion, and . . . we
can reclaim him to virtue and to God."[11] By 1844, a committee reported to
the state legislature that the Jackson penitentiary was admirably carrying
out the "science of penal infliction," so that "the moral sense, blunted if
not obliterated by crime, [would] be put into a course of training calculated to restore its vitality, and give it power again . . . to control action,
and shape the destinies of the once lost, but now renovated human being."[12] With its narrative of perdition and reclamation, the committee's
praise echoed Benjamin Rush's lines, written a half-century earlier, on
the "house of correction" as an institution whose remade subject "was
lost, and is found—was dead and is alive." The solitary cell and the penitentiary regimen, in the eyes of reformers, brought a philanthropic, soul-
transforming discipline to Mississippi. The dream of carceral death and
rebirth, developed by a transatlantic reform movement and monumentalized in Philadelphia and Auburn, had arrived in the frontier South.

The penitentiary was defended both as a stern response to crime and
as a modern, enlightened alternative to older, "savage" punishments. Calling for reform, a newspaper had raised this outraged cry: "Will the pillory
still disgrace a civilized age? Will the branding iron still be exhibited in
the courts of justice to the dishonor of humanity . . . ? Will the thirty-nine
lashes still be prescribed by our bloody criminal code?"[13] Thus the pious
outrage against "bloody" discipline in Mississippi followed the lead of
Euro-American reform, repeating the old slogans of Howard, Roscoe,
and Vaux about the humanity of convicts, the reclamation of lost souls.
But in plantation Mississippi other connotations must also have been
heard, giving an ironic edge to public protests against the lash. The horror of the criminal code was that it treated white convicts like beasts, like
creatures less than human—in other words, like slaves. When both white
and black offenders were made to suffer under the lash, the differences
between them were difficult to discern. The Mississippi penitentiary
would not do away with spectacular and humiliating punishments, but it
would confine them to the plantations, where they would be inflicted only
on the black bodies of slaves. The penitentiary at Jackson served a variety

of purposes, but crucial among them was that it lifted white convicts out of the collective suffering and conspiratorial menace that the popular imagination associated with blackness. With its solitary cells, its industrial labor, its literacy program, and its corrective ambition, the penitentiary defined itself, in part, against the plantation.

Built on plans borrowed from the North, the Southern penitentiary would train its convicts in factory work, and it would achieve its corrective aims through the spiritual action of solitary reflection. This discipline required a penitent conscience and a corrective will, the makings of the cellular soul, which were granted to the white convict in a gesture that reinforced their removal from the black slave. In other words, the Southern penitentiary served, in part, as an institution that reinforced race, rather than class, as the first principle of solidarity and difference in Southern society. In Virginia, where a significant number of "free blacks" were incarcerated, a committee of inspectors put it bluntly: "Although the . . . white persons usually confined to the penitentiary are . . . from the lowest part of society . . . yet the free Negroes and mulattoes are a grade or so below them, and should not be associated with them."[14] In Mississippi, "free" blacks made up only about 1 percent of the prison population, and no slaves were held in the penitentiary. The penal historian Thorsten Sellin observes that "criminal slaves were hanged, mutilated, or flogged," while the penitentiary "was to house criminals from the master class."[15] The white convict might be redeemed through solitude, repenting his way into the "master class." The masses of slaves on the plantations, meanwhile, would continue to suffer under the whip.

The Georgia lawyer Thomas R. R. Cobb, in his authoritative *Inquiry into the History of Negro Slavery*, insisted, "The condition of the slave renders it impossible to inflict on him the ordinary punishments, by pecuniary fine, by imprisonment, or by banishment." The white soul could be renovated by penitence, but the slave, wrote Cobb, "can be reached only through his body."[16] In law and in the public imagination, then, the penitentiary segregated punishment in Mississippi. No longer would white criminals and captive slaves be chained together in the crowded jails. Within The Walls, reformed discipline would move white prisoners toward self-correction; on the plantation, the whip would continue to drive the labor of black bodies. This opposition defined discipline in the Magnolia State from the 1830s until the Civil War, roughly the period when Faulkner's Thomas Sutpen rises from the position of a marginal outsider, eyed with suspicion, to the control of his own plantation.

Toni Morrison has described the "spectacle of enslavement" as the "anodyne to individualism" in Faulkner and other American writers—"individualism is foregrounded," she writes, "when its background is stereotypified, enforced dependency."[17] A similar foregrounding organizes Mississippi's disciplinary structure in the decades just before the Civil War. The penitentiary conjures the cellular soul, a figure of self-binding subjectivity imported from Auburn. The plantation, by contrast, controls an undifferentiated collectivity, a laboring mass almost organic to the fields. It is important to recognize, however, that this is an opposition internal to the larger structure of discipline: the white solitary and the black collective are separate *objects* of containment and control. The plantation and the penitentiary draw from eighteenth- and nineteenth-century Anglo-American culture for their poetics of punishment, but these disciplinary structures are not only the effects of cultural fantasies about racialized subjectivities—as if the convict, thanks to his whiteness, were already a self-governing subject when he entered the solitary cell; or as if the black slave were born without humanity. Rather, the penitentiary and the plantation are the furnaces in which such subjectivities are forged and enforced on convicts and slaves. As the sociologist Loïc Wacquant has observed, such institutions are "major engine[s] of symbolic production" where lines of social distinction are drawn. They do not merely assume difference; they make and mark it.[18]

In its original form, The Walls stood in continuous operation for less than thirty years. It was burned by Sherman's Union troops in 1863. The structure of a perfectly segregated discipline had perhaps never been more than a fiercely pursued fantasy, but when "total war" swept through the South even the fantasy went up in smoke. The Thirteenth Amendment, outlawing slavery except as punishment for a crime, irreparably disturbed the boundary between convict and slave, and Mississippi's government now undertook to police and contain criminals of all colors.[19] In particular, the state became responsible for punishing black offenders who earlier would have been left in the hands of their masters, a potentially overwhelming task for an impoverished administration that was struggling to rebuild its infrastructure and to cope with the sweeping social changes set in motion by Emancipation. The penitentiary at Jackson was repaired and reopened for a while, but it was again used almost exclusively for white criminals serving sentences of more than ten years.[20] The punishment of black convicts on a much larger scale would require new kinds of institutions. Indeed, the state's penal system would expand rapidly and dramatically in the postwar years, as if to rebuild the racist social structure of the plantation era under the sign of criminal justice.

Persuaded by opportunists such as the wealthy planter Edmund Richardson, lawmakers developed the temporary fix known as the "Mississippi Plan" of convict leasing. Under this system, adopted in 1876, the hundreds of (mostly black) convicts sentenced to prison terms were not, in fact, held in prisons; instead, their labor was sold to major landholders and industrialists around the state. Convict leasing brought a modest profit to the state and allowed Richardson and some others to regain the wealth they had lost in the war. It left the convicts themselves exposed to violence and neglect at the hands of new overseers with virtually no obligations toward their well-being.[21]

The historian Alexander Lichtenstein has described convict leasing as a "New South slavery" that retained the racism and brutality of the plantation, reconstituting "a system of forced labor in an age of emancipation."[22] Along similar lines, David Oshinsky records that "in terms of human misery . . . this system could hardly have been worse. The convict now found himself laboring for the profits of three separate parties: the sublessee, the lessee, and the state. There was no one to protect him from savage beatings, endless workdays, and murderous neglect."[23] To convicts, the new slavery of the Mississippi Plan seemed at least as bad as life on the antebellum plantations. Many risked their lives to escape. Many others were murdered or allowed to die of disease or exposure.[24] The anonymous narrator of the short narrative originally published in 1904 as "The New Slavery in the South—An Autobiography, by a Georgia Negro Peon," describes life in the convict-lease system as "a hell on earth" where convicts slept in stables like livestock, worked from dawn until dark in the fields, and were beaten with horsewhips for minor offenses.[25]

The convict-lease system ruled in Mississippi for about a quarter century, into the early 1900s, when the populist and white supremacist James Kimble Vardaman won the governorship and undertook the construction of a vast new prison. Vardaman was driven by several motives.

FIGURE 4. Prisoners working in the fields of the Mississippi State Penitentiary, or Parchman Farm, 1935. Untitled photograph by Estelle Caro, in the collection of the Beinecke Library, Yale University.

A favorite son of the state's poor white population, even a kind of populist, he wanted to reclaim the huge profits generated by convict labor from the elites who had used them to build up an aristocratic wealth and prestige after Reconstruction. In his public attacks on convict leasing, Vardaman even made use of the humanitarian rhetoric of reformers who protested its excessive violence. But he also, and quite explicitly, planned to build into the penitentiary system the segregating and humiliating discipline of the plantation—the structure that, in Vardaman's eyes, had established the racial hierarchy of domination and submission that had undergirded the social order of the Old South. As W. J. Cash notes in *The Mind of the South*, Vardaman belonged to a generation of political demagogues whose race-baiting rhetoric from the stump became legendary. "The way to control the nigger," he announced, "is to whip him when he does not obey without it."[26]

The product of Vardaman's penal scheme was Parchman Farm, a sprawling prison on the grounds of an old cotton plantation in the Yazoo Delta, ninety miles south of Memphis, in William Faulkner's corner of the state (figure 4). After its opening in 1904, the majority of Mississippi's black convicts were no longer leased to private enterprise. They worked in Parchman's cotton fields, owned and managed by the state, which now reaped the profits of their labor. In its discipline, as in its architecture and landscape, Parchman Farm reproduced the old regime of the plantation. Its inmates worked long hours in the fields, where they were watched over by mounted trustees carrying whips and shotguns. Those who failed or refused to work were flogged; those who resisted or attempted to escape were killed. The civil death of felony replaced the social death of chattel slavery, and the work songs of the antebellum fields evolved into the prison blues. As Oshinsky and others have shown, Parchman was a monument to the post-Reconstruction South's efforts to restore the order—and the racist terror—of the past. More than 90 percent of its inmates in the early 1900s were black men, and the small white population was likely to enjoy a position of relative comfort and authority, performing secretarial work in the offices or, in some cases, overseeing the work of the blacks in the fields.[27] Vardaman's dream of an enormous state-owned plantation had been realized.

In the decades after its opening, however, Parchman's racial order underwent a change. As industrializing cities such as St. Louis and Chicago began to recruit their workforce from the South, drawing African Americans to the North and Midwest in the "Great Migration," Mississippi's black population declined. Then, as the Southern agricultural economy collapsed into the Depression, impoverished whites were convicted of crimes in unprecedented numbers: "For the first time since Reconstruction," Oshinsky notes, "significant numbers of [whites] were being convicted for crimes of hunger, not honor, crimes of 'niggers' and slaves."[28] By the mid-1930s, white men made up nearly a third of Parchman's inmates. More and more, their working and living conditions approached those of the abused and degraded African American prisoners. In the late 1920s and early 1930s, the state prison was among the last in the country that still flogged inmates, lashing them with a whip called "Black Annie." As late as 1968, the Southern Regional Council published an attack on Parchman's "brutality, lack of treatment or training programs, very low salaries, continued use of armed convict guards, [and] neglect," all of which constituted "a system . . . far below any reasonable minimum standard."[29]

The reformers of the Southern Regional Council, like Oshinsky and virtually all other critics of the Jim Crow prison farm, emphasize its deep continuities with the antebellum plantation. Indeed, Vardaman had explicitly conceived of Parchman as a zone of penal slavery for the post-Emancipation and post-Reconstruction era. Reflecting on the prison farm's extreme labor exploitation, Faulkner writes of the inmates that "the land they farmed and the substance they produced from it belonged neither to them who worked it nor to those who forced them at guns' point to do so."[30] The prison farm was built on plantation land, devoted to cotton production, and organized, at least in its first few decades, according to a rigid racial segregation. By the 1930s, however, conditions in the prison, as in Mississippi at large, were deeply unstable. Parchman's laboring convicts were no longer exclusively black, and the prison, once an institution for the enforcement of racial difference, was beginning to host a mixed population. The inmates working in its cotton fields were not only the descendants of slaves but also the grandchildren of masters and poor whites.

In *Old Man*, a story written in the late 1930s but set in 1927, Faulkner seems to have taken for granted that punishment in Mississippi was becoming integrated. He writes in the novella's opening passages that "there is no walled penitentiary in Mississippi; it is a cotton plantation where the convicts work under the rifles and shotguns of guards and trusties."[31] The Walls has disappeared. There is only the one great prison farm for Mississippi's convicts, black and white alike. Such conditions begin to disturb the racial opposition enforced by earlier penal systems. Faulkner imagines convicts who are "moved" by the stories they hear of chain gangs working on the levees during the great flood of 1927, "accounts of conscripted levee gangs, mixed blacks and whites working in double shifts against the steadily rising water; stories of men, even though they were Negroes, being forced like themselves to do work for which they received no other pay than coarse food and a place in a mudfloored tent to sleep on."[32] The listeners here are (presumably) white prisoners; the figures in the stories are "mixed blacks and whites." Faulkner describes a growing awareness in the listeners that the conditions of incarceration are the same for all Mississippi convicts, regardless of race, and this awareness allows them to be "moved," to feel a touching and animating connection—"even though they [are] negroes," the men in these accounts share with the white prisoners a common relationship to disciplinary force and labor. As these same listeners are themselves "conscripted" to work on the crumbling levees, they see, in the distance, "a burning plantation house," one of Faulkner's favorite symbols for the passing away of the Old South and its racialized order, "as if a whole civilization were dying."[33]

Mink Snopes, confined to Parchman for murder in Faulkner's *The Mansion*, joins the gangs of prisoners "in the rich black cotton land while men on horses with shotguns across the pommels watched them."[34] In time, Mink comes to suspect that growing cotton may not in fact be the real business of the "farm"—he learns that the guards "neither knew nor cared whether anything came up behind him or not just so he kept moving." "All he had to do now," Faulkner repeats, "was just to keep moving."[35] By the late 1920s, and even more dramatically in the years that followed, Vardaman's original design of a twentieth-century plantation for the containment and discipline of African Americans had given way to something else: Parchman had come to host a mixed population of prisoners whose common, weary but restless sense was that they must "keep moving."

ARRESTING MOTION

In "The Jail," Faulkner describes the cell as a space of stillness, solitude, reflection, and self-expression: "If you would peruse in unbroken—ay, overlapping—continuity the history of a community, look not in the church registers and the courthouse records, but beneath the successive layers of calcimine and creosote and whitewash on the walls of the jail, since only in that forcible carceration does man find the idleness in which to compose . . . the gross and simple recapitulations of his gross and simple heart."[36] In the long hours passed within the walls of the jail, the prisoner comes into the fullest possible self-consciousness, scratching into the stone the record of his true character. This "forcible carceration," for Faulkner as for many generations of penal theorists, transforms and purifies the captive's subjectivity. At the same time, the prison bears more than the marks of the several souls it has confined; the "overlapping . . . history of a community," the secret life of the society that builds this holding chamber for its outcasts and offenders, is buried here, awaiting excavation. Those who wish to understand the community are invited to look into its carceral spaces and practices.

As Faulkner wrote his most famous novels in the 1920s and 1930s, "forcible carceration" became one of his key themes, informing the varieties of history and composition in his fiction. Already we have seen how he imagined the prison farm at Parchman, a zone of labor and discipline, emerging from the rubble of the classic penitentiary and the antebellum plantation, whose multiracial population must "keep moving." Occasionally, scholars have examined the characters of Faulkner's prisoners, from the murderer Mink Snopes to the unnamed "tall convict" of *Old Man* who, adrift in the great flood of 1927, spends most of the story trying desperately to get himself back into the prison that has become his only home.[37] Beyond Faulkner's obvious concern with the prison farm and its laborers, however, the history of punishment in Mississippi may illuminate something deeper about his novels, especially about the kinds of expressive subjectivity they imagine and mobilize.

"The aim of every artist," Faulkner once told an interviewer, "is to arrest motion, which is life, by artificial means and hold it fixed so that 100 years later when a stranger looks at it, it moves again since it is life."[38] When in *Absalom, Absalom!* the outlaw-turned-planter Sutpen wishes to halt and control his slaves, he commands them "with that one word," a word never given in the text because no one but Sutpen and his slaves understands it. The command is spoken "in that language which . . . a good part of the county did not know was a civilized language." Discovering elsewhere that this language is actually "a sort of French" learned in Haiti, however, we can suppose that Sutpen pronounces some version of the imperative "arretez," which means "stop" but has the same root as the English verb "arrest" (44, 27).[39] Spoken but never printed, this keyword connects the novel's poetry of motion and stasis to the theme of discipline and, more broadly, to the history of punishment in the South.[40]

Faulkner's fiction is centrally concerned with solitude and its alternatives, with the possibility of communion among its characters, and with the potential of narrative language to serve as the medium of that communion. As he explores these problems, he turns again and again to images of imprisonment and punishment, not only in stories set in jails and penitentiaries but also elsewhere—in the "voluntary incarceration" of Goodhue Coldfield, for instance, or in the "solitary furnace experience" of Thomas Sutpen. Indeed, the prison farm may have represented to Faulkner, as the penitentiary did to Thoreau and Emerson, a kind of metonym for broader social structures in a period of change that imposed new forms of oppression but also promised new forms of freedom. Fascinated by solitude and collectivity, by the stasis of architecture and the motion of time, Faulkner's novels of the 1920s and 1930s bear the traces of the history of punishment; in their cellular souls and mixed, moving communities, the penitentiary achieves one of its afterlives.

Between 1836 and 1936, in the century before Faulkner composed *Absalom, Absalom!*, the Mississippi penal system had undergone a series of transformations. The classic penitentiary had emerged to bring order and modernity to the frontier, to produce disciplined white subjects through solitude and reflection. Then the Civil War had demolished the penitentiary and its segregating order and, after a series of efforts to reconstitute the old opposition between penitentiary and plantation, the state had allowed the punishment of whites and blacks to be collapsed in the fields and workshops of Parchman. These transformations had been wrought by large-scale historical forces, including the rise of the antebellum plantation, the Civil War, the failure of Reconstruction, the Great Migration, and the Great Depression. For the poetics of punishment, they meant that Mississippi prisoners could no longer be imagined as racially pure cellular souls or as a mass of enslaved and dehumanized bodies; they were becoming a mixed and mobile collectivity. Just as the Great Migration and the Great Depression were leading Parchman toward integration, Faulkner's art underwent a parallel transformation—it passed from a literary experiment based on self-contained, reflexive, and radically alienated selves to the fantasy of a moving, overlapping subjectivity becoming articulate in a "transindividual voice." The passage is clearest in the transition from *The Sound and the Fury* (1929) to *Absalom, Absalom!* (1936).

For all its formal innovations, *The Sound and the Fury* is faithful to certain conventions of late nineteenth-century fiction, elaborating them into new and unfamiliar forms. With its sophisticated handling of perspective, the novel attends to the finest states and movements of consciousness, and its concern for the peculiarities of each character is also a concern for the misunderstandings and missed connections that separate characters. "The salient technical feature of *The Sound and the Fury*," as Cleanth Brooks recognized long ago, "is the use of four different points of view in the presentation of the breakup of the Compson family."[41] The very metaphor of "point of view," borrowed from perspectival painting, implies the separation of individuals and their arrangement in space: "each," as Faulkner writes in the closing line, "in its ordered place."[42] Foregrounding the issue of perspective, *The Sound and the Fury* pushes these tendencies of the modern novel to their limit. Faulkner's 1929 work puts him in the modernist company of Henry James, Virginia Woolf, and James Joyce, where experiments with narrative point of view test the tension between isolation and communion.[43]

In the first three of its four episodes, *The Sound and the Fury* appears to be built around cellular souls. Each of the three character-narrators is locked into an isolated chapter. Distorted echoes, partial repetitions, do connect the chapters, and allow patient readers to reassemble a narrative with some measure of autonomy from the private obsessions of the Compson brothers—but the structure of the book insists that each of them is condemned to solitude. The fence around the Compson property, to which Benjy clings, moaning, in the opening pages, marks this as a novel about bound and bordered selves. Benjy will end up in an asylum in Jackson. Quentin will put iron weights in his clothes and drown himself in a river in Massachusetts. Jason, "a childless bachelor," "rational, contained," will never be reconciled to either of them.[44] Only the novel's fourth and final chapter seems to promise an alternative to this aesthetics of solitude.

As the Compsons' black servant, Dilsey, becomes the center of consciousness in chapter 4, Faulkner shifts from first-person to third-person narration, and from fragments to a more synthetic presentation. The move is, in part, Faulkner's aid to readers whose ability to make sense of the story depends on the old narrative conventions his novel is passing beyond. The prose and the presentation are in the mode of a conventional nineteenth-century novel, with relatively simple sentences attendant to the details of dress and manner: "[Mrs. Compson] wore a quilted dressing gown of black satin, holding it close under her chin. In the other hand she held a red rubber hot water bottle and she stood at the head of the back stairway, calling, 'Dilsey' " (267). The concluding section restores a familiar novelistic style, introducing a "detached, omniscient perspective from which we can assemble the pieces of the story retrospectively."[45] Students encountering Faulkner for the first time greet this prose with a relieved sigh, almost visibly grateful that its defamiliarizing modernism has, at last, relented.

But something else happens in the Dilsey section. Near its end, the novel depicts an escape from deathly isolation that is not simply a return to an older order of shared meaning and narrative synthesis. In the black church on Easter morning, Faulkner imagines an expression and an aesthetic experience opposed to those that have sustained his own novel up to this point:

> "Brethren and sistren," [the voice] said again. The preacher . . . began to walk back and forth . . . a meagre figure, hunched over upon itself like that of one long immured in striving with the implacable earth. "I got the recollection and the blood of the Lamb!" He tramped steadily back and forth beneath the twisted paper and the Christmas bell, hunched, his hands clasped behind him. He was like a worn small rock whelmed by the successive waves of his voice. With his body he seemed to feed the voice that, succubus like, had fleshed its teeth in him. And the congregation seemed to watch with its own eyes while the voice consumed him, until he was nothing and they were nothing and there was not even a voice but instead their hearts were speaking to one another in chanting measures beyond the need for words. (294)

As Shegog preaches his sermon, the borders of selves are lapped, dissolved, and finally washed away by a disembodied voice. The articulation mediates a communion: the voice becomes a vessel whose undulant motion carries its listeners, drawing their energy into the same pattern, the same wave. A single "long moaning expulsion of breath" rises from the congregation (295). Have they been redeemed, ravished, or annihilated? The preacher is devoured by his own sermon; the wave that breaks over and through his listeners recalls Quentin's drowning and, perhaps, the life-devouring flood of the Mississippi River in *Old Man*, a surge of current that creates "a world turned to furious motion."[46]

The escape from the bounds of the ego in *The Sound and the Fury* is, of course, attributed almost exclusively to a mass of African American characters. The estranged "idiot" Benjy, a liminal figure throughout the novel, is the only Compson in the church, the only white person invited to this communion. Perhaps, then, Faulkner is only "playing in the dark" here, using blackness to imagine an ecstatic loss of self while he suppresses the violent history that has made these particular selves so perishable. "The white man's unadmitted—and apparently, to him, unspeakable—private fears and longings are projected onto the Negro," writes James Baldwin in *The Fire Next Time*. "The only way he can be released from the Negro's tyrannical power over him is to consent, in effect, to become black himself, to become a part of that suffering and dancing country that he now watches wistfully from the heights of his lonely power and . . . visits surreptitiously after dark."[47] Faulkner in *The Sound and the Fury* may be indulging in such wistful watching, imagining a release from solitude in the nameless, embodied voices of the oppressed. The novel imposes a structure that isolates each of its three white protagonists and that, in its final section, merges an assembly of black characters into a "moaning" communion.

Seven years later, in the midst of the Great Depression, Faulkner would return to the exploration of a voice that, rather than arising from the individual as an expression of private character, moves through and transcends the boundaries of the self, mediating a communion "in chanting measures." In *Absalom, Absalom!*, however, this voice becomes much more than an afterthought; it dominates the book as a kind of protagonist. In this novel, which carefully explores the history of violence that produced the figures of master and slave in the Old South, the characters through whom the voice moves, haunting them, destroying them, drawing them into its communion, are almost exclusively whites. The Harvard roommates Quentin and Shreve—staying up late on a cold winter night in Massachusetts, taking turns telling the story of Sutpen and his grand, doomed design—come to feel their own dissolution, as the walls of their selves yield to the "successive waves" of narrative voice. The voice that speaks in their room, that questions and answers and pursues the mystery of Sutpen, writes Faulkner, "might have been either of them and was in a sense both: both thinking as one, the voice which happened to be speaking the thought only the thinking become audible, vocal; the two of them creating between them, out of the rag-tag and bob-ends of old tales and talking, people who perhaps had never existed at all anywhere, who, shadows, were shadows not of flesh and blood which had lived and died but shadows in turn of . . . shades too, . . . quiet as the visible murmur of their vaporizing breath" (243). The two young men, one from the Deep South and one from the far North, lose their distinct identities. Like the Easter congregation of *The Sound and the Fury*, they merge into a common speaking voice.

The central character of *Absalom, Absalom!*, the ghost haunting all its interconnected stories, is Thomas Sutpen, a poor white vagrant, marginally criminal, who appears one day in the 1830s and, as if from nothing, builds the grandest plantation in Yoknapatawpha County. As his story is disclosed through conversations held in 1909, the reader comes to understand that his design—his vision of a dynastic House of Sutpen, worked by masses of slaves and ruled over by the successive generations of his white sons—has collapsed. The stately plantation house has rotted for years and finally burned to the ground. But Sutpen has achieved a different kind of immortality. The old colonel, now known as a "demon" and a "ghost," lives in narrative, in "old tales and talking." He persists not in the architecture of the mansion but in the "moving air" of speech, "as if it were the voice that he haunted," writes Faulkner, "where a more fortunate one would have had a house" (4). Breathing life into the Sutpen story, *Absalom, Absalom!* draws an opposition between solitary ambitions and collective destinies, the stasis of architecture and the flow of time, stabilizing designs and the improvisational mobility of oral storytelling. It describes the building of cells and mansions, but it is more concerned with their demolition, their doom; its character-narrators flee from monumental designs into a communion mediated by narrative voice, where "it did not matter (and possibly neither of them conscious of the distinction) which one had been doing the talking" (276).

This ambiguous afterlife, this haunting of voices, is certainly not the kind of immortality Sutpen himself so fiercely pursued. His design was never intended to rest on anything as transient as "moving air." It was supposed to be a monument to the self he had built through will and force. Indeed, the premises of Sutpen's design are very close to those of antebellum Mississippi's segregated system of disciplinary institutions, producing subjectivities in opposition: the white penitent, cloistered in solitude, laboring toward redemption; black slaves, disciplined and circulated in the cotton economy, toiling toward their own disappearance into the productive land. A simple master-slave dialectic will not quite account for the full disciplinary range of this novel. The aspiring master does not generate his selfhood merely by exercising power over his slaves. Instead, his subjectivity is arduously produced through a regimen of willed self-control and "masculine solitude" (30). Sutpen severs himself from his family, from the line of descent that extends back to London's Old Bailey courthouse and a convict transportation ship, and from the wife and son of his West Indian adventure. He appears in Jefferson like an ex-convict released into a strange world, "like a man who had been through some solitary furnace experience," writes Faulkner, "and fought through it at enormous cost not so much physical as mental, alone and unaided" (24). Sutpen disciplines not only his slaves but also, and most feverishly, *himself*.

A crucial and underexplored element of Sutpen's much-discussed "innocence," then, is his faith in the promise of a solitary discipline that reproduces that of the antebellum penitentiary. He believes in remorse and correction: "After more than thirty years," he says, "my conscience had finally assured me that if I had done an injustice, I had done what I could to rectify it" (213). He believes that will and labor are enough to transform him from a suspicious and "origin-less" outsider into the master of a plantation. And he believes that his self-correction will segregate him from the black collective of his slaves, elevating him to a lordship immune from their contagion. Sutpen's design depends on his continuously displayed mastery over the "wild negroes" he has brought from the Caribbean. His heroic figure stands out against the contained mass of his nameless slaves, hauled under the hood of a wagon, "a black tunnel filled with still eyeballs and smelling like a wolfden" (27). His self-discipline sets him against the abject, undifferentiated collectivity that Quentin and Shreve call "the black blood, the black bones and flesh and thinking and remembering and hopes and desires . . . ravished by violence" (202). Sutpen attempts to conjure himself, as if from out of nowhere, through an act of will. The slaves are granted no such self-determination; they are the objects of "two hundred years of oppression and exploitation" (202).

As a spectacular display of his whiteness and his mastery, Sutpen invites an audience of whites and blacks to his barn and stages a ritual combat against a slave: "Yes. It seems that on certain occasions, perhaps at the end of the evening, the spectacle, the grand finale or perhaps as a matter of sheer deadly forethought toward the retention of supremacy, domination, he would enter the ring with one of the negroes himself. Yes. That is what Ellen saw: her husband and the father of her children standing there naked and panting and bloody to the waist and the negro just fallen evidently, lying at his feet and bloody too" (21). Like the slave-breaker Covey in Frederick Douglass's *Narrative*, Sutpen makes the violence of slavery literal and immediate, a contest between white and black bodies.

But, again like Covey's brutality, Sutpen's act of physical domination fails to reinforce the racial lines of power. It creates not difference but a panting, blood-stained union. What Sutpen's "innocence" prevents him from grasping is that, "in getting into the ring . . . he has compromised his own 'domination,' that is to say his own whiteness."[48] The spectators discern no isolated and segregated selves but an embrace that combines "a white one and a black one, both naked to the waist and gouging at one another's eyes as if their skins should not only have been the same color but should have been covered with fur too" (20–21). The segregated spectacle decomposes; rigid difference dissolves, giving way to mixture and mobility.

As Faulkner closes the scene, the reader glimpses "two Sutpen faces," the first of Judith, his daughter by his wife Ellen Coldfield, and the second of Clytemnestra, his daughter by a slave (22). What is revealed in this particular narrative of struggle and blood, then, is not Douglass's revolutionary self-assertion, overturning the relationship between master and slave, but a more intimate violence. Faulkner's contemporary W. J. Cash would describe the plantation as a place of deep, though repressed, interracial intimacy: "The relationship between the two groups was . . . nothing less than organic. Negro entered into white man as profoundly as white man entered into Negro—subtly influencing every gesture, every word, every emotion and idea, every attitude."[49] But Faulkner's vision of the master-slave connection in *Absalom, Absalom!* should not be confused with the sentimental tales of some proslavery advocates or with the nostalgic portrait painted in such works as Margaret Mitchell's *Gone with the Wind*. There, the "family romance" of loving paternalism attempts to bury the cruelty of rape and degrading labor discipline that characterized the plantation order.[50] Faulkner, in the primal scene of conflict between Sutpen and his slave, does not obscure the violence of domination. Indeed, this violence, which compromises the humanity of both, *is* the intimacy of master and slave.

And what is true for Sutpen and his slave in the "ring" of combat is true more generally for Faulkner's narrative of history in *Absalom, Absalom!* The social transformation churning in the novel, erupting into its content and form, is crystallized in *the collapse of a structure of disciplinary counterdefinition*. The figures of subjectivity contained in two opposed disciplinary orders come into violent contact, mutual contagion, blood mixing. If *The Sound and the Fury* escapes, "surreptitiously," from solitude into a fantasy of communal black voices, *Absalom, Absalom!* represents a more profound, intractable relationship, something more like the one Baldwin describes in "Many Thousands Gone": "It is not simply the relationship of oppressed to oppressor, of master to slave, nor is it motivated merely by hatred; it is also, literally and morally, a blood relationship, perhaps the most profound reality of the American experience, and we cannot begin to unlock it until we accept how very much it contains of the force and anguish and terror of love."[51] Faulkner merges the cellular soul into a collective and mobile agency, itself formed by oppression—by diaspora, the mass incarceration of slave ships, plantations, prison farms, and the labor flows that shaped Faulkner's own time. The builders of mansions and cells (Sutpen's French architect also redesigns the local jail) commingle with their slaves. The effect is not so much that master and servant recognize elements of the other in themselves, as in Hegel's classic formulation; rather, a third kind of subject is born from their bonding. The miscegenation of disciplines conceives the transindividual voice.

Faulkner's characters seem to sense and comment on these deep historical changes. Quentin's father, Jason Compson, describes the people of the modern South as "dwarfed and involved," "diffused and scattered creatures" (71). Quentin thinks of himself this way—"his very body was an empty hall echoing with sonorous defeated names; he was not a being, an entity, he was a commonwealth" (7). The critic Stephen M. Ross writes that "Quentin's tragedy, which we hear in *his* voice, is that he can never shut out the myriad voices whirling through his mind."[52] There may be a sense of tragic loss, of aristocratic nostalgia, in such appraisals, but it is the characters' very diffusion that allows them to speak together in chorus. Because Quentin is not locked into a single, "distinct" subjectivity, because he is already a "commonwealth" of voices, he is able to merge with other storytellers, as when he "did not even falter, taking Shreve up in stride without comma or colon or paragraph" (225). Diffused and scattered, complex and mixed, the characters are able through collective recollection to speak a common language, "that meagre and fragile thread," as Faulkner calls it, "by which the little surface corners and edges of men's secret and solitary lives may be joined for an instant now and then" (202).

In the novel's climactic chapters, Quentin and Shreve give themselves over to the "happy marriage of speaking and hearing," a collaborative narrative practice of "loving, violent play."[53] When they do, they find
themselves "as free now of flesh as the father who decreed and forbade,
the son who denied and repudiated, the lover who acquiesced, the beloved
who was not bereaved . . . clattering over the frozen ruts of that December night . . . not two of them there and then either but four of them rid-
ing the two horses through the iron darkness and that not mattering
either: what faces and what names they called themselves and were called
by so long as the blood coursed" (237). The borders of identity, race, gender, even historical time, lose their fixity when the transindividual voice
speaks. The character-narrators dissolve into a communion bound by
blood and recollection. Thus, in the climactic moments of *Absalom, Absalom!* the architectural imagination, the will to design, the static subjectivity of Sutpen encounters a collectivity in motion—structure encounters
flow. The first attempts to contain the second, to arrest its motion and
impose design; but at every turn its boundaries are worn through, over-
flowed, exceeded. This relation is not only one of conflict. The combat-
ants embrace, and their gouging mixes the blood it spills. Oppressor
and oppressed are also lovers, also kin. Recollection is their practice,
blood is their medium, and through this contact they become "brethren
and sistren." It is not one or the other but the bond between them, the
grappling and gouging, the disciplinary embrace, that *speaks* in the
novel.

Faulkner's characters, witnessing the birth of this mixed offspring,
respond in various ways—sometimes with hope but also sometimes
with the lost and bewildered affect Faulkner calls "amazement," sometimes with horror, sometimes with a cold and inflexible rejection. This
is Shreve's attic arithmetic in the closing pages: " 'So it took Charles Bon
and his mother to get rid of old Tom [Sutpen], and Charles Bon and the
octoroon to get rid of Judith, and Charles Bon and Clytie to get rid of
Henry; and Charles Bon's mother and Charles Bon's grandmother to get
rid of Charles Bon. So it takes two niggers to get rid of one Sutpen, don't
it?' Quentin did not answer; evidently Shreve did not want an answer
now; he continued almost without a pause: 'Which is all right, it's fine; it
clears the whole ledger' " (302). Turning away from collaboration—
"evidently Shreve did not want an answer"—and closing the book on the

Sutpen story, Shreve adds and subtracts in black and white. His racist arithmetic divides the Sutpen family, the various intimate "shades" of the past conjured by the act of recollection and speech, into two opposed units, "niggers" and white Sutpens. He is satisfied that the mystery of Thomas Sutpen's doom has been solved, the "ledger" cleared, and at precisely this moment the novel's transindividual voice ceases to move him. Shreve's sentences become short, ironic, and punchy as he loses his capacity to tap into, to join in, the "chanting measures" of the novel's collectivity. His accounting exposes itself as the anxious, defensive gesture of a white Northern subjectivity affronted by miscegenation and by the Great Migration of Southern blacks into the industrial centers: "I think that in time the Jim Bonds are going to conquer the western hemisphere," he trails off, fearing an empire of "African kings" who "spread toward the poles" (302).

Longing for a pure order where white mind and black body are unmingled, Shreve withdraws from the intimacy of the commonwealth into the disembodied, cold, and inflexible language of accounting. The "marriage of speaking and hearing" is over. The possibility of union through collaborative storytelling, through "loving, violent play," is lost, and Quentin is left with his desperate denial of love's opposite: "I don't hate it!" Shreve's effort to "[clear] the whole ledger" recalls Goodhue Coldfield's "balancing of his terrestrial accounts" in his homemade cell. Shreve has repaired, like Coldfield, into an arctic solitude. At the same time, he fixates on the one remaining descendant of Sutpen, Jim Bond, a figure of pure, embodied, moaning, inarticulate voice. The "moving air" of speech, the "murmur of their vaporizing breath" has been the medium of communion in the novel; in the closing paragraphs, Shreve misrecognizes voice, recoiling from it as from a grotesque emanation of the black body. He imposes an untenable segregation, even as he foresees a miscegenated future.

KEEP MOVING

Shreve's vision of black bodies rising from the South and "spread[ing] toward the poles" is not only his private nightmare. It can also be understood as a response to the Great Migration, the mass movement of African Americans from the agrarian South into Northern industrial centers in the early twentieth century. As Shreve speaks in 1909, the migration is just beginning to gather momentum. As Faulkner was writing in the mid-1930s, it was an accomplished fact. The critic Cheryl Lester has argued that the Great Migration was among the profound historical forces that shaped Faulkner's world and his writing. For her, this mass movement of bodies, a response to the rapid mechanization of both Northern industry and Southern agriculture, represents the moment when Southern blacks come into collective agency: "The migration," writes Lester, "demonstrated that African-Americans could participate in the historical process, act in protest against their lot in the South, and change their destiny." Leaving the South in what she calls a "leaderless mass migration," they rose from abjection to become the subjects of their own history.[54] As Faulkner was publishing his best-known novels, African Americans in unprecedented numbers were moving through and out of Mississippi. Like the Haitian Revolution and the Civil War, historical events recalled in *Absalom, Absalom!*, the Great Migration taking place during the novel's composition worked to destabilize the South's racialized power structure. It was a change in the patterns of labor and social life that also opened new forms of mobility and self-assertion.

William Faulkner is not the only artist whose works bear the traces of this history. Meditating on African American migration and its most famous expression, the music called the blues, Houston Baker writes: "Fixity is a function of power. Those who maintain place, who decide what takes place and dictate what has taken place, are power brokers of the traditional. The 'placeless,' by contrast, are translators of the non-traditional. Rather than fixed . . . their lineage is fluid, nomadic, transitional."[55] The voice of the blues, Baker suggests, was no single singer's property; it arose with new ways of being and acting in concert. If so, then it has something in common with the transindividual voice of *Absalom, Absalom!* Thadious Davis has traced the echoes of jazz and blues music in Faulkner's life, in his depiction of black characters, and in several of his novels. Davis notes, for instance, the "blind Negro beggar" in *Sartoris*, "with a guitar and a wire frame holding a mouth-organ to his lips."[56] The musician is emblematic of what Faulkner called, in *Soldier's Pay*, "the crooning submerged passion of the dark race," a force that "swelled to an ecstasy, taking the white man's words as readily as it took his remote God and made a personal Father of him."[57] According to Davis's account, the blues as Faulkner imagines them are a kind of miscegenated form, produced in the encounter between black and white.

"Just to keep moving" is Mink Snopes's task in Parchman Farm. His call is answered, in a sense, by the most famous of Delta bluesmen, Robert Johnson, in "Hellhound on My Trail":

> I've got to keep movin',
> I've got to keep movin',
> Blues fallin' down like hail.

The music Johnson and his contemporaries made was music of restlessness and loss, but it also enabled, by the alchemy of aesthetic mediation, an empowering communion. A voice laments its own solitude—"I was lonesome, I was lonesome, and I could not help but cry"—but to its movements an audience begins to dance. James Baldwin saw this conversion as the essence of the genre. In a little-known essay called "The Uses of the Blues," Baldwin wrote that the blues are the experience of anguish, but that "the acceptance of this anguish . . . and the expression of it, creates, however odd this may sound, a kind of joy."[58] Similarly, Bruce Jackson writes in *Wake Up Dead Man*, a study of the blues music of Texas prison farms, that "the subject [of the songs], always, has to do with making it in Hell," but also that "sometimes, [they] are compellingly beautiful."[59] This is the mystery of the blues: it transmutes the suffering of "bones and flesh . . . ravaged by violence" into a medium of communion, endurance, and "a kind of joy."

Perhaps even more than the famous rambling bluesmen of the Depression-era Delta and the Great Migration, though, the artists of the voice whose project was closest to Faulkner's may have been the prisoners of Parchman Farm. By the 1930s, the Southern prison farms had appeared in journalism, fiction, and other media, beginning to lead the kind of imaginative life in the culture at large that the penitentiary had acquired a century earlier. The speeches of Vardaman and the reformist writings of Parchman's critics contributed to this discourse. So did Faulkner's stories about convicts living and dying there. The most widely circulated and intriguing documents transmitting the meaning and experience of the prison farm to the world at large, though, may have been John and

Alan Lomax's recordings of the prison blues. In Parchman, Alan Lomax remembered, "my father and I had found the finest, wildest, and most complex folk singing in the South."[60] Like *Absalom, Absalom!*, these work songs—built on the rhythm of lockstep marches or hammers breaking rocks, draping a chorus of voices over these abrasive beats—gave voice to the miscegenated subjectivity generated by modern, mixed discipline in the South.

Parchman cobbled together elements of the plantation and of the penitentiary; the music made in its fields and workshops expresses, by turns, the misery of a laboring mass and the loneliness of an imprisoned soul. The songs mediate collective action without any nightmarish turn to undifferentiated collectivity or grotesque embodiment. They are aesthetic instruments of endurance that imagine the possibility of liberation: "Now, fare you well, fare you well, babe," a prisoner sings, "if I can live this business down, babe, I won't be harbored down in prison no more."[61] The Parchman blues, even more than the songs recorded by early stars like Robert Johnson and Bessie Smith, are characterized by a transindividual voice. Sometimes they begin with a call from a "leader" and a response from the laboring gang, but the leader's voice is soon absorbed into the chorus. Indeed, the usefulness of the work song as an instrument of endurance depends on its power to carry the mind of the prisoner away from its private misery. A prisoner called 'Bama, speaking to Alan Lomax on one of the tapes, says that the songs help the singers to pass their hard time because they "keep your mind from being devoted on just one thing." The songs open the walls of the cellular soul so that the self escapes, merging with the chorus—"until he was nothing," as Faulkner writes, "and they were nothing and . . . their hearts were speaking to one another in chanting measures."

The brutal conditions under which the Parchman prisoners toiled were, of course, a long way from Faulkner's house in Oxford. Much more than Faulkner's prose, the prison work songs were practical instruments of endurance, easing the monotony and the anguish of prisoners' lives. The commonwealth of voices in Faulkner's novel might be said to find its unity through a kind of terrified and bewildered racial exclusion, as Quentin and Shreve dream up a dynasty ruined by the secret contamination of "black blood." The blues songs of Parchman Farm, meanwhile, are conceived by some critics and historians as the heritage of slavery and the cultural property of African American laborers enduring the new tyranny of the Jim Crow prison system; like Faulkner's speakers, these singers may have imagined their own unity in opposition to an inimical racial other. At the same time, however, when we listen to these two sets of voices together, a surprising harmony begins to emerge. In each, the architecture of the cellular soul gives way to a moving collectivity. Rising alike from the prison farm along the river and from the stately white house at Rowan Oak are articulations of an unwelcome, irresistible, but also somehow loving communion. Even as law and power impose their paranoid segregating structures, the future seems more and more to mean a life of miscegenation. The modernist novel and the Southern blues resonate with a harmony that unifies not only white and black but also the history of captivity and the dream of liberty.

To the Lomaxes who recorded the Parchman blues and to many who heard them, the work songs seemed almost to come from another world. The voices that sang on the tapes were doubly distant—first because they belonged to the self-enclosed institution of the prison, and second because they belonged to the descendants of slaves. Indeed, listeners fantasized that they were hearing voices not only from another kind of space but also from another time. Governor Vardaman had hoped to remake the antebellum plantation in the twentieth century. Critics and admirers of the Lomax recordings imagined that the famous work songs of the slaves had been revived along with the plantation's conditions of labor and discipline. The *Washington Post*, commenting on the tapes and their origins, noted that the Lomaxes had "spent two years visiting prisons in nine Southern states with the hope that there, if anywhere, they could hear some authentic old-fashioned Negro work songs."[62] A reviewer for the *Chicago Daily Tribune* charted John Lomax's journey "to the prisons, the work farms, the plantations, the construction camps, and the honky-tonks of the south, wherever he could be sure of finding Negro culture relatively undiluted by white."[63] The Parchman blues were understood as a kind of lost treasure, preserving the expressive culture of antebellum slavery. To the Lomaxes, and to the mainly white, Northern audiences who listened to their tapes, the prison songs were the "authentic" and "undiluted" cultural property of the descendants of slaves.

If the anachronistic racial purity of the prison blues was part of their appeal, it generated some peculiar kinds of praise. The most famous of the prison blues artists was Leadbelly, "discovered" in Louisiana's Angola Penitentiary. Promoted by the Lomaxes and touring the United States, Leadbelly became a celebrity and a legend. A wide scar across his throat suggested a dark history of violence. It was said that he had been serving a life sentence for murder when he acquired a pardon by recording a song for the governor of Louisiana—Alan Lomax would call him "a man whose music melted prison bars."[64] The Lomaxes not only recorded his music and arranged his concerts but also "transcribed" a narrative of his life, presented as a commentary on his songs and published under the title *Negro Folk Songs as Sung by Lead Belly*. Alan Lomax called it "the first folksinger biography in English."[65] Readers were delighted to see in the text the same "undiluted" racial expression that they believed they heard in the songs. A certain M. Emmett Kennedy, reviewing the book for the *New York Times*, admired its "simple, graphic vernacular": "For the most part it is a recountment of sordid, semi-savage emotions and episodes revealing a nature endowed with an admirable sense of the dramatic and an insatiable lust for life. Primitive in his mind and heart, his desires and aspirations are likewise primitive and always of the flesh. He is too much of the earth to be concerned with thoughts of the spirit: therefore he never approaches anything resembling a poetic attitude. . . . Even when he sings, his half-inarticulate, groping mind is concerned with thoughts of bodily enjoyment, and he is always the boastful, self-satisfied satyr, conscious of his musical gifts, but proudly aware of his physical force."[66] According to this appraisal, the "primitive" and grotesquely embodied "nature" of Leadbelly, the lusty and "half-inarticulate" "satyr," gave voice to "the common inheritance of his race." Like Faulkner's Shreve, who associates blackness with the terrifyingly meaningless moaning of Jim Bond, the *Times* reviewer recognizes nothing "of the spirit" in the "groping" voice of the blues singer.

Thus Leadbelly and other artists of the prison blues seemed, to some listeners, to be "half-articulate" and not-quite-human creatures, toiling in the Southern mud like slaves and raising a "primitive" cry. Leadbelly's first white audiences, Alan Lomax recalled in an essay written shortly after the musician's death, "could not understand a syllable of his broad southern dialect, but he set them on fire with his sheer power." Yet Leadbelly's life was a complex and surprisingly mobile one. He had acquired his famous twelve-string guitar "from Mexican street singers in Dallas." He had encountered and incorporated a variety of musical traditions, not only "slave dance tunes" and "cotton-picking chants," but also "ragtime" and "the early blues."[67] As he became a celebrity in New York and other Northern cities, his songwriting and performance styles continued to change. His music, Alan Lomax wrote, "was the flower of the southwestern folksong tradition, refined and recreated by a true creative artist."[68] The notion that Leadbelly and his fellow prison blues singers had somehow preserved the purity of slave songs, of an African American voice "undiluted by the white" and unchanged by the upheavals of the late nineteenth and early twentieth centuries, was a primitivist fantasy that misrecognized the hybridity of the music and the creativity of its artists.

Even contemporary scholars of the prison blues have sometimes presented them as a kind of racially "undiluted" expression, the heritage of the plantation passed down through the generations and living on in the neoslavery of the prison farm. Jackson in *Wake Up Dead Man* insists that the work songs of the Texas penitentiary "are the property of black inmates exclusively, and they are clearly in a tradition going back and beyond the importation of the first Negro slaves to the Virginia colonies in 1631."[69] The history of punishment in the Deep South, however, suggests that not only was the prison farm a remade plantation, it also adopted certain disciplines from the antebellum penitentiary, and by the 1930s and 1940s its segregation was beginning to break down. Faulkner, at least, had written of a labor discipline that "mixed blacks and whites" and led to a kind of cross-racial recognition. The poetics of punishment are always contested, but in the vision of the prison farm as a hybrid and miscegenating institution we might discover an alternative to Shreve's racial anxiety about the inarticulate black voice of Jim Bond and M. Emmett Kennedy's primitivist attraction to the "sordid, semi-savage" music of Leadbelly. The prison blues of the 1930s are not a music of pure embodiment or of an "undiluted" African culture but a modern, hybrid art whose voice, to recall Baker's terms, is "fluid, nomadic, transitional." The prison blues recalled the history of slavery, a history of violence but also of intimacy; they arose from the rapidly changing carceral institutions of the twentieth century; and, as the American prison continued to expand, they would resonate with inmates of many colors and many expressive traditions—in a memoir of his time in the jails and prisons of Arizona in the 1970s, the Chicano poet Jimmy Santiago Baca would recall "jamming a Leadbelly blues" on a harmonica in his cell.[70]

CHAPTER SIX

Frontiers of Captivity

IN A 1682 TEXT originally entitled *The Sovereignty and Goodness of God*, Mary White Rowlandson, a Massachusetts Bay colonist and the wife of a Puritan minister, tells the story of her capture by hostile Indians during King Philip's War. Rowlandson depicts the native people of New England as devils and fiends who butcher helpless English settlers in their homes, carrying the survivors into a dismal servitude. "Some in our house were fighting for their lives," she writes, "others wallowing in their blood, the House on fire over our heads, and the bloody Heathen ready to knock us on the head."[1] Removed into the wilderness, nourished by what few scraps she can beg or steal from her savage keepers, Rowlandson must abandon many of her familiar customs and assumptions. She finds herself transformed, adopting the survival techniques of the Indians and behaving in strange ways that would have been abhorrent to her at home. When her six-year-old daughter dies along the way, Rowlandson clings to the corpse. She cradles it in her arms through the night and refuses to allow her captors to dispose of it: "I cannot but take notice," Rowlandson confesses, "how at another time I could not bear to be in the room where any dead person was, but now the case is changed; I must and could ly down by my dead Babe, side by side all the night after" (75). Physical deprivation, intimacy with death, the loss of identity and the emergence of another, somehow savage self—the dark, un-

charted wilderness becomes vivid in Rowlandson's text not as an ex-
panse of freedom but as a space of bondage and servitude. For Rowlandson, and for her many readers on both sides of the Atlantic, the frontier
is discovered through a story of captivity.

In a series of poems composed three centuries later in an Arizona
penitentiary and published under the title *Immigrants in Our Own Land*,
the Chicano writer and activist Jimmy Santiago Baca describes himself
and his people as the survivors of captivity—driven from their homes
and treated as foreign intruders, stripped of sovereignty, confined on
reservations, in detention centers, or in the vast superprisons of the American West, Baca's fellow captives, too, discover an intimacy with death that
remakes the self:

> but so very few make it out of here as human
> as they came in, they leave wondering what good they are now
> as they look at their hands so long away from their tools,
> as they look at themselves, so long gone from their families,
> so long gone from life itself.[2]

Locked away from the known world, alienated from family and identity, the prisoners lose the habits and instruments of culture that once
made them recognizable to themselves as "human." Baca, like Rowlandson and the many other authors of American captivity narratives,
sees the frontier as a zone of bondage and mortification that decomposes identity.

Scholars of American history and culture commonly suggest that
the captivity narrative is the first, and perhaps the most characteristic,
genre of American literature. Christopher Castiglia, for instance, refers
to Rowlandson's narrative as "the first distinctly American best-seller"
and notes the importance of such texts in "creating the cultural mythology of the American wilderness."[3] From Rowlandson in New England
and Cabeza de Vaca in Florida through twentieth-century blockbusters
like John Ford's *The Searchers* and Ron Howard's *The Missing*, frontier
tales of abduction and culture-crossing have held an enduring fascination. They are adventure stories, but also occasions for reflection on violence, on sexuality, and on the cultural and racial identities that have
defined friend against enemy, captor against captive, in the many wars
and other conflicts that shape American history.

Often, the captivity narrative has served as a kind of propaganda, a tale of victimhood and affronted dignity that justifies a furious military reprisal. In a 2007 editorial for the *New York Times*, Susan Faludi argues that Rowlandson's story, like media representations of the terrorist attacks of September 11, 2001, leads us to "bury our awareness of our vulnerability under belligerent posturing and comforting fantasy."[4] The captivity narrative has served to reinforce, perhaps even to create, identities in conflict: white against red, or against black, or against shades of brown. But the captivity narrative has also been turned to some other, perhaps more complex designs. Rowlandson's text includes several stunning passages of self-doubt and self-expression that might have been unspeakable by a Puritan woman in other contexts. In its concluding passages, the author describes herself lying awake at night, haunted by the memory of her experience and ruminating on the new relationship she has found with her God: "Oh! the wonderful power of God that mine eyes have seen, affording matter enough for my thoughts to run in, that when others are sleeping mine are weeping" (111). Like several other captivity narratives by women, Rowlandson's account subverts gender roles and explores the mysterious spaces between cultural identities. Even when it is framed by pious declarations of fidelity to whiteness, Englishness, Christianity, and so on, a text like Rowlandson's also makes itself available to other interpretive desires, some of them illicit and transgressive.[5] In the hands of Baca, a contemporary captive of mixed ethnicity, the potential to disturb boundaries and upset hierarchies is exploited to the extreme. The captivity narrative becomes a genre of protest against the forms of imprisonment and dislocation that have expanded the power and territory of the imperial United States.

As Frederick Jackson Turner's classic study established decades ago, the myth of the open wilderness has been an important set of ideas and stories for the imagination of U.S. expansion, from the earliest phase of "discovery" through the age of Manifest Destiny and beyond. What has been less clearly understood, perhaps, is the reality of captivity, containment, and disenfranchisement involved in the "opening" of the West. The history of the American frontier includes the Indian Wars of the Massachusetts Bay Colony in the seventeenth century, Indian Removal and the creation of the reservation in the nineteenth (contemporary with the erection of the great model penitentiaries in Philadelphia and New

York), and the explosion of the prison-industrial complex in the contemporary suburban and rural West. Emerging from these sometimes hidden or forgotten spaces, the captivity narrative has become much more than a genre of wartime propaganda. Conceived in the early periods of European encounter with the new world, developing through several centuries and eventually taken up by Native American writers such as Jimmy Santiago Baca and Simon Ortiz, it records the violent history essential to the expansion of U.S. territory.

At the same time, the captivity narrative exposes the precarious contingency of identity, even when it attempts to draw solid boundaries between two warring communities. A premise of the genre is the controversial idea—often repressed in the explicit claims of captors and captives—that captivity breaks down and remakes the self. The captivity narrative shows that practices of violence are not merely effects of irreconcilable racial identities meeting at the wartime front; rather, the schematics of war actually help to bring such identities into being. Even as the captivity narrative depicts battles waged along racial lines, it suggests that those lines are provisional and unstable, wrought by massacre and dislocation. The literature of the frontier thus discloses some surprising kinds of connection and hybridity. And, like the literature of the ever-expanding American prison, it finds in the hard realities of captivity the material for a dream of liberty.

ANIMAL AND MENTAL CONSTITUTIONS

"It is a solemn sight," declares Mary Rowlandson, "to see so many Christians lying in their own blood . . . like a company of Sheep torn by Wolves. All of them stript naked by a company of hell-hounds, roaring, singing, ranting and insulting, as if they would have torn our very hearts out" (70). The reader of such lines may have the impression that Rowlandson and her fellow colonists were enjoying days of peace and security before the pack of "black creatures of the night" came roaring out of the woods to terrorize them (71). But the attack on Lancaster was one of many such conflicts between Indians and English colonists in New England in the 1670s. The story of Rowlandson's captivity belongs to the larger, more complex history of King Philip's War, a struggle for power and land that would also come to redefine the identities of the Indians and of the colonists.

As the historian Jill Lepore has shown, King Philip's War was a turning point in the development of the Massachusetts Bay Colony, when relations of relative interdependence and tolerance between the Indians and the English hardened into a stark, dangerous enmity. In accounts such as Rowlandson's, printed and circulated to a transatlantic audience, the colonists, whose "greatest cultural anxiety . . . was that they were becoming Indianized," used language and imagery that "defined themselves against the Indians' savagery."[6] Thus Rowlandson, as she disappears deeper and deeper into the wilderness, insists ever more fiercely upon her own "civilization," a quality of character and culture that includes literacy in English, the use of European technologies, and Puritan Christianity. Her efforts to draw durable oppositions between Indians and English are most explicit, and most strained, in certain moments of confusion: "In that time came a company of *Indians* to us, near thirty, all on horse-back. My heart skipt within me, thinking they had been *English men* at the first sight of them, for they were dressed in *English* Apparel, with Hats, white Neckcloths, and Sashes about their waists, and Ribbonds upon their shoulders: but when they came near, there was a vast difference between the lovely faces of Christians, and the foul looks of these Heathens, which much damped my spirit again" (94). Here, Rowlandson approaches a racialized language that locates civilization, and with it the possibility of redemption, in the very bodies of the English. The "lovely faces of Christians" are somehow of a singular character in the eyes of God and man, not to be confused with the "foul looks of . . . Heathens." But the insistence on difference comes just after the confession that Rowlandson herself, at least for a fleeting moment, has been unable to distinguish Indians from English. There is a sense of contradiction and anxiety in this passage, especially since it is embedded in the narrative of Rowlandson's own gradual assimilation to the ways of her captors. If *The Sovereignty and Goodness of God* participates in the invention of an irreconcilable difference between "Heathen" and "Christian," then, it also worries about the security of its own cultural borders.

Indeed, as Rowlandson is captured, humiliated, and removed into the wilderness, what she discovers is that civilization does not, after all, inhere in the body or in the soul. Deprived of English food, she will savor groundnuts and steal a gnawed piece of meat from a child's mouth. Traumatized and grief-stricken, she will lie all night with her daughter's lifeless body. These are not expressions of any durable racial or cultural character. They are the acts of one transformed by hardship in an unknown landscape, and they reveal the power of captivity to remake subjectivity, to produce something akin to the character of the savage.

As the U.S. frontier shifted to enclose a wider and wider swath of territory, the captivity narrative would continue to be animated by its defining tension, at once marking and blurring the lines between savage and civilized. Rowlandson's narrative ends with her "redemption"; her husband negotiates to buy her freedom from the Indians for the sum of twenty pounds, and she returns to Puritan society. But other captivity narratives would tell different stories, some of death, some of violent resistance, some of a more radical assimilation. The 1824 narrative of Mary Jemison's capture and life among the Seneca people of Pennsylvania and New York, for example, begins with a preface by James Seaver, the editor who transcribed and published her text, in which Seaver insists on the profound differences between the two classes of humanity he calls the "vile" and the "virtuous": "Without a knowledge of the lives of the vile and abandoned," he claims, "we should be wholly incompetent to set an appropriate value upon the charms, the excellence and the worth of those principles which have produced the finest traits in the character of the most virtuous."[7] Seaver presents the narrative as a lesson in the depravity of the savage and the noble refinements of Christian civilization. Jemison's tale itself, however, refuses to uphold such oppositions. It tells the story of the captive's initiation into a Seneca family and, eventually, her full membership in the Seneca community, including two marriages and several children.

Of Jemison's many episodes of culture-crossing, perhaps the most striking is the ritual through which she is adopted to replace a fallen warrior. "Oh! she is our sister," say the members of her new family, "and gladly we welcome her here. In the place of our brother she stands in our tribe."[8] To her Seneca sisters, Jemison—renamed Dickewamis—represents one of the dead restored to the company of the living. Given a series of opportunities to return to white society, Dickewamis decides instead to remain among the Senecas. She has passed too deeply into the territory of a new identity. Even her editor concludes that Jemison's narrative "shows what changes may be effected in the animal and mental constitution of man" through the "cruelties" and "pain" of captivity.[9]

By the 1820s and 1830s, the cruelties and pain of captivity had been built into the foundations of the American social order. New York State, where Dickewamis had given the interviews that became her 1824 narrative, had recently undertaken its first experiment in the solitary confinement of convicts at Auburn Prison, resulting in mass death, illness, and scandal—and, eventually, in the reforms that produced the celebrated Auburn system, the new standard in American prison discipline. In the South, slavery was approaching its fullest and most violent form in the age of the large-scale plantations. At many frontiers, the long history of conflict between Native Americans and European Americans over land, resources, and sovereignty was moving toward another crisis as U.S. military forces prepared to drive the remaining Eastern tribes beyond the Mississippi River into Oklahoma and elsewhere. Alongside the penitentiary and the plantation, the reservation was emerging as a third major zone of enclosure, divestment of rights, and identity transformation on the American scene.

The arguments for Indian Removal in the Jacksonian age were based on some of the same Enlightenment theories that had contributed to the conception of the modern prison in the works of Beccaria, Bentham, Rush, and others. Since English colonists had used a "forfeiture argument" to justify the enslavement of hostile Indians during King Philip's War, Anglo-American jurists had continued to draw from Locke and other philosophers of the social contract and the state of nature, distinguishing between the civilized, whose cultural practices entitled them to rights and property, and those uncivilized wanderers who could properly be driven from their homelands.[10]

Theorizing what came to be known as the Law of Capture, "Locke positions the Indian as lacking even a territorial claim because the Indian knows no enclosure. In Locke's script, the Indian is a drifter with claims only to the food that nourishes him at the moment he gathers it."[11] In a book on law, sovereignty, and the conflicts of the nineteenth century, the legal historian Tim Allan Garrison shows how such arguments prepared the way for Indian Removal. From the beginning, civil rights, including property rights, followed the social contract. People who appeared to be living without such codes had not yet ascended to humanity—they remained the "stupid, limited animal" of Rousseau's formulation—and could therefore be driven from the land by force. As early as 1629, the

Puritan governor John Winthrop would invoke such a theory in New England, and by the mid-eighteenth century, Enlightenment philosophers and political authorities had come to take it for granted that lands inhabited by the native peoples of the new world did not properly belong to them, because often they had not established systems of planting or civil government recognizable to the Europeans. Even the ordinarily cheerful and tolerant Benjamin Franklin, recalling the French and Indian War in his *Autobiography*, speculated that it might be "the Design of Providence to extirpate these Savages in order to make room for Cultivators of the Earth."[12]

Franklin's potentially genocidal thinking echoes the more formal and widely influential work of the Swiss theorist Emmerich de Vattel. People who "though dwelling in fertile countries, disdain the cultivation of the soil and prefer to live by plunder," wrote Vattel in his 1757 *Law of Nations*, "deserve to be exterminated like wild beasts of prey."[13] Nearly a century later, as the cotton gin and other historical forces brought the conflict between white planters and Native American tribes into the crises that would lead to the Trail of Tears and the Indian Wars of the antebellum period, American lawyers and lawmakers continued to invoke Vattel's concepts. Widely cited by such authorities as John Marshall and Joseph Story, *The Law of Nations* was "accepted as the preeminent treatise on Indian rights in the nineteenth century."[14] Like the architects of the emerging penitentiary system, the advocates of Indian Removal adapted Enlightenment ideas of natural rights to the purposes of disenfranchisement and captivity at the margins of the U.S. body politic.

Two schools of legal thought took shape. The Southern state judiciaries argued that Native Americans living within their borders were subjects of those states. Such a claim might appear to draw the Cherokees and others into the body politic, offering them the protections of citizenship. Instead, the racialized legal codes of the antebellum South were used to deprive them of land and property and, if they resisted, to try them in local and state courts hostile to their cause. Meanwhile, the federal Supreme Court under Marshall moved toward a recognition of Indian "sovereignty," defining the tribes first as a set of "domestic dependent nations" and then as independent nations capable of negotiating treaties with the United States.[15] This recognition of sovereignty, too, was turned against Native American communities: excluded from the U.S. body politic, they could be met as enemies in war, driven from their land and made to "resettle" in territories of little value to U.S. agricultural interests. The radically uneven force relations between federal armies and Native American nations led to a legal reality in which either conception of their subjectivity—as citizens of the states or of their own independent governments—could serve the project of removal. Nor did these conflicts stop at the Appalachians, or at the Mississippi River. After the wars against the Creeks and Seminoles in the Southeast and the devastation of the Cherokee Trail of Tears, conflicts between U.S. troops and Native Americans continued in the West. Even as federal armies were drawn into the Civil War, some continued to fight the Indian Wars. It was the time of Sand Creek and many other famous massacres, battles, and captures. It was the age when the frontier lands between the Mississippi River and the Pacific Ocean began their transformation into the modern, militarized, "carceral West."[16]

TO MAKE THESE MEN POSSIBLE

"Passing through, one gets caught into things; this time it was the Veterans Administration Hospital, Ft. Lyons, Colorado, 1974–75."[17] In the opening lines of *from Sand Creek*, the poet Simon J. Ortiz gestures toward the place and time of his writing. "Passing through," a vagabond self drifting across a landscape, "one" is "caught into things"—arrested, ensnared, and locked away for a while inside the hospital. Thus the poet presents his book as a record of captivity. As it unfolds, *from Sand Creek* meditates on the speaker's life in the psychiatric institution, among men damaged by the war in Vietnam, contained and managed, not healed, by their keepers. It also reflects on the history of the institution where it was composed. Confined at Fort Lyon, Ortiz discovers a site of many struggles, prowled by diverse ghosts.

Ortiz's title, *from Sand Creek*, excavates the deep history of the hospital and the land it occupies. The story goes back at least to 1860, when the U.S. Army began construction of a sandstone compound in Southern Colorado, designed to protect traders, and others traveling between Kansas and Santa Fe, from hostile Indians. In 1861, as the Civil War broke out, the place was named Fort Lyon, in honor of Nathaniel Lyon, a Union brigadier general killed in battle. During the early years of the war, while most of the fighting played out in the East, Fort Lyon was held

by a small number of soldiers who were involved in occasional skir-
mishes with local tribes. It would become famous in November 1864,
when Colonel John M. Chivington and his regiment of irregulars
stopped there during their campaign against Indians resistant to U.S.
military and business interests in the Western territories.

On a freezing cold day, Chivington and his troops rode from Fort
Lyon to a temporary settlement of Cheyenne and Arapaho Indians at
Sand Creek. Though the Indians believed they were at peace with the
United States—a U.S. flag and a smaller white flag were flying above
their encampment—Chivington's men attacked, killing more than a
hundred, mostly women and children, and driving the survivors out
across the snowy plains. "The reverend Colonel Chivington and his Vol-
unteers and Fort Lyon troops," Ortiz records, "numbering more than
700 heavily armed men, slaughtered 105 women and children and 28
men" (8). Even in the context of the Civil War and Indian Removal, the
Sand Creek Massacre was a scandal. It provoked a federal investigation
and many expressions of mourning and protest. To some, Fort Lyon began to seem like a cursed site in the Western landscape.

According to the journalist Alan Prendergast, "some taint of the
mass murder . . . seemed to find its way back to Fort Lyon" in the decades following the Sand Creek Massacre. Soon after the end of the Civil
War, an ice dam caused the nearby Arkansas River to flood. The bodies
of soldiers were washed up from the cemetery; in time, they would be
gathered, loaded onto rail cars, and shipped to Fort Leavenworth for re-
burial. The old fort was ruined, and briefly abandoned. Fort Lyon was rebuilt in 1867 but fell out of use until the early 1900s, when the navy
acquired the site and converted it into a sanitarium for tuberculosis patients. The navy then turned it over to the Veterans Bureau, which oper-
ated the hospital for most of the twentieth century. Prendergast notes
that the VA hospital was at its best in the immediate postwar years of the
1950s, but that it declined in the 1960s and 1970s. When Simon Ortiz
arrived, then, Fort Lyon was becoming outdated, even neglected. By the
1990s, it was considered one of the two worst VA facilities in the United
States, and in 2001 the federal government sold it to the state of Colorado, for use as a prison, for the price of one dollar. A former hospital
and residential facility for psychiatric patients, Fort Lyon seemed to be
well suited for use as a prison, and the state planned to house some of its

infirm inmates there. Since the opening of the prison, however, officials and inmates have discovered that the old facilities, built with asbestos and lead paint, may be causing more health problems than they are curing. "Something about the place," an inmate named Anthony Swift told Prendergast in 2007, "made me feel sick, fatigued, a little loopy. Seems like I've been sick since I got here."[18]

As he was writing *from Sand Creek* in the 1970s, Simon Ortiz was troubled by a different kind of lingering malevolence. He was haunted by the knowledge that he was sleeping and waking within virtually the same structure that had housed Chivington's soldiers a century before. Ortiz's book of poems thus emerged from his "sudden realization that . . . the cavalry who massacred the Cheyenne and Arapaho rode forth from this very place."[19] Chivington had envisioned what he called the "Battle of Sand Creek" as more than an isolated skirmish over territory; he saw it as part of a far-reaching project of racial extermination. His own correspondence reveals that his ambition was not only to defeat the Indians but to annihilate them.[20] Discovering himself in a site so deeply connected to the historical devastation and dislocation of Native Americans, Ortiz devotes much of his book to their memory. In his preface, he presents himself as the spokesperson for a people—"We, the Natives of the Western Hemisphere"—who have suffered a virtual double erasure from America. He observes that the material violence of killing, scattering, and relocating native people has been supplemented by an intellectual removal, the deletion of their lives from the historical record: "We had been made to disappear. We were invisible. We had vanished. Therefore we had no history" (6).

In one of the first poems in the volume, Ortiz attacks official histories that repress the realities of violence, blotting out the names and numbers of the dead:

> In 1969
> XXXX Coloradoans
> were killed in Vietnam.
>
> . . . .
>
> In 1864,
> there were no Indians killed. (15)

"Repression," writes Ortiz, "works like a shadow," casting the dead into obscurity (14). How can we, in the present, connect across time and geography with these lost figures? Ortiz's strategy of resistance against the repressions of official histories is the trope, common in multiculturalist discourse, of historical memory. "Remember Sand Creek," he writes (15). Like many who would speak for lives lost and silenced, Ortiz contends that a memory preserved in the culture of a minority people can be used to resist the authority of a dominant, imperialist narrative of "Conquest" and "Destiny" (43).[21]

Ortiz calls on Indians to become "insistent upon the value and integrity of their own human cultural existence." In essays and public speeches, he has called for a nationalist "Indian Literature" based on "authenticity" and rootedness in the land, and as a public intellectual he has worked to publish and promote emergent Native American writers.[22] At times, he uses a model of difference that depends not just on cultural memories but on the sense of a blood continuity. *From Sand Creek* celebrates "something precious in the memory and blood" and, whispering a promise of violent uprising after centuries of suffering, declares that "Warriors will keep alive in the blood" (33). In such moments Ortiz echoes N. Scott Momaday's writings on the concept of "blood memory," signaling at once his connection to the generations of American Indians and to a specific tradition of American Indian literature.[23]

Like many American Indian authors, however, Ortiz is a contested cultural property, pulled in different directions by the various readers who wish to claim him. His biographer, Andrew Wiget, notes that Ortiz's poetry has been read according to two "alien and antagonistic" critical frameworks.[24] Faithful to Ortiz's public declarations about his identity, most critics who have examined *from Sand Creek* have placed it in a tradition of American Indian literature, recognizing Ortiz as a central figure in what some call the "Native American Renaissance"; as recently as 2005, for instance, Patricia Clark Smith insisted that the "land, language, and oral traditions [of his native Acoma Pueblo] ground Ortiz's writing."[25] Meanwhile, however, a few readers have connected Ortiz to other, related interpretive frameworks such as trauma theory, class conflict, and postcolonial critique.[26] By expanding the range of interpretive and contextual approaches to Ortiz's work, they suggest that racial and cultural differences, while they are deeply important to the author, are not the only ways of reading the poetics of violence and resistance in *from Sand Creek*.[27]

In his preface, Ortiz writes that modern Americans' relationship to history is trapped in a "schematic of 'victors and victims' " (7). Ortiz himself has often imagined history as a conflict of white against red, but the poems in *from Sand Creek* also present alternative "schematics," other ways of seeing the lines of solidarity and difference. They explore not only the identities and allegiances that lead human subjects to make war on one another, such as Chivington's genocidal design, but also how violence itself makes humans into certain kinds of subjects. "Wars," he writes, "were to make / these men possible" (87). In these arresting and unsettling lines, Ortiz calls attention to the creation of new identities through conflict and suffering. Like other captivity narratives, then, Ortiz's volume defines Native Americans against European Americans, but in its careful attention to the remaking of captive selves it destabilizes the borders of identity, opening some surprising possibilities of contact and recognition.

Alluding to the captivity narrative with his phrase about getting "caught into things," Ortiz does not specify why he was committed to Fort Lyon, but he does represent his condition as one of unwilling confinement in a military prison-hospital. There, he encounters several other inmates, many of whom are soldiers recovering from traumas suffered in Vietnam. "Look at me and the hospital," he writes; "stricken men and broken boys / are mortared and sealed / into its defensive walls" (83). For Ortiz, the war in Asia was in some ways an extension of the U.S. imperial project that had begun in Puritan New England several centuries before, expanding across Colorado and his native New Mexico to the Pacific Ocean and beyond. He invokes the My Lai massacre as an echo of Sand Creek. But Ortiz, living with the other veterans, does not only represent himself as the descendant of "victims." He also sees himself as one of the soldiers, caught in the same material structure, driven by the same unrelenting historical forces. Soldiers shaken by the terror of war—"shallow eyes / called men"—do not appear in *from Sand Creek* as imperial victors with the blood of innocents on their hands. They are themselves captives, conscripted and transformed:

> They knew
> we would be mad,
> and so they gave us plenty.
> Little paper cups
> so full of knowledge. (37)

These soldiers are no "victors": they are devastated, divested of spirit and humanity: "his life / and the swirl of his mind," Ortiz writes of one fellow patient, "have become lead" (93).

For first-time readers, one of the most bewildering features of Ortiz's poetry in *from Sand Creek* is the ambiguity it introduces into fixed racial schemes of conquerors and vanquished. In many instances, we are unable to discern the identities of the characters in the conflicts Ortiz stages because the poet "often chooses not to characterize [them] in racial or ethnic terms."[28] A poem about how intellectual systems destroy people's capacity to feel anger and compassion, for instance, begins with an ambiguous pronoun: "Anger meant nothing to them" (59). As the poem develops, it declines to reveal who "they" are:

> Their scholars set them
> away from it
>   and deemed
> that they should be systematic. (59)

Several lines later, when "they" are described as people whose "blood [has] diminished" over time, some readers will feel that the puzzle has been solved. Recollecting that Ortiz received his earliest public education in schools run by the U.S. Bureau of Indian Affairs, we might see "blood" as the clue that reveals this as a poem about the assimilation of native people into a rationalizing "Euro-American" society that robs them of their "most precious treasure: / their compassion, their anger" (59).[29]

Other pieces of *from Sand Creek*, however, give a different resonance to these lines about stolen compassion. Just a few pages earlier, Ortiz considers the European immigrant populations recruited into the project of U.S. expansion. Again, the poem begins with an ambiguous pronoun, but this time its ambiguity is short-lived:

> They were simple enough.
> Swedes, Germans,
> Mennonites, Dutch,
> Irish, escaping
> Europe.
>   Running. (51)

Drawing on a familiar narrative of American history, Ortiz imagines downtrodden people in flight from oppression in the old world, crossing the Atlantic in search of a new life. There "should have" been, he suggests, a natural sympathy between these people and the natives: "They should have eaten / whole buffalo," he writes, "like the People wanted for them." But such a communion never takes place, because the immigrants make the mistake of "stopp[ing] / and listen[ing] to Puritans" who indoctrinate them with imperial designs, teaching them "that mountains were chains / to be crossed like breaking / something." The immigrants, writes Ortiz, are "humble hard-working folk" whose "hearts and minds" are "stole[n]" by "senators, bishops, presidents, missionaries, [and] corporation presidents" (50). They begin "simpl[y]," with only a desire to escape brutality, but they are soon organized by U.S. authorities into a colonizing force, their "hearts and minds" transformed until they become "complex liars" (51). Thus the other poem about subjects robbed of their ability to feel "anger" and "compassion," converted into "systematic" intellects, can be seen as a poem not only about the assimilation of natives but also about the recruitment of European peasant and working-class immigrants into the project of American conquest.[30]

Ortiz keeps both possibilities open by manipulating the pronoun, using *them* without securing its reference to any "native" or "European" subject. The trick of grammar enacts, quite subtly, a radical shift in the representation of the history of violence. It implies that the identities of victor and victim may not be anyone's birthright; they might instead be vacant positions in a structure of violence, like pronouns whose zone of reference is indeterminate. Thus Ortiz introduces a second "schematic of 'victors and victims' " in which each subject position is available to virtually anyone, regardless of culture or "blood," because each belongs to the dynamics of imperial war itself. This second schematic challenges us to reverse our conventional understanding of causes and effects, to grasp violence as a force not *created by* subjects predisposed to conflict but *creative of* human subjects in a "schematic" or structure of opposition. Here, power is not something wielded by one group against another but, in a sense, a subject of history that arranges populations into schematics of victims and victors.

In his *Discourse on Colonialism*, the political theorist Aimé Césaire conceives of the moment of colonial "contact" as a scene where, because of an uneven distribution of power and the exercise of force, both the colonizer and the colonized undergo a radical transformation. Neither remains what he was before; rather, what emerges are "relations of domination and submission which turn the colonizing man into . . . an army sergeant, a prison guard, a slave driver, and the indigenous man into an instrument of production."[31] In similar terms, Achille Mbembe has depicted colonialism as a "circle" from which "neither the colonist nor the colonized people emerge . . . unharmed."[32] Suturing the present of Vietnam onto the past of Sand Creek, spending his days among the "broken" agents of war, Ortiz, too, imagines that imperial violence creates a schematic, a structure of opposition ("domination and submission"), then draws people into that structure, converting them into newly created subjectivities (the "slave driver" and the "instrument of production"). When he writes that "wars . . . make / these men possible," he suggests not that war expresses the identities or desires of the warriors but that war is a transformative process for all involved. When violence erupts, victors and victims are created simultaneously in a structure that does not depend on their previous identities. The "real winner or culprit," writes Ortiz, "is the imperial one; the agents and men are only agents and men" (72). Both groups of subjects are the secondary objects of a primary exercise of power.

Such an unorthodox view of violence and subjectivity opens up some surprising kinds of cross-cultural identification, even of the charged connection Ortiz calls "compassion" or togetherness in suffering. The grammatical ambiguities of the poetry are exercises in a kind of connection by structural homology, where Ortiz is surprisingly able to extend his sympathetic identification to diverse groups "broken and scattered" by imperial violence (56). Even as he demands that readers remember the lives lost, the people massacred in places like Sand Creek and My Lai, he carefully explores how the people who committed these massacres were themselves the manipulated, "robbed," and devastated objects of imperial designs. The very "agents" who made war at Sand Creek, those who "rode like steel, / blades flashing," become, in Ortiz's vision, "stalwart victims" (21, 29). The pioneers of westward expansion are remembered not only as killers but also as the objects of violence, rendered monstrous by discipline and conflict. Their bodies and minds deteriorate; their speech is fractured:

Wasted.
Spots appeared on their lungs.
Marrow dried
    in their bones.
They ranted. (43)

Here, a schematic based on force relations allows Ortiz to extend "compassion" across the divides of racial and cultural difference. Such is the promise of a schematic of victors and victims liberated from the confines of racial or cultural identity.

Ortiz must recognize, however, that such liberation is not easy; even as the poetry frees itself to extend its compassionate voice not only to the colonized but also to the colonizing armies, it becomes haunted by ambiguity. Perceiving that "victor" and "victim" are structures produced by violence, that any human life might be drawn into either position, leaves the poet unmoored from the security of cultural belonging. Although such schematics enable Ortiz's extension of compassion to Euro-American soldiers, they interrupt other patterns of solidarity to which the poet is also committed. *From Sand Creek* is no utopian celebration of multicultural harmony or cross-cultural sympathy; it is a tortured, riven work. A painful tension is expressed at the heart of the book in one of Ortiz's most sophisticated poems on power and resistance.

The piece begins with an epigraph that seems to surge with hope, ascending toward a vision of escape from confinement: "There is an honest and healthy anger," declares Ortiz, "which will raze these walls, and it is the rising of our blood and breath which will free our muscles, minds, spirits" (84). In the opening lines of the poem that follows this epigraph, the reader is led to expect that the fulfillment of such a dream is about to be depicted. We hear the sound of a man locked away from his family and losing his identity, crying "for his mother":

His anger
was so ferocious it rang
and cracked
through the hospital
walls. (85)

Hearing the cries of the man who longs to reunite severed generations, Ortiz's speaker feels a compassionate response; the expression of pain and desire seems even to draw his body into readiness for some insurgent action: "my / shoulders hunched," he says, "in secret." In the next few lines, he seems to declare his readiness to strike, as if the "rising of our blood and breath" were really about to animate a riot or a jailbreak:

> I could have flown
> through the wall
> his anger had opened. (85)

At this point, the unifying and liberating "anger which will raze these walls" seems to be erupting. Almost as soon as it introduces this incipient revolt, however, Ortiz's poem turns against it. The reader sees that the desire stirred in the speaker is not for collective uprising but for a murderous and oppressive violence against the crying man: the speaker "could have flown" through the walls, he continues, "And strangled him / to soothed finality" (85). The shift, emphasized by unconventional punctuation that splits one sentence into two, is devastating. In the space of a line break, the poem turns from a vision of liberating collective action to the nightmare of one hospital captive recruited into the silencing and killing of another.

Readers are able to anticipate a kind of compassion between Ortiz's speaker and the man who cries for his mother because we recognize that they are both held within the same structure; they have the common schematic position of "victim." But at the same time Ortiz shows how such hope can be frustrated by any structural schematic of victors and victims, which must refuse continuity over time, through the generations (severing the captive from his parentage), and by the structure of Fort Lyon in particular, which is designed to produce subjects of violence. In the final lines of the piece, Ortiz continues to explore the collapse of solidarity, the confusion of the positions of victor and victim. "I could only cry," he writes—the speaker does experience a kind of solidarity with the other crying man, but it is a wounded solidarity. In the end, Ortiz's speaker is not stirred to collective resistance. He is battered, "mangled / like his anger," as if the violence he wished on the crying man has been turned on him instead. At once pulled toward the solidarity of victimhood and disciplined toward becoming an instrument of imperial violence, he is paralyzed, undone and "dismayed" (85).

From Sand Creek begins by promising a kind of captivity narrative in reverse, as if it would restore to the myth of the frontier the real history of massacre, displacement, and enclosure. Recollecting imperial violence and reflecting on his own captivity, however, Ortiz develops a more complex, more ambivalent account. The project of subversion, of reversing the imperial logic of conventional captivity narratives, is drawn into the same doubts and suspicions about the fixity of identity that have characterized the genre itself over the past several centuries. Grasping the character of the self as an effect, not a cause, of conflict and confinement, Ortiz's poetry imagines the dissolution of an ideological schematic of victors and victims, but it does not easily welcome the emergent possibilities of intimacy and hybridity. Like Rowlandson at the end of her narrative, Ortiz's speaker in *from Sand Creek* lies awake at night, troubled by the distant voices that reach him, unmade by captivity but also unredeemed.

NO CONNECTION TO THIS LIFE

Ortiz's *from Sand Creek* is addressed to the reader from within a site shaped and reshaped by the violence of the American frontier: a nineteenth-century military fort, then a twentieth-century veterans' hospital, then a twenty-first-century prison. There, Ortiz attempts to recover an unbroken, continuous American Indian heritage but, at the same time, perceives the frailty of any identity, witnessing the ways captivity "mangles" the self. The book is a testimony not only of endurance but also of loss and deep uncertainty; beneath the schematic of victors and victims, it discovers a common precariousness. Ortiz is especially concerned with the relationship between militarism and the science of the mind in the VA hospital, but his poetry also joins a tradition of writing about captivity from other dark territories, including the prison. Indeed, the dehumanization of Ortiz's hospital is seen, in a more extreme form, by Ortiz's contemporaries in the modern prisons of the American West.

In a collection of autobiographical writings entitled *Working in the Dark*, Jimmy Santiago Baca recalls his time in solitary confinement in a Florence, Arizona, penitentiary. Like Ortiz's speaker, Baca experiences captivity as an unmaking of the self: "There was a place in my heart where I had died. My life had compressed itself into an unbearable dread of being. The strain had been too much. I had stepped over that line where a human being has lost more than he can bear, where the pain is too intense, and he knows he is changed forever. I was now capable of killing, coldly and without feeling. I was empty. . . . I had no connection to this life."[33] Composed in prison, Baca's first volume of poetry, *Immigrants in Our Own Land*, is in part a record of this experience of dread and disconnection. It presents Baca and his fellow inmates as men captured and transformed, "long gone from this life" in a dehumanizing institution.[34] Baca's work echoes many other literary dispatches from the prison, among them Harry Hawser's lines about the solitary cell as a "living tomb" and, closer to Baca's own time, George Jackson's description of imprisonment as "the closest thing to death that one is likely to experience in this life." Reflecting on the long history of conflicts and negotiations that have defined the relations between European Americans and Native Americans in the Western United States, Baca's memoirs and poems of prison life join the captivity narrative to the imaginative literature of the penitentiary. They explore how internment breaks down the self through the administration of pain, terror, and alienating solitude; they imagine what remains of a life deprived of civil rights and subsisting at the limit point of human capacity. They also tell stories of resurrection, as the prisoner discovers in language the possible awakening of new selves capable of previously unthinkable modes of experience and expression.

In "Coming into Language," the opening essay of *Working in the Dark*, Baca refers to his childhood as a time of confusion in a society of "Anglo" "outsiders." Only in late adolescence, when he begins to learn some of the complexities of American border history and gets to know a group of Chicano prisoners, does he begin to find a sense of belonging. When the police find him in the street, his bloody arm wrapped in a T-shirt, they lock him in the Montessa Park jail on suspicion of murder, and he waits four months before the charges are dismissed.[35] There in the holding cells he encounters the literate inmates who welcome him into a language that is at once strange and mysteriously resonant: "And when they closed the books, these Chicanos, and went into their own Chicano language, they made barrio life come alive. . . . I began to learn my own language, the bilingual words and phrases explaining to me my place in the universe." Baca's first experience of captivity, a brief period in jail on a false charge, involves the discovery of a new language that seems to animate an identity which, though inborn, had lain dormant and repressed until this moment. The young Baca's persona—"intimidated and vulnerable, ridiculed and scorned"—drops away, and he welcomes the emergence of a new self enlivened by a new sense of belonging.[36]

In this early episode, Baca's story resonates with a number of other twentieth-century narratives in which prisoners are reborn into politicized minority identities. George Jackson's letters from Soledad and San Quentin, for instance, describe his transformation from a petty criminal into a militant in the cause of Marxist Pan-Africanism. Jackson in his solitary cell learns to control his body and his impulses, hardening himself into a kind of model soldier. "I do heavy exercises," he writes to his mother, "I enjoy almost perfect health and great reserves of energy and strength."[37] Similarly, in *The Autobiography of Malcolm X*, the young derelict previously known as "Satan" acquires discipline, education, and a new kind of dignity in the Nation of Islam. "In fact," he claims, "up to then, I had never been so truly free in my life."[38] In some ways, these stories of personal transformation seem oddly to conform to the ideals of the reformers who built the great penitentiaries of the nineteenth century: in the prison interior, the convict learns to govern his body, acquires a redemptive faith, and is accepted into a community. At the same time, of course, such prisoner-authors insist that their community, the collective into which the reborn self is adopted, is not the dominant society that builds the prisons. It is a minority group whose project is one of resistance, even revolution. Like African identity in the work of Jackson and Malcolm X, Chicano identity allows Baca to insist that his narrative, though it may appear to reproduce the logic of penitentiary discipline, actually *subverts* that logic, pushing it to unintended consequences. Identity here is, in part, a rhetorical strategy that gives new meaning to old stories, rewriting a narrative of confinement as one of liberation. Thus the monster engendered by the prison, in Jackson's account, returns to torment its maker.

About two years after his release from jail, Baca was incarcerated again, this time on serious drug charges. (In a memoir, *A Place to Stand*, Baca discusses his involvement in distributing Mexican marijuana for sale in Arizona and California, but insists that he was innocent of the heroin charges of which he was convicted.) In the Florence, Arizona, penitentiary, he is sent to what he calls "deadlock maximum security in a subterranean dungeon," spending many of his days and nights in solitary confinement. Like several generations of prisoners before him, Baca finds isolation unbearable: "I was frayed like a rope carrying too much weight." The walls of the cell lead him not into repentance but into dissolution. "My face," he recalls, "was no longer familiar to me."[39] In another essay, "Lock and Key," Baca describes what happens, in solitude, to the prisoner's capacity for reflection: "When a man leaves prison, he cannot look into the mirror for fear of seeing what he has become. In the truest sense, he no longer knows himself. Treated like a child by the guards, forced to relinquish every vestige of dignity, searched at whim, cursed, beaten, stripped, deprived of all privacy, he has lived for years in fear; and this takes a terrible toll."[40] The penitentiary as Baca describes it is no space of self-examination, certainly not of correction. It is a lair of "scaly demons, their claws primed for secret and unspeakable brutalities."[41] Thus Baca's captivity narrative invokes the language and tropes of the carceral gothic, depicting the solitary cell as a chamber of terror that divests its inmate of humanity—the house of the living dead.

Baca finds himself confined in "the dehumanizing environment of a prison intended to destroy me."[42] As he understands it, the Arizona penitentiary has no interest in his rehabilitation, or even his survival. It is a "tomb of concrete and iron" that "stripped me down to nothing."[43] In emphasizing that the prison is *intended* to dehumanize, Baca calls attention to the emergence, in the 1970s, of new criminal justice policies that abandoned the ideal of correction and imposed a more openly vengeful model of imprisonment. As a number of studies have shown, state and federal policies in the 1970s, inspired largely by the Arizona Republican Barry Goldwater, sought to redefine the business of punishment in "tougher" language. The dream of redemption began to fade as political rhetoric—and penal practice—became more openly vengeful and violent. Sentences were lengthened, paroles were less readily granted, and funding for job training and other educational programs was slashed, even as the total budget for building and operating prisons was dramatically expanded. Indeed, most scholars trace the origins of the sprawling twenty-first-century American prison system, which has become the largest in the world, to the policies of Goldwater, Johnson, and especially Nixon in the 1970s.[44] While Baca's writing expresses a view from inside the transforming prison system of that decade, however, he does not represent it as an unprecedented novelty but also—like Simon Ortiz—links the new prison to the long history of incarceration and wartime captivity that has shaped American history in its capitals and along its frontiers.

As he endures his second, more radically dehumanizing period behind bars, Baca undergoes a second rebirth. This time, though, the self that emerges is not the bearer of any recognizable human identity. Baca has "quit talking," relinquishing the spoken language that had been his connection to the Chicano inmates in the jail. He has turned, instead, to writing, a practice whose discovery is described as a resurrection from the abyss: "I crawled out of stanzas," Baca recalls, "dripping with birth-blood, reborn and freed from the chaos of my life." The newborn self of the prisoner-poet writes, according to Baca, "with a deep groan of doom in my blood, bewildered and dumbstruck"; but it also finds, in the condition of its doom, a surprising form of "compassion" beneath, or beyond, humanity. "I cracked out of the shell wide-eyed and insane," Baca writes. "Trees grew out of the palms of my hands, the threatening otherness of life dissolved, and I became one with the air and sky, the dirt and the iron and concrete. There was no longer any distinction between the other and I." In the profound isolation of his cell, Baca seems to escape the confines of the embodied and captive self; his captivity narrative reaches its climax in a moment of transcendence. He merges with the physical world, and "threatening otherness" gives way to communion.[45]

"I became one with the air and sky"—Baca's moment of escape, his transformative experience of perception-as-being, recalls some of the most rhapsodic passages of American Romanticism. It is a disembodied and all-encompassing vision akin to that of Emerson's "transparent eyeball" or to Whitman's conversion of himself into a medium for the voices of the downtrodden, even for the lowliest of vermin:

> Through me many long dumb voices,
> Voices of the interminable generations of prisoners and slaves,
> Voices of the diseas'd and despairing and of thieves and dwarfs,
> . . . .
> And of the rights of them the others are down upon,
> Of the deform'd, trivial, flat, foolish, despised,
> Fog in the air, beetles rolling balls of dung.[46]

Perhaps, then, we might understand Baca's turn to poetry as a kind of compensation for the rigors and indignities of confinement. Like Dickinson's speaker in "No Rack can torture me," Baca may be invoking the inviolable freedom of the poet's soul, its capacity to fly from the walls of any merely physical prison, even to feel its own liberty most intensely when the body is bound and wounded.

But the kind of transformation imagined in Baca's captivity narrative is not quite the same kind of Romantic escapism after all. Baca's imagery of transcendence is shot through with the imagery of his imprisonment. He does not just ascend to the sky; he merges with the material and filth of the prison world, with "the dirt and the iron and concrete," a phrase that recalls his description of the prison as a "tomb of concrete and iron." This merger of the self with the world, too, comes only after the long, nearly unbearable mortifications of captivity. In other words, Baca is no leaning and loafing Whitman, musing on the beautiful interconnectedness of man and nature. He will never suggest, as Whitman does, that "agonies" are merely "one of my changes of garments."[47] Rather, Baca approaches those other, darker Romantics—Dickinson in her verses on obliteration or Melville's Bartleby in his turning away from the lawyer's sentimental embrace—who represent the prison interior as a dungeon of creatures beyond the pale of humanity. No detached and speculative ego remains. Instead, Baca undergoes a radical unmaking, losing the humanity and the identity he carried into the penitentiary. He is literally dehumanized—"stripped . . . down to nothing" and "empty," recognizing "no connection to this life"—and in the condition of dehumanization he is one with the material world, with the air and with the iron.

"I sought to remain human," Baca remembers in "How We Carry Ourselves," a poem dedicated "To Others in Prisons." But the speaker seems not to have achieved the kind of endurance he had hoped for. He sees prisoners' bodies, his own among them, mauled and incorporated into the machinery of the institution. Again, the image is of a broken ligature:

We are steel hunks of gears and frayed ropes,
    our hands the toolsheds,
    our heads the incessant groan

of never ending revolving wheels
in an empty, gaunt warehouse
our blood dripping from steel joints
like grease and oil onto granite floors.[48]

Such figures are virtually beyond human recognition, beyond any reformist sympathy. What binds them together is no common ethnic or
racial identity—"Chicanos, Blacks, Whites, Indians," writes Baca in the
same poem, "we are all here, our blood all red"—but their common vulnerability: their common capacity to be unmade by the violence of captivity. At its most radical, Baca's poetry leaves behind sentimentalism to
articulate, as the common ground of carceral life and prison critique, a
kind of inhuman condition.

"If the humanities has a future as cultural criticism," writes Judith
Butler in *Precarious Life*, "and cultural criticism has a task at the present
moment, it is no doubt to return us to the human where we do not expect
to find it, in its frailty and at the limits of its capacity to make sense."[49] In
Baca's poetry, we might attend to a language that emerges after the unmaking of the subject, the poetry of a frailty, a vulnerability, hardly intelli-
gible according to conventional categories of the human. For Baca, as for
Ortiz, "compassion" means not the sympathy of the free subject for the
suffering object but the discovery of a unity in the precariousness of
human life. It does not allow the poetic subject any lofty integrity, any
power to watch and pity the misery of the other; nor does it ask for the
other's recognition in terms of any immaterial, transcendent humanity. It
insists, instead, that mutual recognition comes only after the discovery
that the self, like the other, is made and unmade by violence.

Like Simon Ortiz, Jimmy Santiago Baca is a contested cultural property. Does he belong to the canon of Native American literature, of Chicano literature, of a multicultural American literature? Roland Greene
suggests that Baca might be a major voice for the emergent critical project of a hemispheric "New World Studies," since his work, rising from a
culturally complex border area, "absorb[s] both national and transna-
tional perspectives."[50] For other critics and anthologists, such as H. Bruce
Franklin and Bell Gale Chevigny, Baca belongs to a distinct, though heterogeneous and expanding, canon of prison literature—that is, writings
produced by prisoners and ex-prisoners.

There is no doubt that Baca's poetry and its critical reception have been deeply informed by his experiences in prison, but the poetry may belong to a more expansive field than such categories allow. The presumption behind the genre of prison literature is that, unlike any others who might write about the prison—sociologists, penologists, journalists, novelists, and poets at large—the incarcerated have actually seen the institution from the inside and can therefore depict its realities in ways no one else is able to imagine, perhaps even to understand. In the introduction to his landmark collection *Prison Writing in Twentieth-Century America*, Franklin writes that "modern American prison writings constitute a coherent body of literature with a unique historical significance and cultural influence."[51] Similarly, the journalist Tom Wicker, in his preface to Franklin's volume, observes that its authors "disclose the nasty, brutish details of the life within—a life the authorities would rather we not know about, a life so far from conventional existence that the accounts of those who experience it exert the fascination of the unknown, sometimes the unbelievable."[52] As Angela Davis notes in a review of prison anthologies, such books insist "that this aggregate of writings comprises a literary genre whose significance resides not so much in its formal qualities, but rather in the alternative knowledges it is able to generate about the prison."[53] The category of prison literature rests on a premise of authenticity, on the belief that prisoners' real experiences give them a unique identity and a privileged point of view.

Thus the power and allure of prisoners' writings are understood as arising from a contradiction: though convicts are removed from the ordinary world, our world, and locked away in a dungeon-tomb of civil death and material dehumanization, they become peculiarly gifted subjects, able to expose the dark realities of the prison and to speak a semiforeign language of survival and resistance to an audience of outsiders. This critical centering of the incarcerated author receives its most sophisticated and compelling defense in Dylan Rodriguez's *Forced Passages: Imprisoned Radical Intellectuals and the U.S. Prison Regime*. Rodriguez insists that the prison unmakes subjectivity through "technologies of human immobilization and bodily disintegration." At the same time, however, the institution "reconstitutes" the inmate, sometimes in unanticipated ways: "technologies of incarceration do not *only* repress or delimit the praxis of imprisoned activists—this programmatic violence inhabits, occupies, and interpellates political and historical subjects within a specific structure of historical confrontation." In other words, the prison makes its own prisoners, but it does not make them just as it pleases. It incubates the agents of its own critique and resistance, prisoner-authors who open a "pathway of radicalism and insurgency."[54]

The critical approaches of Franklin and Rodriguez help to illuminate the peculiar achievement of Baca's refashioned captivity narratives. Baca's writing, like that of Rodriguez's canon of imprisoned intellectuals, is deeply "inscribed by the very logic of violence, disappearance, and death that forms the regime from which it is produced."[55] Thus Baca discovers a kind of liberation in the dismantling of humanity, in the reduction of the captive to the condition of mere flesh (or dirt) and blood (or oil). Unlike his first rebirth into Chicano identity, Baca's second awakening is not a subversion of the dominant narrative of carceral resurrection from a minority point of view; rather than subverting the story, it interrupts and dismantles it, stalling it in the phase of living death. It imagines the radical divestment of humanity as a condition of escape from the prison's subject-making regime. Somewhat like Melville's Bartleby, Baca refuses reform's sentimental—humanizing yet paralyzing—embrace.

Baca's work is, in part, a narrative of his own captivity. It describes his progressive disappearance from the known world, into a dark and alien territory. It depicts the disintegration of his old identity and his discovery of new selves and new languages. It crafts its imagery of communion and transcendence from the materials of the soul-destroying carceral system. Yet Baca himself insists that the effect of his captivity has been to collapse the separation between himself and all that once seemed alien—"There was no longer any distinction," he writes, "between the other and I." He imagines that his poetry creates "bridges of fire" between his solitary cell and the outside world.[56] He thinks of the readers who pick up his poems as interlocutors in a kind of secret and sustaining conspiracy.

Even if Baca did not present himself as such a translator, his most compelling articulations of resistance—his expressions of a common vulnerability, frailty, and inhumanity—bring him into the company not only of Ortiz and Jackson but also of Dickinson and Melville. He speaks not only from within the prison but also, even more powerfully, as part of a wider tradition of imaginative writing on captivity in America. He taps into the story of death and rebirth around which reformers like Benjamin Rush imagined the revolutionary house of corrections; he speaks of the living death encoded in the penal law and performed in the prison rituals of two centuries; and though this complex of images and narrative patterns may circumscribe the limits of his self-expression, it also gives him a structure to inhabit and, within limits, to rebuild. Prisoners do not occupy a zone of exile outside the circle of juridical and philosophical humanity; the prison that holds them is one of the primary sites through which the very idea of modern humanity is imagined and contested. One central project of this book, therefore, has been to disclose connections that link the writings of inmates to other texts and discourses concerned with the American prison, assembling an archive and an interpretive approach to its imaginative representations. The prison raises a wall between the captive and the world at large, but it is also the medium of their contact, of their common cause.

Epilogue

IN THE AGE OF GUANTÁNAMO, Abu Ghraib, and a sprawling do-mestic prison-industrial complex, the American prison looms vast and awful on the social horizon, an international scandal and a humanitar-ian disaster. The problems of mass captivity and of its consequences for the meaning of humanity, partly buried since the riots and radical move-ments of the 1970s, are again forcing themselves into public and critical consciousness. Today, however, the prison no longer promises to correct criminals or to train citizen-subjects. Instead, it appears as a kind of grotesquely violent warehouse whose inmates have been divested of rights, even of humanity, and condemned to a living death.

Perhaps the most notorious of the contemporary institutions, the war prison at Guantánamo Bay, has often been described as a monstrous "exception" to long-standing modern codes and procedures, an island of secret violence in a juridical void, created by a sovereign power that sus-pends the law under the pretense of a wartime state of emergency. Don-ald Pease describes Guantánamo's detainees as "persons outside the existing juridical categories and refused the basic dignities of legal pro-cess"; these are not the rights-bearing subjects of political modernity but "exceptions to the human condition" reduced to mere "animated flesh."[1] In similar language, Judith Butler writes that, according to the authority that holds them, "the prisoners indefinitely detained in Guantanamo

Bay are not considered 'subjects' protected by international law, are not entitled to regular trials, to lawyers, to due process"; "the humans who are imprisoned in Guantanamo," Butler goes on, "do not count as human."[2] And Susan Willis refers to the detainees as "humans who are less than chattel," men without a country "who have no status."[3] Guantánamo is not a conventional modern prison, designed to discipline and punish; it is a "camp" whose inmates have lost the protections of citizenship and now endure, suspended in an "indefinite" time and space, beyond the pale. In short, the prevailing account of the "new war prison" in the critical humanities represents it as an anachronism in modern history, a violation of the established national and international order that inaugurates a terrifying new state. Guantánamo is the prison that appears when detention, interrogation, and punishment are conducted outside the bounds of the law; its inmate is the vulnerable life exiled from the circle of juridical humanity.

Much has been illuminated by such interpretations. We see, especially, how the tremendously influential thesis of Foucault's *Discipline and Punish*—that prisons produce self-governing subjects through isolation and surveillance—loses its explanatory power in the age of Guantánamo. The urgent questions for the critique of captivity no longer seem to be those of a private, inward-looking subjectivity or of a managerial "governmentality"; instead, the old, undead issues of sovereignty and war have reawakened in a new century. In the war prison, we find none of the techniques of training, labor discipline, or rehabilitation associated with the penitentiary of the Enlightenment reformers. In place of such humanizing disciplines, we confront a violent captivity that strips away rights and mortifies subjectivity, a policy and practice of dehumanization.

The scholarly and theoretical critique of dehumanization responds not only to the conditions in the war prisons, so far as they have come to light, but also to their official justification in the law. Legal and military authorities, in developing the concepts behind indefinite detention and interrogation, have carefully discriminated their captive, the terrorist "illegal enemy combatant," from other, conventionally protected categories. Under the standards of criminal procedure, the accused offender would be entitled to habeas corpus and due process rights. Under the terms of the Geneva Convention and other international accords, the prisoner of war would require a minimum standard of decent treatment. The third category invented by the White House is a shadowy figure whose humanity is not so protected. Bearing neither the rights ensured by the criminal law nor those nominally recognized on the modern battlefield, the illegal enemy becomes the object of virtually unlimited violence. It is this dangerous form of legal nonrecognition that critics such as Butler and Pease mean to address when they use the language of dehumanization. Their studies aim to diagnose the legal and political discourse of exclusion that enables the violence of indefinite detention, secrecy, and torture.

The difference between the official language of nonrecognition and the critics' position, of course, is that the critics see dehumanization not as a justifiable necessity but as a scandal and a crime. Their implicit or explicit claim is that those who "do not count as human" nonetheless are human, and ought to be recognized as such by the U.S. institutions that hold them. Without such an imperative, the analysis of the war prison as a scene of dehumanization would be more or less a repetition of official policy, a description without the force of protest. Finally, then, the critique of the war prisons advances a human rights claim. It points to a dark space where the universal field of humanity exceeds the restricted circle of citizenship (or legal personhood)—and it calls for a wider inclusion. It holds up figures dehumanized through their exclusion, neglect, and exposure to violence, and it insists upon their humanity. "Claims for humanity," as Butler has written elsewhere, "are always made for those who mark the limits of juridical status."[4] In a sense, the human rights claim is always made by or in the name of figures who appear monstrously inhuman from another point of view.[5] As a kind of ethical and imaginative language, it has something in common with the sentimental mode in literature: it represents the suffering of the abject in order to embrace them, to draw them into the protective circle of humanity. It echoes the cries of such great reformers as Harriet Beecher Stowe, Charles Dickens, and William Roscoe: *These*, it declares, *are our fellow creatures*.

On the one hand, such a declaration is an obvious statement of fact. On the other hand, it has its imperative force because of conditions that deny the humanity of those for whom human rights are being claimed. The human rights claim is a speech act that attempts to change the world in order to make itself true.[6] As Hannah Arendt famously perceived in her study of the refugees displaced after the Second World War, human rights may be imagined as natural and inviolable, but the protection of humanity in the historical world depends on laws and institutions: "The Rights of Man . . . had been defined as 'inalienable' because they were supposed to be independent of all governments," writes Arendt, "but it turned out that the moment human beings lacked their own government and had to fall back upon their minimum rights, no authority was left to protect them and no institution was willing to guarantee them."[7] Thus, for those who lack citizenship or other forms of juridical recognition, for those who have nothing but their natural humanity, human rights become "unenforceable."[8]

In response to this gap between living humanity and the institutions that protect it, the human rights claim calls for an ethical recognition, even a sympathetic identification with the victim's humanity, and an extension of institutional safeguards to secure us all within the same juridical community.[9] The understanding of "humanity" as a certain "status conferred by the protective work of the law" is precisely what "enables the renaming of human rights violations as practices of dehumanization."[10] Critics call attention to an exclusion from a rights-bearing humanity that would otherwise, presumably, shelter everyone within its circle from such extreme, transfiguring violence. Thus human rights activists and lawyers argue that the standards of due process and habeas corpus, among other safeguards, should apply not only to U.S. citizens arrested for crimes but also to the captives held by the U.S. military as part of the ongoing, indefinite war on terror. Both the legal cases and the political activism surrounding Guantánamo have devoted themselves to this expansion of juridical humanity. In response to widespread protests, the Bush administration has begun to build several state-of-the-art prisons in the war zones overseas.[11]

Human rights claims and the organizations that advance them have a vital political urgency. Their appeals to U.S. and international legal standards have been perhaps the only effective vocabulary of protest against indefinite detention, torture, and other abuses in the war prisons. After a long study of the history and representations of the American prison, however, my conclusion is that carceral dehumanization is neither a novelty nor an "exception," and the mere expansion of the kind of juridical humanity encoded in the criminal law will not end it. The news from

Guantánamo is disturbing, but such captivity has a national and international history. With its promise of human recognition, the prison has, from the beginning, claimed the power to dehumanize, to sentence its inmates to the exile of living death. The imaginative writing arising from its cells suggests that its peculiarly mortifying form of humanization must not simply be enlarged; it must be decomposed and refashioned from within. The disasters of the war prisons and warehouses of incapacitation emerge during a profound transformation in the relationship between human subjects and the powers that govern them. The very foundations of citizenship and sovereignty seem to be at stake. Might it be possible, in such a moment, to imagine a concept of humanity that opposes the virtually unlimited violence of indefinite war without attempting to defend the old concepts on which the prison itself has always depended?

Provoked by Guantánamo and Abu Ghraib, scholars have offered several accounts of the historical and legal conditions that have made the war prisons possible. In "Where Is Guantánamo?" for instance, Amy Kaplan explores how a hundred years of imperialism established a legal framework that enabled American military and administrative powers to control populations without granting them constitutional rights. This internalizing exclusion, Kaplan demonstrates, set the precedent for the Bush administration's designation of the "enemy combatant," a person "codified as less than human and less deserving of human, international, or constitutional rights."[12] Turning from the periphery to the "homeland," Michelle Brown connects the spectacular degradations of Abu Ghraib to a domestic prison complex that, over the past few decades, has itself devolved toward a violent inhumanity. The connections between the war camps and the prison at home are not only rhetorical. Brown traces the specific biographical and material lines from the war prison back to "the penal system at home."[13] In the case of Guantánamo, there is an even more precise repetition: the solitary confinement units of the military camp are literally modeled on the "super-max" prisons first built to hold U.S. offenders.[14] A common theory of captivity finds its concrete manifestation in such architecture, and we cannot fully understand the war prisons as exceptions to the ordinary, domestic practice of legal captivity. If they are key sites in the new war on terror, producing such new juridical categories as the enemy combatant, they are also knots in a heterogeneous but continuous prison network that extends from the homeland across the globe.

The "ominous discretionary powers used to justify [abuse and torture at Abu Ghraib]," according to Colin Dayan, "are not exceptional; they are routine and entirely familiar to those who follow the everyday treatment of prisoners in the United States."[15] A common set of discourses and practices, Brown concludes, is "apparent in the precedents and policies reformulating and restricting the rights of prisoners, not just in war zones abroad, but in the domestic interior."[16] Both Dayan and Brown emphasize the dramatic expansion of imprisonment, along with the severe curtailment of prisoners' rights and rehabilitation programs, since the 1970s. These transformations have turned U.S. prisons into what radicals in the prison abolition movement sometimes call "domestic war zones."[17] In response, a growing movement of activists, lawyers, and critics, both inside and outside the prison system, carries on a campaign in the name of the human rights of the incarcerated.

In September 1971, the inmates of New York's Attica Prison rose up in what would become one of the most notorious riots in American history. They were provoked, in part, by the news that George Jackson had been killed in California, but their revolt was not only an occasional expression of mourning and rage; it was a protest against the inhumane conditions in which they were being held. The inmates felt they had endured too long the racism and abuses of their keepers. They resented the cramped, unsanitary conditions of their confinement. They grieved the restrictions on their rights of political expression and religious observance. "We are men," they declared in the opening lines of their published demands. "We are not beasts and we do not intend to be beaten and driven as such." Much like contemporary critics who protest the dehumanizing force of the American prison abroad and at home, the Attica inmates began their demands with the question of humanity. Their call for reform was founded on a human rights claim.[18]

By 1981, legal scholars had begun to observe the "decline of the rehabilitative ideal" in American penal policy. In place of the reformist ambitions that had traditionally defined the penitentiary, they foresaw the resurgence of a "war theory" of punishment. The prison seemed to be losing its interest in reclaiming the convict's humanity, regressing to an ancient code of vengeful violence against enemies of the state. In the decades since those prophesies, the transformation has accelerated, creating circumstances widely called a "crisis."[19] The ideology of toughness, of retribution, or of mere containment displaces the enlightened, reformist language of mercy and healing. The asylum degenerates into the warehouse. The house of corrections becomes the domestic war zone.

When did the American prison lose its humanity? The response to the decline of rehabilitation and the rise of the warehouse prisons has been, in the main, a defensive one: an attempt to recover the legal protections that the courts have taken from prisoners or to preserve those precious few rights that are still recognized. Critics call for decent living conditions, improved health care, drug and alcohol rehabilitation, job training, and other reforms. Reacting against the warlike and inhumane violence of the new carceral system, they call for a return to humanity. Indeed, in many ways, the campaign for prisoners' rights is a renewal of the movement that abolished the horror of the scaffold and sought to reclaim the offender for the modern marketplace and civil society—in other words, to the movement that built the prison system in the first place.

The critical project of exposing and resisting dehumanization in the American prison is not a novelty of the twenty-first century. The scandals of the war prisons today, like the riots of the 1970s, have made deathly conditions spectacularly visible, but such conditions are both older and more far-reaching than the periodic scandals might suggest. One lesson of my work on this book is that a certain outraged reaction against cruel and degrading punishments in the late eighteenth century—against the "loathsome" overcrowding of jails and the "disgraceful" violence of the scaffold—motivated the reforms that created the prison as the new standard in punishment. Political theorists such as Beccaria and Rush argued that the scaffold wrongfully spilled the blood of the condemned, violating the standards of the social contract. Reformers such as Howard and Smith were appalled by the dangerous, unsanitary conditions of dungeon-prisons where convicts were neglected, corrupted, and exposed to unregulated violence. Like many in today's human rights movements, the Enlightenment reformers were especially troubled by the idea that the innocent—children and the wrongly accused—might be enduring the horrors of the oubliette. The penitentiary was designed to provide a humanitarian solution to such terrifying abuses.

What actually emerged, however, was a new pattern of violence in which civil death and ritualized mortification were justified as ways of preparing the convicted offender for a restoration to humanity. In place of the dark pit stood an ascetic discipline of silence and penitence. In place of the capricious spectacle of the scaffold stood the exemplary mortification of the solitary cell. "Dehumanization" of one kind or another has thus been fundamental to the American prison since its conception, and it continues to follow wherever the prison goes. Perceiving the range and depth of carceral mortification, moreover, is not only a matter of the maps we draw of the carceral network or of the historical narratives we tell about when the prison gained or lost its humanitarian ways. It is a matter of how we understand the profound relationship between imprisonment and the very concept of humanity enshrined in the laws, institutions, and imaginative world of our modernity.

The American prison has always been a monument to a certain ideal of juridical humanity, even of human rights, resting on a foundation of violent dehumanization. The subjection of the inmate to a ritualized unmaking and remaking dramatizes a myth of the social contract in which the criminal law claims the power to mortify citizens in order to resurrect them. The cell is designed to quarantine the inmate from dangerous and corrupting influences, to provide a clean space for reflection and the recomposition of the mind, but it is also a tomb of abjection that breaks the will and severs the inmate's ties to the known world. Imprisoned convicts in the United States—whose most enduring image, over the past two centuries, has been that of the dead held captive by the living—are not outside the law. Far from it: the inhuman punishment they endure is within the purview of penal law, which, since the founding of the penitentiary, has assumed the power to harm and deprive offenders as part of the project of reclaiming their humanity. There is no suspension of the law, no state of emergency declared; penal violence is meticulously scripted and managed by legislatures, judges, and prison administrators. It is the subject of reformist debates and is explicitly approved, either as a necessary evil or as a disciplinary good in the service of rehabilitation. Perhaps more than any other institution, the prison manifests the power of the law to disfigure and kill those within its circle of rights, in the name of humanity.

If the archive I have assembled and interpreted in this book has some value in addressing the critical problems of the age of the new war prison, it may be that, at its best, it provides a language of critique—directed not against the inhuman violence done to those outside juridical humanity but against the mortification of those whose predicament is that they are inextricably ensnared within the law. The various works of the American carceral imagination compose a gothic alternative to the sentimental language of reform. These are the voices of figures dying so that a new humanity might be born:

> I prefer not to . . .
> Fated to a living tomb . . .
> This monster they've engendered in me . . .
> I know no way but through the grave . . .
> Alone, I cannot be . . .
> He was not a being, an entity; he was a commonwealth . . .
> Passing through, one gets caught into things . . .
> One with the dirt and the iron and concrete.

These monstrous apparitions, these semilegible utterances do not come from beyond the pale, calling for recognition. They do not speak in the sentimental mode that would draw the abject other into the protective circle of humanity. Instead, their gothic imagination confronts humanity with the monstrousness it creates, not through exclusion but through the most profound, and most mortifying, burial within itself. They represent the ghosted inhumanity whose ruins the sovereign subject of humanity has not quite transcended—the presence of the other that the self continuously bears. Their secret is that it is not enough to expand humanity, if the promise of humanity claims the power of mortification; we must also unmake and recompose our concept of the human to divest it of its dehumanizing power. In the end, it is not the inmate but the prison, with its harrowing forms of resurrection, that must be sacrificed in order to be redeemed.

NOTES

INTRODUCTION

1. Dickinson, poem 303. Throughout, Dickinson's poems are cited according to their numbers in Thomas H. Johnson's edition of *The Complete Poems*.
2. On the invention of Dickinson as a lyric sensibility and the consequences of that invention for the interpretive history of her texts, see Jackson, *Dickinson's Misery*.
3. See, for example, Fuss, "Interior Chambers."
4. Hanway, *Distributive Justice and Mercy*; Beaumont and Tocqueville, *Report*, 55.
5. In his preface to the U.S. edition of Beaumont and Tocqueville's *Report*, the legal scholar Francis Lieber made this point explicit, arguing that women were incapable of the reasoned reflection necessary for rehabilitation: "The two sexes have been destined by the Creator for different spheres of activity, and have received different powers to fulfill their destiny. The women destined for domestic life, and that sphere in which attachment and affection are most active agents, has been endowed with more lively feeling and acute sensibility: she feels; man reasons (10). The gender ideology of separate spheres is part of reform's deep relationship with sentimentalism, a connection I explore in detail, especially in chapter 2.
6. Foucault, *Discipline and Punish*, 233.
7. See Melossi and Pavarini, *The Prison and the Factory*; and Ignatieff, *A Just Measure of Pain*.
8. See Adorno and Horkheimer, *Dialectic of Enlightenment*; Dumm, *Democracy and Punishment*; and Rothman, *The Discovery of the Asylum*.
9. Adorno and Horkheimer, *Dialectic of Enlightenment*, 187–188. Cited as quoted, in a variant translation, in Dumm, *Democracy and Punishment*, 4.

10. Hawser, "The Captive," in *Buds and Flowers*, 70.

11. Baca, *Working in the Dark*, 10.

12. Goffman, *Asylums*.

13. Dayan, "Legal Slaves."

14. Rush, *Essays*, 91.

15. Spierenburg, "The Body and the State," 55.

16. Foucault, *Discipline and Punish*, 48–49.

17. Shoemaker, "The Problem of Pain," 15. See also Greg T. Smith, "The Decline of Public Physical Punishment," which argues that eighteenth-century "public executions in the metropolis had developed into a highly ritualized 'cultural' event" (27–28).

18. Evans, *Fabrication of Virtue*.

19. Spierenburg, "The Body and the State," 55–57.

20. Hoffer and Scott, quoted in Friedman, *Crime and Punishment*, 26.

21. Friedman, *Crime and Punishment*, 26.

22. Evans, *Fabrication of Virtue*, 75.

23. Spierenburg, "The Body and the State," 58.

24. Evans, *Fabrication of Virtue*, 75.

25. Spierenburg, "The Body and the State," 58–59.

26. Spierenburg, "The Body and the State," 59–60.

27. Meranze, "A Criminal," 307.

28. Rush, *Essays*, 81.

29. See Foucault, *Discipline and Punish*, 63.

30. See Meranze, "A Criminal."

31. See Rothman, *The Discovery of the Asylum*.

32. Beaumont and Tocqueville, *Report*, 52.

33. Dumm, *Democracy and Punishment*, 113.

34. Beaumont and Tocqueville, *Report*, 50.

35. Dayan argues that "if Foucault's metropolitan world of public torture . . . died out by the eighteenth and the beginning of the nineteenth century, the punitive spectacle and the requisite bodies were resurrected in the colonies" ("Legal Slaves," 12). Similarly, Jason Haslam, though he draws heavily from Foucault's work, criticizes its "lack of discussion of the impact of slavery on the formation of the early prison—a connection which . . . has a significant impact on any understanding of the prison as a modern institution and of its use of both physical and societal violence" (*Fitting Sentences*, 10). For a discussion of how Foucault's thoughts on the history of punishment might be extended to include colonial projects of "modernization" and "humanization," see Asad, *Formations of the Secular*, 102–113.

36. While the history of slavery in the United States goes back to the earliest days of the Republic, historians cite the period between 1820 and the Civil War as the fullest development of the plantation system—"It was actually 1820," notes W. J. Cash, "before the plantation was fully on the march, striding over the hills of Carolina and Mississippi" (*The Mind of the South*, 10). See also Berlin, *Generations of Captivity*.

37. Roscoe, *Observations*, 51.

38. Morrison, *Playing in the Dark*, 38.

39. This connection is made by Orlando Patterson in his classic study, *Slavery and Social Death*, and by others, including Colin Dayan in "Legal Terrors" and "Legal Slaves and Civil Bodies." I explore it in greater detail in chapter 1.

40. See, for example, Asad's discussion of the decline of torture in *Formations of the Secular*.

41. Rousseau, *Social Contract*, 151.

42. These lines from Blackstone are quoted by Dayan, who elaborates their meaning into a theory of civil sacrifice: "In this duality of civil and natural, the natural person who existed before the social contract haunts the margins of the formal community. The resurrection of the individual as civil person depends on sacrifice: the old nature takes on the skin of the civil" (Dayan, "Legal Slaves," 4).

43. C. Taylor, *Modern Social Imaginaries*, 6, 23, 27.

44. Asad, *Formations of the Secular*, 101. In similar terms, Mark Canuel has described the movement away from the scaffold, toward incarceration, as "a species of humanitarian reform that simultaneously—and more importantly—aimed to redefine the relationship between political subjects and legal structures" (*Shadow of Death*, 12).

45. Hawthorne, *The Scarlet Letter*, 45. Subsequent references are cited parenthetically in the text.

46. As Robert Shulman observes in "The Artist in the Slammer," *The Scarlet Letter* "is not . . . an accurate portrayal of the seventeenth century . . . but rather an image that emerges from the depths of [Hawthorne's] contemporary experience" (83). Similarly, Richard Brodhead writes that the "system" of punishments explored in the novel "is exactly that . . . kind of discipline the mid-*nineteenth* century [felt] compelled to look in the face" ("Sparing the Rod," 77).

47. Cover, "Nomos and Narrative," 100.

48. White, *Heracles' Bow*, 199, 205. See also Crotty, *Law's Interior*.

49. See Rothman, *The Discovery of the Asylum*.

50. I am grateful to Hazel Carby for her provocation to see the prison and the plantation, especially, as "mutually constitutive" institutions.

51. See Miller, *The Novel and the Police*; and Grass, *The Self in the Cell*.

52. See Franklin, *The Victim as Criminal and Artist*; Haslam, *Fitting Sentences*; and Rodriguez, *Forced Passages*.

53. Butler, *Precarious Life*, 140.

54. Cheah, *Inhuman Conditions*, 3.

55. Rodriguez, *Forced Passages*.

CHAPTER 1. CIVIL DEATH AND CARCERAL LIFE

1. Jackson, *Soledad Brother*, 19–20.

2. Genet, "Introduction," 1.

3. Hawser, "The Captive," in *Buds and Flowers*, 70.

4. Rothman, *The Discovery of the Asylum*, 86.

5. For Foucault, the penitentiary is an "apparatus" that trains deviants to monitor and control themselves, creating "docile bodies" by ensuring the disciplinary power of the "soul." For Marxist critics such as Dario Melossi and Massimo Pavarini, the penitentiary is a factory for the making of perfect workers who will stop thieving and looting, and accept the logic of wage work in the factory. For Thomas Dumm, following Adorno and Horkheimer, the prison turns out ideal citizens who will submit to the isolation and hierarchy of the modern political order. I address these arguments in more detail in the Introduction and in chapter 3.

6. Colin Dayan's critical work is the most important exception to this trend in prison studies. I discuss Dayan's ideas at length in the concluding pages of this chapter.

7. "Civil Death Statutes," 968.

8. Johnston, *Forms of Constraint*, 18.

9. Pollock and Maitland, *History of English Law*, 1:434.

10. Itzkowitz and Oldak, "Restoring the Ex-Offender's Right to Vote," 721–723; Von Bar, *History of Continental Criminal Law*, 24–25.

11. Ewald, " 'Civil Death,' " 1059; Rusche and Kircheimer, *Punishment and Social Structure*, 21.

12. Pollock and Maitland, *History of English Law*, 2:449. See Itzkowitz and Oldak, "Restoring the Ex-Offender's Right to Vote," 722–723 and Ewald, " 'Civil Death,' " 1059.

13. For similar accounts of the origins of modern civil death and disenfranchisement penalties, see "Civil Death Statutes," 969–970; "Disenfranchisement of Ex-Felons," 1301–1302; Itzkowitz and Oldak, "Restoring the Ex-Offender's Right to Vote," 721–727; and Ewald, " 'Civil Death,' " 1058–1064.

14. Agamben, *Homo Sacer*, 105.

15. An English-language version of Beccaria's *Of Crimes and Punishments* was printed by William Young in Philadelphia in 1793, where it informed the growing reform movement led by Benjamin Rush, Benjamin Franklin, and others. Wai Chee Dimock, in *Residues of Justice*, notes that long sections of Beccaria's work were also copied into Thomas Jefferson's *Commonplace Book*, informing the legal codes he drafted for Virginia (15).

16. For Beccaria's account of the social contract and how it "places obligations on both" individual and society, see *Of Crimes and Punishments*, 10–13.

17. Beccaria, *Of Crimes and Punishments*, 66.

18. Beccaria, *Of Crimes and Punishments*, 67.

19. Beccaria, *Of Crimes and Punishments*, 68.

20. Beccaria, *Of Crimes and Punishments*, 58.

21. "And that they may be known from others," Monson continued, "they must be shaved both head and face, and marked in the cheek with a hot iron, for men to take notice of them to be the king's labourers, for so they should be termed and not slaves." M. Oppenheim, ed. *The Naval Tracts of Sir William*

Monson (London: Navy Records Society, 1923), 4:109. Quoted in Linebaugh and Rediker, *The Many-Headed Hydra*, 57.

22. Ekirch, *Bound for America*, 21.

23. Quoted in Ekirch, *Bound for America*, 21.

24. In "Legal Terrors," Dayan describes a "transatlantic domain of penance, punishment, and possession" (45) that began to take shape in the seventeenth century and continues into the present. For example, she connects the early history of punishment in New England to the forms of legal exclusion and torture involved in Caribbean slavery (43–46). She goes on to explore the changing conception of the penal soul in the early era of penitentiary discipline, by way of an intellectual tradition that includes John Locke, Jonathan Edwards, and Benjamin Rush.

25. Ekirch, *Bound for America*, 19.

26. A. E. Smith, *Colonists in Bondage*, 131.

27. A. E. Smith, *Colonists in Bondage*, 124.

28. A. E. Smith, *Colonists in Bondage*, 125.

29. A. E. Smith, *Colonists in Bondage*, 118.

30. Ekirch, *Bound for America*, 152–153. Ekirch fully recognizes that "colour mattered a great deal in eighteenth-century life," and that white servants, unlike black slaves, were not doomed to "perpetual" servitude based on "blood"; still, he shows how convicts, "in the eyes of fearful colonists, embodied the most repugnant features of human society," and how closely their legal and material condition resembled those of the slaves (151–156).

31. A. E. Smith, *Colonists in Bondage*, 117–119.

32. A. E. Smith, *Colonists in Bondage*, 133–166.

33. Franklin told the story of one who "laid his Left-hand on a Block, cut it off, and threw it at [his mistress], saying, *Now make me work, if you can*" (Franklin, "On Transported Felons"). The same story was reported in the *Maryland Gazette* in the spring of 1751 (Ekirch, *Bound for America*, 157).

34. Ekirch, *Bound for America*, 138.

35. Chapin, *Criminal Justice in Colonial America*, 52–55.

36. Lepore, *The Name of War*, 155.

37. A 1641 text known as the "Body of Liberties" had established the legal terms: "There shall never be any Bond-slavery, Villenage or Captivity amongst us," it declared, "unless it be lawful Captives taken in just Wars" (quoted in Lepore, *The Name of War*, 162). The fullest and best-known version of the "just war" theory would be made by John Locke in his *Two Treatises on Government* (see Farr, " 'So Vile and Miserable an Estate' ").

38. Quoted in Lepore, *The Name of War*, 163.

39. Lepore, *The Name of War*, 159.

40. Hanway, *Distributive Justice and Mercy*, 45.

41. G. W. Smith, *Defence of the System of Solitary Confinement*, 75.

42. Boston Prison Discipline Society, 1846 *Report*, 35

43. Foucault, *Discipline and Punish*, 74, my emphasis.

44. Bouvier, *Institutes of American Law*, 94.

45. Bouvier, *Institutes of American Law*, 95.

46. "Civil Death Statutes," 971.

47. "Civil Death Statutes," 968.

48. See "Disenfranchisement of Ex-Felons," 1302.

49. Ewald, " 'Civil Death,' " 1045

50. Dayan, "Legal Slaves," 3.

51. Dayan, "Legal Slaves," 16.

52. Goffman, *Asylums*, 15–16, 35.

53. Goffman, *Asylums*, 16.

54. Goffman, *Asylums*, 14.

55. Hassine, "How I Became a Convict," 16.

56. Hassine, "How I Became a Convict," 15.

57. Johnston, *Eastern State*, 48–49.

58. Dickens, *American Notes*, 91. Dickens's horrified reaction to the solitary prison was widely circulated in its time and continues to be cited as a sign that some nineteenth-century authorities were not fooled by reformers' professions about humane correction. See, for example, Dayan, "Legal Slaves," 16; and Rusche and Kircheimer, *Punishment and Social Structure*, 136–137. For their part, the men who built and oversaw Eastern State Penitentiary sought to defend it against Dickens, claiming that the novelist had let his fictional imagination get the better of his "power of detection" and that his "account . . . may be presumed to be exaggerated or untrustworthy" (Richard Vaux, *Brief Sketch*, 112). I return to Dickens at greater length in chapter 2.

59. Haslam, *Fitting Sentences*, 27.

60. Quoted in Rothman, *The Discovery of the Asylum*, 95.

61. Beaumont and Tocqueville, *Report*, 84.

62. The age of the prison, the plantation, and the reservation was also the age of other emergent institutions of captivity, such as the asylum and the reformatory. See Rothman, *The Discovery of the Asylum*, and Reiss, *Theaters of Madness*.

63. These lines are quoted and refuted in Roscoe, *Observations*, 50–51.

64. Exploring the relations between punishment and slavery, several critics have noted the connection between civil death and social death. The most complex historical study is Sellin's *Slavery and the Penal System*, published in 1976. For more recent accounts, see Dayan, "Legal Slaves," and Wacquant, "From Slavery to Mass Incarceration." For a reading of these problems in relation to Douglass's *Narrative*, see A. Y. Davis, "From the Prison of Slavery to the Slavery of Prison."

65. Patterson, *Slavery and Social Death*, 5.

66. Douglass, *Narrative*, 135.

67. Douglass, *Narrative*, 105.

68. Douglass, *Narrative*, 47–48.

69. Patterson, *Slavery and Social Death*, 51.

70. Douglass, *Narrative*, 49.

71. Mbembe, "Necropolitics," 21.

72. Douglass, *Narrative*, 105.

73. Andrew M'Makin, untitled poem accompanying a painting of Eastern State Penitentiary in Wild, *Panoramas and Views of Philadelphia*, n.p.

74. Patterson, *Slavery and Social Death*, 41–43, 5.

75. James Boyd White, in his analysis of the language of criminal law, suggests that such arguments are almost always a "cruel joke," a rhetoric used to "reassure an audience" about the use of "the power of discretionary punishment." White, *Heracles' Bow*, 201.

76. Meranze, "A Criminal."

77. Rothman, *The Discovery of the Asylum*, 102.

78. Beaumont and Tocqueville, *Report*, 164.

79. Beaumont and Tocqueville, *Report*, 163.

80. Allen, *Examination of the Remarks*, 4; my emphasis.

81. Roscoe, *Observations*, 47–49.

82. Roscoe, *Observations*, 10.

83. Roscoe, *Observations*, 49.

84. Foucault, *Discipline and Punish*, 235. Similarly, Ruth Gilmore notes that many well-meaning "remedies . . . get caught in the logic of the system itself, such that a reform strengthens, rather than loosens, prison's hold" (*Golden Gulag*, 242).

85. Rush, *Essays*, 90.

86. Dumm, *Democracy and Punishment*, 87–88; see also Meranze, *Laboratories of Virtue*.

87. See Dumm, *Democracy and Punishment*, 87–112.

88. Rousseau, *Social Contract*, 151.

89. Quoted in Warner, *Letters of the Republic*, 100.

90. Roach, *Cities of the Dead*, 3.

91. Dayan, "Legal Slaves," 15.

92. Dayan, "Legal Slaves," revised version, 54.

93. Dayan, "Legal Terrors," 45–55.

CHAPTER 2. CADAVEROUS TRIUMPHS

1. Beccaria, *Of Crimes and Punishments*, 68–69.

2. Blomfield, "The Christian's Duty Towards Criminals," 6.

3. Foucault, *Discipline and Punish*, 108.

4. Beccaria, *Of Crimes and Punishments*, 68–69.

5. Rush, *Essays*, 81.

6. Rush, *Essays*, 83.

7. Rush, *Essays*, 88.

8. On Rush's concept of a mediated terror, see Meranze, "A Criminal." For a fuller discussion of the role of fiction in the early phase of reform, see Okun, *Crime and the Nation*. Okun, noting the simultaneous development of the first American penitentiaries and the first American novels in Philadelphia in

the late eighteenth century, compellingly reads them side by side to reveal a series of common concerns, including "the division of labor and the commodification of bodies; the inculcation of virtue and the thrills of transgression; the construction and replication of identity; the moral allegories of domestic space" (Okun, *Crime and the Nation*, xx).

9. Johnston, *Eastern State*, 36.

10. Thomas M'Elwee and George W. Smith, quoted and reproduced in Richard Vaux, *Brief Sketch*, 56–61.

11. The Tombs, a structure including not only prison cells but also courtrooms and police facilities, was built between 1835 and 1838. Haviland had also used an Egyptian-style façade for the New Jersey Penitentiary at Trenton, constructed between 1833 and 1836. See Johnston, *Forms of Constraint*, 85–86.

12. John McGinn, *Ten Days in the Tombs* (New York: P. F. Harris, 1855), 5–6. Quoted in Berthold, "Prison World," 237.

13. Dickens, *American Notes*, 75.

14. Dayan, "Poe, Persons, and Property," 406. In an essay that appeared as I was completing my revisions on this book, Jason Haslam compellingly argues that Poe's "The Pit and the Pendulum" addresses the new forms of publicity and mediation that arose when the prison system displaced the scaffold as the scene of punishment. Drawing from Meranze and Dayan, Haslam argues that, for reformers, "the spectacle would . . . continue to exist—and have an impact on society—in publicly circulated narrative forms, including literature"; Haslam goes on to show how the reformist debate "about punishment and publicity is thematized—even analyzed—in Poe's 'The Pit and the Pendulum'" (Haslam, "Pits, Pendulums, and Penitentiaries," 269).

15. Poe, *Complete Tales*, 250.

16. Halttunen, "Gothic Mystery," 42.

17. Many of the founders of the penitentiary system, from Beccaria to Rush, expressed their hope that it would haunt the public imagination, spreading fear especially among the poor and semiliterate populations that seemed, to authorities, most disposed to crime. Of course, they also took pains to assure themselves and their enlightened colleagues that the prison was not really a dungeon or a tomb. Their vision of the institution might be understood as an appeal to a divided audience: to the dangerous public, they spun a gothic tale designed to inspire dread; to their fellow reformers, they offered the sentimental story of lost souls reclaimed.

18. Louis S. Gross identifies the central concern of the gothic as "the singularity and monstrosity of the Other: what the dominant culture cannot incorporate within itself, it must project outward onto this hated/desired figure" (Gross, *Redefining the American Gothic*, 90; see Martin and Savoy, *American Gothic*, 4–6). On the gothic as a "complex," see Anne Williams, *Art of Darkness: A Poetics of Gothic* (Chicago: University of Chicago Press, 1995).

19. Marianne Noble has argued, for instance, that sentimentality has a "gothic core," that the pleasures of sympathy are bound up with the thrill of watching

another's misery. Laura Hinton takes an even more cynical view, proposing that sentimental sympathy always directs a "perverse gaze" at its victims. See Noble, "An Ecstasy of Apprehension," and Hinton, *The Perverse Gaze of Sympathy.*

20. Fiedler's critical method traded in archetypes, but I do not mean to suggest that it tended toward empty formalism. Fiedler's book, as even recent revisionist studies of the gothic recognize, was a pioneering effort to combine the energies of historicism and psychoanalysis (Martin and Savoy, *American Gothic*, viii).

21. Noble provides a concise synthesis of this view: "It is no coincidence, critics agree, that the gothic arose at the moment when Enlightenment thinkers were idealizing the human being as a coherent, rational self. The gothic represents the underside of this ideal, exposing both the illicit desires and the tactics of terror used to repress them during the construction of hegemonic subjectivities" (Noble, "An Ecstasy of Apprehension," 165).

22. Poe, *Complete Tales*, 258.

23. The best-known treatment of these issues is Toni Morrison's *Playing in the Dark: Whiteness and the Literary Imagination.* Among many other examples are the essays collected under the heading "Racial Politics in Gothic Texts" in Martin and Savoy, *American Gothic*; and Dougherty, "Foucault in the House of Usher."

24. Richard Vaux, *Brief Sketch*, 111.

25. See Johnston, *Eastern State.*

26. Dickens, *American Notes*, 91. Subsequent quotations are cited parenthetically in the text.

27. Dickens did not give the names of the prisoners he saw at Eastern State, but he mentions a man who "wrote verses about ships (he was by trade a mariner), and the 'maddening wine-cup,' and his friends at home" (*American Notes*, 94). Hawser's "To the Sailor" includes a warning against "the poison'd wave / Of the madd'ning bowl" (71). In Joseph Adshead's *Prisons and Prisoners* (1845), the poet mentioned by Dickens is identified as Hawser and defended against Dickens's dismissive treatment (104–113).

28. Foucault famously described the ways in which prisons create and profit by a sort of managed "deviancy" (*Discipline and Punish*, 257–292). The anthropologist Lorna Rhodes, in *Total Confinement*, a study of super-max prisons, argues that the derangement caused by "total confinement" distorts the logic of rational action and consequences according to which the institution is supposed to operate.

29. Goffman, *Asylums*, 61.

30. Roscoe, "Brief Statement," 25–26. The lines are quoted and rebutted by Roberts Vaux in his *Letter on the Penitentiary System*, 8.

31. I discuss these two rival systems in detail in chapter 3.

32. Hawthorne, *House of the Seven Gables*, 76. Subsequent quotations are cited parenthetically in the text.

33. Shulman briefly mentions Clifford in relationship to Hawthorne's treatment of punishment ("Artist in the Slammer," 87); Carol Colatrella, in *Literature and Moral Reform*, gives a more extensive reading, considering Clifford a model for some of Melville's characters.

34. For a survey and historicist reconsideration of the critical tradition that opposes Hawthorne's work to the sentimental work of Stowe and others, see Tompkins, "Masterpiece Theater: The Politics of Hawthorne's Literary Reputation," in *Sensational Designs*, 3–39.

35. Melville, *Bartleby*, 3. Subsequent quotations are cited parenthetically in the text.

36. The most extensive version of the autobiographical reading is made by Leo Marx, who reads the novella "as a parable having to do with Melville's own fate as a writer" (602). Michael Paul Rogin, though he recognizes that Bartleby is crucially a character without "history," connects him to Melville's friend James Ely Murdock Fly, who, Rogin writes, "supplies the missing history of *Bartleby*" (*Subversive Genealogy*, 193–194). Later, Rogin suggests that Bartleby is a projection of "the lawyer's interior, impoverished by a lifetime in contracts and deeds" (199). H. Bruce Franklin, devoting a few pages to the novella in *The Victim as Criminal and Artist*, considers Bartleby a Christ-figure (58–59), a "version" of Melville (57), and above all a figure of "rebellion" against "the sterile world of capitalism" (57, 56). Curiously, Franklin does not take up Melville's allusions to the penitentiary. In "Guantánamo's Symbolic Economy," Susan Willis offers a brief but fascinating discussion of Bartleby in the context of the contemporary war on terror (129–130).

37. Deleuze, "Bartleby," 68

38. Melville, letter to Hawthorne, April 16, 1851, reprinted in Levine, ed., *The House of Seven Gables*, 318–320.

39. Deleuze, "Bartleby," 73.

40. Colatrella, *Literature and Moral Reform*, 52.

41. Colatrella, *Literature and Moral Reform*, 11–14, 24.

42. The connection between *Bartleby* and the prison system was made earlier by Michael Berthold in "The Prison World of Melville's *Pierre* and *Bartleby*" and by Michael Paul Rogin in *Subversive Genealogy* (190–201).

43. As Rogin argues, building his reading on the political lives of Melville and his family, *Bartleby* is set at a moment of transition in the history of disciplinary paradigms, the passage from bodily harm to spiritual correction, from torture to incarceration, from "the whip" to "the wall" (*Subversive Genealogy*, 192). Colatrella, pursuing the same line, writes that "the lawyer deliberately creates a separate cell that Bartleby is meant to work in" (*Literature and Moral Reform*, 41). Colatrella mentions the Auburn system and the panoptic constructions of some European prisons, but not the skylights of Eastern State.

44. Dickens, *American Notes*, 76.

45. Johnston, *Eastern State*, 40.

46. Beaumont and Tocqueville, *Report*, 41.

47. Beaumont and Tocqueville, *Report*, 57, my emphasis.

48. Reprinted in Melossi and Pavarini, *The Prison and the Factory*, 166–168.

49. Melossi and Pavarini, *The Prison and the Factory*, 163.

50. Rogin, *Subversive Genealogy*, 195–196. "Bartleby's mysterious strike," as H. Bruce Franklin notes, "shatter[s] all [the lawyer's] customary assumptions, first about the relations between employers and employees, then about private property itself, and finally about the entire human condition in this society" (*The Victim as Criminal and Artist*, 57).

51. Ngai, *Ugly Feelings*, 32.

52. In "Sparing the Rod," Brodhead shows how the passage from spectacular punishment to corrective discipline was accompanied in the American North by the development of a theory and practice of training based on the bonds of familial love. According to the discourse of disciplinary intimacy, children should learn to embrace right principles and polite behavior by learning, first of all, to love the person who instructed them in those virtues. The emergent philosophy, which Brodhead identifies as "the middle class's greatest creation, absorption, and self-identifying badge," had its anchor in mother-child relations, but it shaped institutions outside the home as well, such as the public schools reformed by the Massachusetts administrator Horace Mann. Disciplinary intimacy, Brodhead writes, meant "a purposeful sentimentalization of the disciplinary relation . . . and a conscious intensification of the emotional bond between the authority figure and its charge," features that Brodhead sees explored not only in pamphlets and magazine articles but also in popular fiction (Brodhead, "Sparing the Rod," 70–72, 77–92). The sentimental home, then, may represent the perfect "house of correction," a completely reformed scene of subject-making through sympathy and love, without violence.

53. See Dickens, *American Notes*, 77. If the reference is to the site of the scaffold, then there is some subtle irony in the lawyer's romantic feeling that the grass represents the triumph of a softening nature over the hard cruelties of the prison.

54. Adorno and Horkheimer, *Dialectic of Enlightenment*, 178.

55. Rogin, *Subversive Genealogy*, 201.

56. Coviello, "The American in Charity," 158–165.

57. Coviello, "The American in Charity," 156. Along the same lines, Sianne Ngai praises the "antisentimental aesthetic" of *Bartleby* as the grounds of "a politics . . . very different . . . from the direct activism supposedly incited, according to what has now become American folklore, by Harriet Beecher Stowe's poetics of sympathy and the genre of sentimental literature as a whole" (Ngai, *Ugly Feelings*, 32, 9).

58. Coviello, "The American in Charity," 173.

59. Stowe, *Uncle Tom's Cabin*, 348–349. Subsequent quotations are cited parenthetically in the text.

60. Castronovo, "Political Necrophilia," 121.

61. My readings in this section follow the lead of Joseph Roach's *Cities of the Dead* and Sharon Patricia Holland's *Raising the Dead*.
62. On the fugitive slave as a hunted outlaw, see Sellin, *Slavery and the Penal System*, 137.

CHAPTER 3. THE MEANING OF SOLITUDE

1. Johnston, *Forms of Constraint*, 75–76.
2. Howard, *State of the Prisons*, 24.
3. G. W. Smith, *Defence of the System of Solitary Confinement*, 36, 37.
4. Beaumont and Tocqueville, *Report*, 41. Subsequent quotations are cited parenthetically in the text.
5. G. W. Smith, *Defence of the System of Solitary Confinement*, 24.
6. Bentham, *Panopticon*, 50.
7. Meranze, *Laboratories of Virtue*, 327.
8. Foucault, *Discipline and Punish*, 236; Dumm, *Democracy and Punishment*, 101.
9. Foucault, *Discipline and Punish*, 232.
10. Boston Prison Discipline Society, 1846 *Report*, 28.
11. Blomfield, "The Christian's Duty Towards Criminals," 12; emphasis original.
12. Richard Vaux, *The Convict*, 30.
13. Beaumont and Tocqueville, *Report*, 163.
14. The idea of the carceral "soul" has been explored by a long and rich critical tradition, but it still has some obscure dimensions, especially concerning the peculiar history of captivity in the American context. For thirty years, the great theoretical authority on how prisons remake their inmates has been Foucault's *Discipline and Punish*. Foucault's work reveals much about the prison reform movement and its place in the advent of Enlightenment modernity, with its new regimes of knowledge, power, and subjectivity. I will draw from it, and from several scholars for whom Foucault is a guiding light. I wish, however, to depart from Foucault in a few important ways. In exploring prison architecture and its designs on the soul, I will emphasize not the surveillance that has fascinated many of Foucault's readers but solitude and the architecture of mind. In describing the institutional and political transformations that brought the penitentiary onto the historical scene, I will also disagree with Foucault's narrative, according to which the old spectacle of the scaffold gives way, in time, to the modern discipline of the penitentiary. In the United States, the rise of the prison was actually contemporary with the rise of the full-scale plantation order and its grotesquely spectacular punishments: the difference between cell and scaffold is one not of chronology but of geography, economy, and especially race. Finally, I will emphasize how the making of subjects in the penitentiary, the rise of the modern soul, remained deeply bound to a myth and practice of sacrifice—a desire, in Blomfield's words, "to quicken those who were dead" (12). The cultivation of the prisoner's new life depended upon the ritual enactment of his death and burial.

15. See, for example, Johnston's chapters "Makeshift Prisons" and "Prisons in the Early Modern Period" in *Forms of Constraint*.

16. Evans, *Fabrication of Virtue*, 89–91. Johnston dates the construction of the Warwick pit to 1680 (see *Forms of Constraint*, 28).

17. Evans, *Fabrication of Virtue*, 94.

18. Evans, *Fabrication of Virtue*, 96.

19. Howard, *State of the Prisons*, 6.

20. Evans, *Fabrication of Virtue*, 95.

21. Bentham, *Panopticon*, 46–47.

22. Howard, *State of the Prisons*, 8.

23. Evans, *Fabrication of Virtue*, 115.

24. Quoted in Brodie, Croom, and Davies, *English Prisons*, 10.

25. Woven into the discourse of "contagion," into all the disgusted complaints about the "free intercourse" of prisoners and the vice that festered in such an arrangement, was the shocking discovery of sex in the prisons, which has been an unspoken but a crucial theme in prison reform since its earliest days. As late as 1934 an American reformer recorded his frustration with the silence and euphemisms surrounding the question: "Vitally important as the sex problem is in prison, involving as it does various aspects of immorality and perversion, the undermining of discipline, and the ravages upon the mental, physical, and emotional make-up of the prisoner . . . the subject is never discussed openly" (Fishman, *Sex in Prison*, 18).

26. Quoted in Evans, *Fabrication of Virtue*, 66.

27. Howard, *State of the Prisons*, 8.

28. Bentham, *Panopticon*, 50–51.

29. G. W. Smith, *Defence of the System of Solitary Confinement*, 11.

30. Some early reformers attempted to combat the two types of conspiracy with improved ventilation. Leading this version of reform in England was Stephen Hales, a doctor of divinity and a fellow of the Royal Society who had been pursuing projects in philanthropy and engineering for several decades. Hales proposed "to furnish ships, gaols, hospitals . . . with the wholesome breath of life in exchange for the noxious air of confined places" (quoted in Evans, *Fabrication of Virtue*, 100). Around 1749, he built and installed ventilators for Savoy Prison and the Wincester County Gaol, among others, and was planning with French authorities to bring his technology to their institutions. Between 1750 and 1755 he completed his most ambitious work, an enormous respiration machine for London's Newgate Prison, a combination of windmills and bellows that "functioned like a gigantic . . . lung" for the building. See Evans, *Fabrication of Virtue*, 101–102.

31. Earlier experiments in the solitary confinement of civil offenders had been made by the local bishops of Bamberg, Germany, in 1627 and by the Florentine priest Filippo Franci in 1677. See Johnston, *Forms of Constraint*, 34–35.

32. Evans, *Fabrication of Virtue*, 60.

33. See Johnston, *Forms of Constraint*, 36.

34. Quoted in Evans, *The Fabrication of Virtue*, 60.

35. See G. W. Smith, *Defence of the System of Solitary Confinement*, 8–9.

36. Evans, *Fabrication of Virtue*, 59.

37. Johnston, *Forms of Constraint*, 39.

38. See G. W. Smith, *Defence of the System of Solitary Confinement*, 8–9.

39. Howard, *State of the Prisons*, 116. Howard was disappointed when, upon later visits to Ghent, he found the Maison de Force in decline, its cells crowded with more than one prisoner, its manufacturing equipment sold or fallen into disrepair, its inmates hungry and unclean (117–118).

40. Howard, *State of the Prisons*, 26. Subsequent quotations are cited parenthetically in the text.

41. *The State of the Prisons* belongs to the first phase of reform in England, the era when Newgate Prison was rebuilt (1769–1780) according to a plan that separated debtors, female felons, and male felons; and when Parliament passed the Penitentiary Act of 1779, the Hard Labour Bill, which called for classification of inmates, solitude by night, and supervised work by day. The Hard Labour Bill came close to enacting Howard's ideal plan—but no national penitentiary was built according to its rules, and most local and regional institutions carried on as they had before. See Johnston, *Forms of Constraint*, 34, 43.

42. Evans, *Fabrication of Virtue*, 75.

43. Hanway, *Distributive Justice and Mercy*, 96.

44. G. W. Smith, *Defence of the System of Solitary Confinement*, 8.

45. King James Version, Matthew 6:33 and 25.

46. Chadwick, *Western Asceticism*, 15–21.

47. Vivian, *Life of Onnophrius*, 156.

48. Chadwick, *Western Asceticism*, 25.

49. On the anchorite's civil death, see Johnston, *Forms of Constraint*, 18.

50. Chadwick, *Western Asceticism*, 24.

51. Chadwick, *Western Asceticism*, 25; see also Johnston, *Forms of Constraint*, 18.

52. Chadwick, *Western Asceticism*, 293–294.

53. Chadwick, *Western Asceticism*, 311.

54. Howard, *State of the Prisons*, 25.

55. Foucault, *Discipline and Punish*, 123.

56. Hanway, *Distributive Justice and Mercy*, ii–iii; emphasis original. Subsequent quotations are cited parenthetically in the text.

57. Bentham, *Panopticon*, 34.

58. Bentham, *Panopticon*, 44.

59. Barnes, *Evolution of Penology*, 31–35.

60. Richard Vaux, quoted in Barnes, *Evolution of Penology*, 72.

61. Rothman, *The Discovery of the Asylum*, 60.

62. Rush, *Essays*, 90.

63. Johnston, *Forms of Constraint*, 67–68.

64. Richard Vaux, *Brief Sketch*; see also Johnston, *Forms of Constraint*, 70–72.

65. Roberts Vaux, *Letter on the Penitentiary System*, 10

66. Quoted in Meranze, *Laboratories of Virtue*, 294

67. G. W. Smith, *Defence of the System of Solitary Confinement*, 75; see Rothman, *The Discovery of the Asylum*, 85

68. Quoted in Meranze, *Laboratories of Virtue*, 294.

69. Foucault, *Discipline and Punish*, 239.

70. G. W. Smith, *Defence of the System of Solitary Confinement*, 71.

71. See Dumm, *Democracy and Punishment*, 110.

72. Hawser, *Buds and Flowers*, preface.

73. Rothman, *The Discovery of the Asylum*, 85.

74. Rush, *Essays*, 90.

75. Rush, *Essays*, 93.

76. Cobb, *Inquiry*, 266.

77. Jefferson, *Notes on Virginia*, 238–239.

78. See Meranze, *Laboratories of Virtue*, 296–300.

79. Coates, "Effects of Gloomy Imprisonment," 96.

80. Dumm, *Democracy and Punishment*, 127.

81. Sutton, *The New York Tombs*, 591.

82. Richard Vaux, *The Convict*, 17.

83. Roscoe, *Observations*, 57–58.

84. Melossi and Pavarini, *The Prison and the Factory*, 129.

85. Rothman, *The Discovery of the Asylum*, 88.

86. Rothman, *The Discovery of the Asylum*, 71.

87. Johnston, *Forms of Constraint*, 77.

88. Dumm, *Democracy and Punishment*, 3.

89. "Surrounding the controversy over the way in which criminals should be punished," Thomas Dumm explains, "was a set of questions concerning the nature of democratic citizenship in the United States" (*Democracy and Punishment*, 113–114). For nineteenth-century sources other than Tocqueville, see the works of Francis Lieber, the essays of Benjamin Rush, and Thomas Jefferson's writings on the question of punishment.

90. See, for example, Dumm, *Democracy and Punishment*, 128–140.

91. Tocqueville, *Democracy in America*, 507–508.

92. Dumm, *Democracy and Punishment*, 111–112. Along similar lines, the historian Michael Meranze sees the penitentiary as a symbol of "a new ethics of governance and submission": "Inmates shorn of their contagious and vicious community, would look inward, internalize Christian morality, and meekly submit. . . . The spirit of redemption would reign" (Meranze, *Laboratories of Virtue*, 293).

93. Blomfield, "The Christian's Duty Towards Criminals," 12.

94. Dumm, *Democracy and Punishment*, 8.

CHAPTER 4. CAPTIVITY AND CONSCIOUSNESS

1. Rush, *Essays*, 88, 89. On the importance of secrecy in Rush's plan, see Meranze, *Laboratories of Virtue*.

2. Haynes, *Historical Sketch*, 215.

3. Beaumont and Tocqueville, *Report*, 79.

4. Beaumont and Tocqueville, *Report*, 6.

5. Roscoe, *Observations*, 49.

6. Foucault, *Discipline and Punish*, 233.

7. Adorno and Horkheimer, *Dialectic of Enlightenment*, 226.

8. Tocqueville, *Democracy in America*, 255.

9. Tocqueville, *Democracy in America*, 255–256.

10. "There is no significance to a chain," writes Colin Dayan in "Held in the Body of the State," "other than its ability to stigmatize" (191).

11. Thoreau, "Civil Disobedience," 129. Subsequent quotations are cited parenthetically in the text.

12. Haslam, *Fitting Sentences*, 24.

13. Matthiessen, *American Renaissance*, 8.

14. Several Emerson scholars, notably Barbara Packer and Christopher Newfield, have connected Emerson to institutional histories, but so far they have focused on other institutions: religious organizations, businesses, universities, and so on. I hope my reading of the penitentiary in Emerson's imagination can collaborate with, rather than displace, such accounts. I will draw from Packer's work in some detail below. Newfield's study, *The Emerson Effect*, based mainly on hierarchical corporate structures, is a nuanced treatment of how Emerson's rhetoric of individual liberty enfolds within itself a logic of "submission." The penitentiary provides an especially rigid, concrete instance of a similar reversal, where Emerson's call for self-reliance smuggles in the imagery of penitentiary "correction." Benjamin Reiss's recent work connects Emerson's life and work to another great reformed institution of the antebellum period, the insane asylum. For a fuller version of the argument that follows, see my "Emerson and Incarceration."

15. Emerson, *Letters*, 107.

16. See Fuller, "Charities," 374.

17. Emerson, *Essays*, 144–45. Subsequent quotations are cited parenthetically in the text.

18. Emerson, *Letters*, 92.

19. Emerson, *Journal*, 66.

20. See Lewis, *Development of American Prisons*, 151.

21. Lewis, *Development of American Prisons*, 149.

22. Lewis, *Development of American Prisons*, 150.

23. See "Plain truths."

24. New Hampshire House, *Journal*, 112.

25. New Hampshire Senate, *Journal*, 90.

26. New Hampshire House, *Journal*, 112.

27. New Hampshire House, *Journal*, 113.

28. New Hampshire House, *Journal*, 113.

29. Lewis, *Development of American Prisons*, 151.

30. In its 1831 *Report*, the Boston Prison Discipline Society recorded that the New Hampshire State Prison "has no solitary dormitories and corresponding discipline; and if this evil is not remedied, old convicts will soon . . . flee to New Hampshire, where . . . they may enjoy each other's society in the State Prison" (sixth *Report*, 1831, 13).

31. David Bromwich, among others, notes how "liberty" and "solitude" are joined in Emerson's discourse. See *A Choice of Inheritance*, 143. Russ Castronovo, in "Political Necrophilia," criticizes Emerson (and Bromwich) for his embrace of an abstract model of freedom that can never be realized in the heterogeneously embodied social world (120).

32. Richardson, *Emerson*, 298–300. Richardson's phrase is a paraphrase of Emerson's: "For nonconformity the world whips you with its displeasure" (182).

33. Barbara Packer notes that Emerson, suddenly feeling power wielded against him, took a renewed interest in what she calls "the contours of social and political history" (*Emerson's Fall*, 133). His conflict with the Unitarian establishment, experienced as a sort of trial and punishment, led him to consider the life cycles of radical movements. By 1841, he had arrived at an account of reform and reaction in a dialectical cycle, an alternation of explosive energy and containing order where, as Packer summarizes, "the boldest speculation of one era becomes the reactionary obstruction of the next" (135). Emerson had seen radical Unitarians, ascendant to power, become judges and censors. He perceived that the force of reform, once it establishes a new system, quickly ossifies; its bones become the cage against which the next generation must rail and fight—the hard, confining circle which the individual must break through.

34. Emerson, *Essays*, 178. On the evolution of the passage from a journal entry to a piece of "Self-Reliance," see Richardson, *Emerson*, 299–300. A century later, Sigmund Freud would describe the formation of the "super-ego" in a passage that translates Emerson's insights about social life into the language of developmental psychology: "Young children," writes Freud, "are amoral and possess no internal inhibitions against their impulses striving for pleasure. The part which is later taken on by the super-ego is played by an external power, by parental authority." Freud goes on: "It is only subsequently that . . . the external restraint is internalized and the super-ego takes the place of the parental agency and observes, directs and threatens the ego in exactly the same way as earlier the parents did with the child" ("Dissection of the Psychical Personality," 526).

35. Emerson, *Journal*, 181.

36. Richardson, *Emerson*, 343.

37. Emerson, *Letters*, 244–245, my emphasis.

38. Castronovo, "Political Necrophilia," 120.

39. Reprinted in Haynes, *Historical Sketch*, 215.

40. Bentham, *Panopticon*, 50–51.

41. Norton, "Arrival," 22.

42. Genet, *Miracle of the Rose*, 5.
43. Whitman, *Poems*, 91, 123.
44. Whitman, *Poems*, 87.

CHAPTER 5. MISSISSIPPI VOICES

1. Faulkner, *Absalom, Absalom!*, 47. Subsequent quotations are cited parenthetically in the text.
2. The female poet's seclusion in the Civil War years recalls Emily Dickinson, whose meditations on solitude and subjectivity are discussed in the Introduction and in chapter 4.
3. P. Brooks, *Reading for the Plot*, 294.
4. See, for example, Angela Davis's "Race and Criminalization: Black Americans and the Punishment Industry": "With the passage of the Thirteenth Amendment, slavery was abolished for all except convicts—and in a sense the exclusion from citizenship accomplished by the slave system has persisted within the US prison system" (*Angela Y. Davis Reader*, 72). For a critique of the prison-as-plantation narrative, see Gilmore, *Golden Gulag*, 20–21.
5. Faulkner, "The Courthouse," 24.
6. Thompson, "Reforms in the Penal System," 51–52
7. Faulkner, "The Courthouse," 21.
8. Thompson, "Reforms in the Penal System," 53–54; my emphasis.
9. J. D. Shields, quoted in W. B. Taylor, *Brokered Justice*, 10.
10. Quoted in W. B. Taylor, *Brokered Justice*, 15.
11. Quoted in Ayers, *Vengeance and Justice*, 60.
12. Mississippi Committee on the Penitentiary, *Report*, 3.
13. Quoted in Thompson, "Reforms in the Penal System," 59.
14. Quoted in Ayers, *Vengeance and Justice*, 61–62.
15. Sellin, *Slavery and the Penal System*, 140.
16. Cobb, *Inquiry*, 266.
17. Morrison, *Playing in the Dark*, 56, 64.
18. Wacquant, "From Slavery to Mass Incarceration," 57. In practice, of course, the distinctions between disciplinary practices were never absolute. As I have suggested, the penitentiary depended on bodily coercions, including whips and chains, to enforce silence and obedience. The plantation, meanwhile, was not only a scene of spectacular bodily violence but also dominated slaves by granting them certain limited and dependent kinds of subjectivity. See Hartman, *Scenes of Subjection*.
19. The connections between slavery and incarceration in the United States have been the subject of many studies and arguments. See, for example, Sellin, *Slavery and the Penal System*; Meranze, "A Criminal"; and Colvin, *Penitentiaries, Reformatories, and Chain Gangs*. See also Dayan's "Legal Slaves" and Wacquant's "From Slavery to Mass Incarceration," both of which explore the closely related processes of "social death" for the slave and "civil death" for the convict, noting how the Thirteenth Amendment conflates convict and slave.

20. Oshinsky, *Worse Than Slavery*, 41.

21. In Mississippi and elsewhere in the South, convict leasing also provided large-scale employers with a powerful advantage in their dealings with free labor. Workers who organized and threatened to strike were made to understand "that if they pressed too hard for higher wages, they could easily be replaced" with a readily available supply of bonded laborers from the prison system (Oshinsky, *Worse Than Slavery*, 81).

22. Lichtenstein, *Twice the Work of Free Labor*, 3.

23. Oshinsky, *Worse Than Slavery*, 44.

24. Oshinsky, *Worse Than Slavery*, 31–53.

25. Reprinted as "Autobiography of an Imprisoned Peon" in Franklin, *Prison Writing in Twentieth-Century America*, 21–29. Convict leasing and the forced labor of the chain gangs are remembered in a few of Faulkner's stories as scenes of forced black labor. The narrator of the gothic tale "A Rose for Emily" describes a chain gang working on the roads of Jefferson, while the foreman Homer Baron oversees "the niggers singing in time to the rise and fall of picks" (*Portable Faulkner*, 396). Uncle Job, in *The Sound and the Fury*, remarks that, if being a fool were a crime, "all chain gangs wouldn't be black" (231).

26. Quoted in Cash, *The Mind of the South*, 253.

27. Parchman's population also included a very small minority of women inmates. Oshinsky records that, between 1870 and 1970, women were never more than 5 percent of Mississippi's incarcerated (*Worse Than Slavery*, 168–169). In *Old Man*, Faulkner describes life on the prison farm as a "monastic existence of shotguns and shackles," far from "all pregnant and female life" (462).

28. Oshinsky, *Worse Than Slavery*, 164.

29. Southern Regional Council, *The Delta Prisons*, 8.

30. Faulkner, *Old Man*, 440.

31. Faulkner, *Old Man*, 435.

32. Faulkner, *Old Man*, 439.

33. Cowley, introduction to *The Portable Faulkner*, xxv.

34. Faulkner, *The Mansion*, 49.

35. Faulkner, *The Mansion*, 92.

36. Faulkner, "The Jail," 598.

37. See Newhall, "Prisons and Prisoners."

38. Meriwether and Millgate, *Lion in the Garden*, 253. As early as 1968, Richard P. Adams took these lines as a philosophical and aesthetic manifesto for Faulkner, reading his major novels through the themes of motion and stasis. "The proposition that 'Life is motion,' " writes Adams, "committed Faulkner to the imagination of a world in which the concrete experience of humanity is continual change." Yet such a "proposition" creates an aesthetic problem, "extremely hard to conceive, and quite impossible to formulate, because all formulas are static" (Adams, *Faulkner*, 4). The tension is dramatized in the story of Sutpen, whose design for a static monument is continually eroded by time

and change, forces of motion beyond the maker's control. More recently, critics have understood that in Faulkner mobility is not only a philosophical interest but also a way of abstracting and imagining social and material deterritorializations. For an extensive reading of these aesthetic tendencies that grounds them in economic history, see Carolyn Porter's "William Faulkner: Innocence Historicized" in *Seeing and Being*. Porter presents a modernizing South characterized by the tension between plantation agriculture and modern market capitalism. She argues that Faulkner's poetics abstract or "reify" this tension, as in *Absalom, Absalom!*'s opposition between static monumentalism (Sutpen's design) and the modulations of oral narrative (Porter, *Seeing and Being*, 259–268).

39. Sutpen might also use a dialect term with a different root, such as "estop"— but given the deep importance Faulkner assigns to the idea of "arresting," and given his knowledge of standard French, it seems reasonable to me to assume that the word he puts (or doesn't put) in Sutpen's mouth is either "arretez" or a dialect form like "retez." I am grateful to Srinivas Aravamudan for his help with nineteenth-century Haitian dialect.

40. Foucault described penitentiary discipline in terms that echo Faulkner's aesthetic theory: "Discipline fixes; it arrests or regulates movements; it clears up confusion; it dissipates compact groupings of individuals wandering about the country in unpredictable ways; it establishes calculated distributions. It must also master all the forces that are formed from the very constitution of an organized multiplicity; it must neutralize . . . agitations, revolts, spontaneous organizations, coalitions" (219). Like Faulkner's experimental narrative art, then, the prison is a site of tension between stasis and flow, architecture and movement, disciplined solitude and dangerous collectivity. Just as the folks of Jefferson County misapprehend Sutpen's Haitian French, however, most critics have not attended to the full implications of "arresting" in *Absalom, Absalom!* Richard Godden's widely cited *Fictions of Labor* is seriously concerned with discipline as an element of Southern economic history, and includes a chapter entitled "*Absalom, Absalom!,* Time, and Labor Discipline." A recent paper by Susan V. Donaldson uses the Foucault-inflected vocabulary of Robyn Wiegman's *American Anatomies* to explore the optics of power and control in *Go Down, Moses*. These studies have opened the way to a new understanding of how Faulkner engages history, and of how his aesthetics emerge from that engagement. Pursuing their provocations, my own research suggests some different conclusions. For instance, Mississippi disciplinary history, as I understand it, will not fit into a racialized dialectic of white subjects and black objects—the dialectic that, so far, organizes each study of discipline in Faulkner. History, and its invocations in Faulkner, suggests an even more primary role for discipline, whose white and black objects become subjects through its processes and distributions.

41. C. Brooks, *William Faulkner*, 325.

42. Faulkner, *The Sound and the Fury*, 321. Subsequent quotations are cited parenthetically in the text.

43. Here I am drawing from an account of modernist style developed by Frederic Jameson: "The great modernisms were . . . predicated on the invention of a personal, private style, as unmistakable as your fingerprint, as incomparable as your own body. But this means that the modernist aesthetic is . . . linked to the conception of a unique self and private identity . . . which can be expected to generate its own unique vision of the world and to forge its own unique, unmistakable style" (Jameson, "Consumer Society," 114).

44. Faulkner detailed the fates of the Compson brothers in the appendix he wrote for *The Portable Faulkner*.

45. Porter, *William Faulkner*, 64.

46. Faulkner, *Old Man*, 464.

47. Baldwin, *The Fire Next Time*, 96.

48. Godden, "*Absalom, Absalom!*, Haiti, and Labor History," 690.

49. Cash, *The Mind of the South*, 49–50. The founders of Jefferson, Faulkner writes elsewhere, "had grown from infancy among slaves, breathed the same air and even suckled the same breast with the sons of Ham: black and white, free and unfree, shoulder to shoulder in the same tireless lift and rhythm" (Faulkner, "The Courthouse," 46).

50. See Hartman, *Lose Your Mother*, 76–83.

51. Baldwin, "Many Thousands Gone," 42.

52. Ross, "The 'Lost World' of Quentin Compson," 255.

53. Matthews, *The Play of Faulkner's Language*, 150.

54. Lester, "Racial Awareness," 128–129.

55. Baker, *Blues, Ideology, and Afro-American Literature*, 202.

56. See T. Davis, "From Jazz Syncopation to Blues Elegy," 87.

57. See T. Davis, "From Jazz Syncopation to Blues Elegy," 83. Davis resists the temptation to dismiss the blues or spirituals as escapist flights from the real world of history and oppression. For Faulkner, Davis argues, "sound in the human voice evokes a particular cluster of emotions communally felt and centered in the material rather than spiritual configurations of a secular world" (83).

58. Baldwin, "The Uses of the Blues" (241). See also Albert Murray, who describes blues music as a piece of "equipment for living," an "artful and sometimes seemingly magical combination of idiomatic incantation and percussion that creates . . . dance-oriented good-time music (*Stomping the Blues*, 16–17).

59. Jackson, *Wake Up Dead Man*, xx.

60. A. Lomax, "Saga," 178.

61. The lines are from "Prison Blues" as performed by an inmate called "Alex." The Lomax recordings were recently rereleased as *Prison Songs: Historical Recordings from Parchman Farm* (2 volumes, Rounder Records, 1997).

62. H. R. Miller, "Folk Song Curator."

63. MacFall, "Lomax Finds Treasures."
64. Lomax, "Leadbelly's Songs," 199.
65. Lomax, "Saga," 176.
66. Kennedy, " 'King of the Twelve-String Guitar Players.' "
67. Lomax, "Leadbelly's Songs," 198–199.
68. Lomax, "Leadbelly's Songs," 199.
69. Jackson, *Wake Up Dead Man*, xix.
70. Baca, *A Place to Stand*, 111.

CHAPTER 6. FRONTIERS OF CAPTIVITY

1. Rowlandson, *The Sovereignty and Goodness of God*, 69. Subsequent quotations are cited parenthetically in the text.
2. Baca, *Immigrants in Our Own Land*, 13.
3. Castiglia, *Bound and Determined*, 1–2.
4. Faludi, "America's Guardian Myths."
5. See Castiglia, *Bound and Determined*.
6. Lepore, *The Name of War*, 129, xiv.
7. Seaver, *Narrative of the Life of Mrs. Mary Jemison*, 122.
8. Seaver, *Narrative of the Life of Mrs. Mary Jemison*, 143.
9. Seaver, *Narrative of the Life of Mrs. Mary Jemison*, 123.
10. On King Philip's War, see Lepore, *The Name of War*, and my chapter 1.
11. VanderVelde, "The Role of Captives," 657–658.
12. Franklin, *Autobiography*, 135–136.
13. Quoted in Garrison, *The Legal Ideology of Removal*, 70–71.
14. Garrison, *The Legal Ideology of Removal*, 75.
15. On these debates, see Garrison, *The Legal Ideology of Removal*.
16. The historian Stephen Pitti uses the phrase "carceral West" to revise the myth of the open frontier and call attention to the many kinds of violence and captivity that have characterized the history of the region, including the recent development of vast networks of federal and state prisons in California, Arizona, and Colorado.
17. Ortiz, *from Sand Creek*, 10. Subsequent quotations are cited parenthetically in the text.
18. Prendergast, "The Poisoned Pen of Fort Lyon Prison," n.p. On the history of Fort Lyon, see also the official Web site of the Colorado Department of Corrections.
19. P. C. Smith, "Simon Ortiz," 230.
20. On Chivington's genocidal ambitions, see Svaldi, *Sand Creek and the Rhetoric of Extermination*, especially pp. 289–296.
21. "Recollecting and re-imagining history," explains Robin Riley Fast, "Ortiz speaks as a witness to the past . . . and demands that his audience witness" (" 'It Is Ours to Know,' " 53). Ortiz shares a metaphorics of memory with many other writers who confront the history of violence, dislocation, racism, and mass death. The critical literature on Toni Morrison's novels, to take the

most famous example, is largely devoted to what she calls processes of "re-memory" in relation to the enslavement of Africans and African Americans. Fast's reading of *from Sand Creek* makes connections to trauma theory and the testimony of Holocaust survivors. For a controversial critique of such "memory," see Michaels, "You Who Never Was There."

22. See, for instance, Ortiz's "Towards a National Indian Literature" and his edited collection *Speaking for the Generations*.

23. On blood memory and its significance in these traditions, see C. Allen, *Blood Narrative*.

24. Wiget, *Simon Ortiz*, 5.

25. P. C. Smith, "Simon Ortiz," 227.

26. See, respectively, Fast, " 'It Is Ours to Know' "; Libretti, "The Other Proletarians"; and C. Allen, *Blood Narrative*.

27. The dispute over who can claim American Indian literatures has been long and, at times, somewhat ugly. David L. Moore, for example, sharply divides Ortiz from Euro-American literary theory, attacking "romantic" ideas about "the death of the author" (a reference to an essay by Foucault) and the "prison of language" (a dig at Frederic Jameson's critique of structuralism) as he celebrates Ortiz's indigenous "warrior courage" (Moore, " 'The Story Goes Its Own Way,' " 35). While Moore's position seems to lack the "generosity" he praises in Ortiz, it is not as aggressive as the stance taken by some critics on the other side. Arnold Krupat, for instance, seems to indulge in a kind of primitivism when he writes that scholars of Native American literature who don't draw from literary theory are "carrying on their analyses . . . at a virtually pretechnological level of sophistication" (Krupat, "Post-Structuralism and Oral Literature," 113). This academic tug-of-war is motivated by the false sense that poetry as complex in its aims as *from Sand Creek* can belong to only one readership, one tradition, one university department. Contemporary American Indian experience is at once distinctive and integrated into global circuits of power, capital, and ideas. Without neglecting its singularity, we can recognize that, as Chadwick Allen argues, American Indian texts arise from "multiple motivations" and help to create "multiple contexts for their reception—local, national, and global" (*Blood Narrative*, 12).

28. Fast, " 'It Is Ours to Know,' " 53.

29. Ortiz reflects on his early education in his introduction to *Woven Stone* (8–9).

30. Moore, " 'The Story Goes Its Own Way,' " 43.

31. Césaire, *Discourse on Colonialism*, 42.

32. Mbembe, *On the Postcolony*, 22.

33. Baca, *Working in the Dark*, 10.

34. Baca, *Immigrants in Our Own Land*, 13.

35. See Baca, *A Place to Stand*, 36–42.

36. Baca, *Working in the Dark*, 4–5.

37. Jackson, *Soledad Brother*, 86.

38. Malcolm X, from *The Autobiography of Malcolm X*, in Franklin, *Prison Writing in Twentieth-Century Anerica*, 154.
39. Baca, *Working in the Dark*, 8–9.
40. Baca, *Working in the Dark*, 17.
41. Baca, *Working in the Dark*, 13.
42. Baca, *A Place to Stand*, 5.
43. Baca, *A Place to Stand*, 117, 5.
44. See, for example, Parenti, *Lockdown America*, and J. Q. Whitman, *Harsh Justice*. I return to this narrative of decline in the Epilogue.
45. Baca, *Working in the Dark*, 7–11.
46. Whitman, *Complete Poems*, 87.
47. Whitman, *Complete Poems*, 102.
48. Baca, *Immigrants in Our Own Land*, 43.
49. Butler, *Precarious Life*, 151.
50. Greene, "Wanted," 337.
51. Franklin, *Prison Writing in Twentieth-Century America*, 1.
52. Wicker, preface to Franklin, *Prison Writing in Twentieth-Century America*, xi.
53. A. Y. Davis, "Writing on the Wall," 428.
54. Rodriguez, *Forced Passages*, 1–7.
55. Rodriguez, *Forced Passages*, 2.
56. Baca, *Working in the Dark*, 9.

EPILOGUE

1. Pease, "Global Homeland State," 14–15.
2. Butler, *Precarious Life*, xv, xvi. The language of this critique is drawn from Carl Schmitt's theories of sovereign power and from Giorgio Agamben's concept of "bare life," especially as developed in *Homo Sacer*. Agamben, in turn, cites Butler's account with approval (*State of Exception*, 4).
3. Willis, "Guantánamo's Symbolic Economy," 124.
4. Butler, "Afterword," 1659.
5. See Cadava, "The Monstrosity of Human Rights."
6. "Why," asks Thomas Keenan in his study of human rights claims, "is the noise, the clamor, of the speech act required?" Drawing his terms from the philosopher of language J. L. Austin, Keenan goes on to explain that the human rights claim "superimposes a performative and a constative in a way which renders the difference very difficult to make out"; it is thus a "declaration [that] aims at producing the condition it requires as its condition" (Keenan, *Fables of Responsibility*, 40–41).
7. Arendt, *Origins of Totalitarianism*, 291–292.
8. Exploring Arendt's arguments, Ian Balfour and Eduardo Cadava write that "it is precisely when the noncitizen appears, when the human is divorced from citizenship . . . that rights are lost" (Balfour and Cadava, "Introduction: The Claims of Human Rights," 281).

9. On the ideal of recognition in contemporary debates about ethics and politics, see Patchen Markell's remarkable recent work of political critique, *Bound by Recognition*.

10. Esmeir, "On Making Dehumanization Possible," 1544. See also Asad, "Redeeming the Human through Human Rights," in *Formations of the Secular*, 127–158.

11. Brown, " 'Setting the Conditions,' " 974.

12. Kaplan, "Where Is Guantánamo?" 853.

13. Brown notes that "several of the reservists at the center of the abuse scandal"—including Charles Graner and Ivan Frederick—"were assigned to Abu Ghraib precisely because they had experience working in prisons" in the United States. In the "sociopolitical economy" of the world of Abu Ghraib, she concludes, "the prison-industrial complex and the military-industrial complex converge" (" 'Setting the Conditions,' " 982–983).

14. Conover, "In the Land of Guantánamo."

15. Dayan, *The Story of Cruel and Unusual*, 5.

16. Brown, " 'Setting the Conditions,' " 982.

17. See Rodriguez, *Forced Passages*.

18. On the Attica uprising and the inmates' demands, see Wicker, *A Time to Die*.

19. F. Allen, *The Decline of the Rehabilitative Ideal*. Over the last several years, scholars have elaborated and refined the narrative of "decline." James Q. Whitman's *Harsh Justice*, for example, explores the increasing severity of punishment in the United States over the past few decades, showing how, after "the last quarter century of deepening harshness, we are no longer clearly classified in the same categories as the other countries of the liberal West" (4). Ruth Wilson Gilmore's *Golden Gulag* shows how a political and economic "crisis" in the late twentieth century leads to an explosion of prisons whose main function is the mere containment, or "incapacitation," of offending bodies. For a history of the political and social transformations that produced the contemporary prison, see Parenti, *Lockdown America*.

Adams, Richard P. *Faulkner: Myth and Motion*. Princeton: Princeton University Press, 1968.

Adorno, Theodor W., and Max Horkheimer. *Dialectic of Enlightenment*. Ed. Gunzelin Schmid Noerr. Trans. Edmund Jephcott. Stanford, CA: Stanford University Press, 2002.

Adshead, Joseph. *Prisons and Prisoners*. London: Longman, Brown, Green, and Longman, 1845.

Agamben, Giorgio. *Homo Sacer: Sovereign Power and Bare Life*. Trans. Daniel Heller-Roazen. Stanford, CA: Stanford University Press, 1998.

———. *State of Exception*. Trans. Kevin Attell. Chicago: University of Chicago Press, 2005.

Allen, Chadwick. *Blood Narrative: Indigenous Identity in American Indian and Maori Literary and Activist Texts*. Durham, NC: Duke University Press, 2002.

Allen, Francis. *The Decline of the Rehabilitative Ideal: Penal Policy and Social Purpose*. New Haven: Yale University Press, 1981.

Allen, Stephen. *An Examination of the Remarks on the Report of the Commissioners*. New York: Totten, 1826.

———. *Observations on Penitentiary Discipline: Addressed to William Roscoe, Esq., of Liverpool, England*. New York: Totten, 1827.

Arendt, Hannah. "On Violence." In *Crises of the Republic*, 103–184. San Diego: Harvest Books, 1972.

———. *The Origins of Totalitarianism*. New York: Harcourt Brace, 1975.

Asad, Talal. *Formations of the Secular: Christianity, Islam, Modernity*. Stanford, CA: Stanford University Press, 2003.

Ayers, Edward L. *Vengeance and Justice: Crime and Punishment in the Nineteenth-Century American South*. New York: Oxford University Press, 1984.

237

Baca, Jimmy Santiago. *Immigrants in Our Own Land*. Baton Rouge: Louisiana State University Press, 1979.

———. *A Place to Stand: The Making of a Poet*. New York: Grove, 2001.

———. *Working in the Dark: Reflections of a Poet of the Barrio*. Santa Fe: Red Crane, 1992.

Bache, Franklin. *Observations and Reflections on the Penitentiary System: A Letter from Franklin Bache, M.D. to Roberts Vaux*. Philadelphia: Jesper Harding, 1829.

Baker, Houston. *Blues, Ideology, and Afro-American Literature: A Vernacular Theory*. Chicago: University of Chicago Press, 1984.

Baldwin, James. *The Fire Next Time*. New York: Vintage, 1993.

———. "Many Thousands Gone." In *Notes of a Native Son*, 24–45. Boston: Beacon, 1957.

———. "The Uses of the Blues." *Playboy*, January 1964, 241.

Balfour, Ian, and Eduardo Cadava, eds. *The Claims of Human Rights*. Special issue of *South Atlantic Quarterly* 103, nos. 2–3 (Spring/Summer 2004).

Barnes, Harry Elmer. *The Evolution of Penology in Pennsylvania*. Indianapolis: Bobbs-Merrill, 1927.

Beaumont, Gustave de, and Alexis de Tocqueville. *On the Penitentiary System in the United States and Its Application in France* (1833). Trans. Francis Lieber. Carbondale, IL: Southern Illinois University Press, 1964. (Cited as *Report*.)

Beccaria, Cesare di. *Of Crimes and Punishments and Other Writings*. Ed. Richard Bellamy. Trans. Richard Davies. Cambridge: Cambridge University Press, 1995.

Bender, John. *Imagining the Penitentiary: Fiction and the Architecture of Mind in Eighteenth-Century England*. Chicago: University of Chicago Press, 1987.

Bentham, Jeremy. *The Panopticon Writings* (1787). Ed. Miran Bozovic. London: Verso, 1995.

Berlin, Ira. *Generations of Captivity: A History of African-American Slaves*. Cambridge, MA: Belknap Press of Harvard University Press, 2003.

Berthold, Michael. "The Prison World of Melville's *Pierre* and *Bartleby*." *Emerson Society Quarterly* 33, no. 4 (1987): 227–252.

Blomfield, Charles James. "The Christian's Duty Towards Criminals: A Sermon Preached in St. Philip's Chapel, Regent Street, for the Benefit of the Society for the Improvement of Prison Discipline and for the Reformation of Juvenile Offenders, on Sunday, June 22, 1828." London: Philanthropic Society, 1828.

Boston Prison Discipline Society. *Annual Report of the Board of Managers*. Boston: Prison Discipline Society, 1831, 1841, 1846.

Bouvier, John. *Institutes of American Law*. Philadelphia: R. E. Peterson, 1851.

Brodhead, Richard H. "Sparing the Rod: Discipline and Fiction in Antebellum America." *Representations* 21 (Winter 1988): 67–96.

Brodie, Allan, Jane Croom, and James O. Davies. *English Prisons: An Architectural History*. Swindon, U.K.: English Heritage, 2002.

Bromwich, David. *A Choice of Inheritance: Self and Community from Edmund Burke to Robert Frost*. Cambridge, MA: Harvard University Press, 1989.

Brooks, Cleanth. *William Faulkner: The Yoknapatawpha Country.* New Haven: Yale University Press, 1963.

Brooks, Peter. *Reading for the Plot: Design and Intention in Narrative.* Cambridge, MA: Harvard University Press, 1984.

Brown, Michelle. " 'Setting the Conditions' for Abu Ghraib: The Prison Nation Abroad." *American Quarterly* 57, no. 3 (September 2005): 973–994.

Buck-Morss, Susan. "Hegel and Haiti." *Critical Inquiry* 26, no. 4 (Summer 2000): 821–864.

Butler, Judith. "Afterword." Pages 1658–1661 in "The Humanities in Human Rights: Critique, Language, Politics," *PMLA* 121, no. 5 (October 2006): 1518–1661.

———. *Precarious Life: The Powers of Mourning and Violence.* London: Verso, 2004.

Cadava, Eduardo. "The Monstrosity of Human Rights." Pages 1558–1565 in "The Humanities in Human Rights: Critique, Language, Politics," *PMLA* 121, no. 5 (October 2006): 1518–1661.

Canuel, Mark. *The Shadow of Death: Literature, Romanticism, and the Subject of Punishment.* Princeton: Princeton University Press, 2007.

Cash, W. J. *The Mind of the South.* New York: Vintage, 1969.

Castiglia, Christopher. *Bound and Determined: Captivity, Culture-Crossing, and White Womanhood from Mary Rowlandson to Patty Hearst.* Chicago: University of Chicago Press, 1996.

Castronovo, Russ. "Political Necrophilia." *boundary 2* 27, no. 2 (Summer 2000): 113–148.

Césaire, Aimé. *Discourse on Colonialism.* Trans. Joan Pinkham. New York: Monthly Review Press, 1972.

Chadwick, Owen, ed. and trans. *Western Asceticism.* Library of Christian Classics, volume XII. Philadelphia: Westminster Press, 1958.

Chapin, Bradley. *Criminal Justice in Colonial America, 1606–1660.* Athens: University of Georgia Press, 1983.

Cheah, Pheng. *Inhuman Conditions: On Cosmopolitanism and Human Rights.* Cambridge, MA: Harvard University Press, 2006.

Chevigny, Bell Gale, ed. *Doing Time: Twenty-Five Years of Prison Writing.* New York: Arcade Publishing, 1999.

"Civil Death Statutes." *Harvard Law Review* 50 (1937): 968–977.

Coates, Benjamin H. "On the Effects of Gloomy Imprisonment on Individuals of the African Variety of Mankind in the Production of Disease." Philadelphia: John C. Clark, 1843.

Cobb, Thomas R. R. *Inquiry into the Law of Negro Slavery in the United States of America* (1858). Athens: University of Georgia Press, 1999.

Colatrella, Carol. *Literature and Moral Reform: Melville and the Discipline of Reading.* Gainesville: University Press of Florida, 2002.

Colvin, Mark. *Penitentiaries, Reformatories, and Chain Gangs: Social Theory and the History of Punishment in Nineteenth-Century America.* New York: St. Martin's, 1997.

Conover, Ted. "In the Land of Guantánamo." *New York Times Magazine*, June 29, 2003.

Cover, Robert. "Nomos and Narrative." In *Narrative, Violence, and the Law: The Essays of Robert Cover*. Ed. Martha Minow, Michael Ryan, and Austin Sarat. Ann Arbor: University of Michigan Press, 1995.

Coviello, Peter. "The American in Charity: 'Benito Cereno' and Gothic Anti-Sentimentality." *Studies in American Fiction* 30, no. 2 (2002): 155–180.

———. *Intimacy in America: Dreams of Affiliation in Antebellum Literature*. Minneapolis: University of Minnesota Press, 2005.

Cowley, Malcolm, ed. *The Portable Faulkner*. New York: Penguin, 2003.

Crotty, Kevin M. *Law's Interior: Legal and Literary Interpretations of the Self*. Ithaca: Cornell University Press, 2001.

Davis, Angela Y. *The Angela Y. Davis Reader*. Ed. Joy James. Cambridge, MA: Blackwell, 1998.

———. "From the Prison of Slavery to the Slavery of Prison: Frederick Douglass and the Convict Lease System." In *The Angela Y. Davis Reader*, 74–95.

———. "Writing on the Wall: Prisoners on Punishment." *Punishment and Society* 3, no. 3 (2001): 427–431.

Davis, Thadious. "From Jazz Syncopation to Blues Elegy: Faulkner's Development of Black Characterization." In Doreen Fowler and Ann J. Abadie, eds., *Faulkner and Race*, 70–92. Jackson: University of Mississippi Press, 1988.

Dayan, Colin (Joan). *Fables of Mind: An Inquiry into Poe's Fiction*. New York: Oxford University Press, 1987.

———. *Haiti, History, and the Gods*. Berkeley: University of California Press, 1995.

———. "Held in the Body of the State: Prisons and the Law." In Austin Sarat and Thomas R. Kearns, eds., *History, Memory and the Law*, 183–247. Ann Arbor: University of Michigan Press, 1999.

———. "Legal Slaves and Civil Bodies." *Nepantla* 2, no. 1 (December 2001): 3–39.

———. "Legal Slaves and Civil Bodies" (revised version). In Russ Castronovo and Dana D. Nelson, eds., *Materializing Democracy: Toward a Revitalized Cultural Politics*, 53–93. Durham, NC: Duke University Press, 2002.

———. "Legal Terrors." *Representations* 92 (Fall 2005): 42–80.

———. "Poe, Persons, and Property." *American Literary History* 11, no. 3 (Fall 1999): 405–425.

———. *The Story of Cruel and Unusual*. Cambridge, MA: MIT Press, 2007.

Deleuze, Gilles. "Bartleby; or, The Formula." In *Essays Critical and Clinical*, trans. Daniel W. Smith and Michael A. Greco, 68–90. Minneapolis: University of Minnesota Press, 1997.

Dickens, Charles. *American Notes and Pictures from Italy*. London: Macmillan, 1903.

Dickinson, Emily. *The Complete Poems of Emily Dickinson*. Ed. Thomas H. Johnson. Boston: Little, Brown, 1961.

Dillon, Elizabeth. "Sentimental Aesthetics." *American Literature* 76, no. 3 (September 2004): 495–523.

Dimock, Wai Chee. *Residues of Justice: Literature, Law, Philosophy.* Berkeley: University of California Press, 1996.

"Disenfranchisement of Ex-Felons." *Harvard Law Review* 102 (1989): 1300–1317.

Dougherty, Stephen. "Foucault in the House of Usher: Some Historical Permutations in Poe's Gothic." *Papers on Language and Literature* 37, no. 1 (Winter 2001): 3–24.

Douglass, Frederick. *Narrative of the Life of Frederick Douglass.* Ed. Houston A. Baker, Jr. New York: Penguin, 1982.

Dumm, Thomas. *Democracy and Punishment: Disciplinary Origins of the United States.* Madison: University of Wisconsin Press, 1987.

Ek, Auli. *Race and Masculinity in Contemporary American Prison Narratives.* New York: Routledge, 2005.

Ekirch, A. Roger. *Bound for America: The Transportation of British Convicts to the Colonies, 1718–1775.* Oxford: Clarendon, 1987.

Emerson, Ralph Waldo. *Emerson in His Journals.* Ed. Joel Porte. Cambridge, MA: Belknap Press of Harvard University Press, 1982.

———. *Selected Essays.* Ed. Larzer Ziff. New York: Penguin, 1982.

———. *Selected Letters of Ralph Waldo Emerson.* Ed. Joel Myerson. New York: Columbia University Press, 1997.

Esmeir, Samera. "On Making Dehumanization Possible." Pages 1544–1551 in "The Humanities in Human Rights: Critique, Language, Politics," *PMLA* 121, no. 5 (October 2006): 1518–1661.

Evans, Robin. *The Fabrication of Virtue: English Prison Architecture, 1750–1840.* Cambridge: Cambridge University Press, 1982.

Ewald, Alec C. " 'Civil Death': The Ideological Paradox of Criminal Disenfranchisement Law in the United States." *Wisconsin Law Review* (2002): 1045–1132.

Faludi, Susan. "America's Guardian Myths." *New York Times,* September 7, 2007.

Farr, James. " 'So Vile and Miserable an Estate': The Problem of Slavery in Locke's Thought." *Political Theory* 14, no. 2 (May 1986): 263–289.

Fast, Robin Riley. " 'It Is Ours to Know': Simon J. Ortiz's *From Sand Creek.*" *Studies in American Indian Literatures* 12, no. 3 (Fall 2000): 52–63.

Faulkner, William. *Absalom, Absalom!* New York: Vintage, 1986.

———. "The Courthouse." In *The Portable Faulkner,* 19–50.

———. "The Jail." In *The Portable Faulkner,* 597–631.

———. *The Mansion.* New York: Random House, 1959.

———. *Old Man.* In *The Portable Faulkner,* 435–524.

———. *The Portable Faulkner.* Ed. Malcolm Cowley. New York: Penguin, 2003.

———. *The Sound and the Fury.* New York: Vintage, 1990.

Fiedler, Leslie. *Love and Death in the American Novel.* New York: Anchor, 1992.

Fishman, Joseph F. *Sex in Prison: Revealing Sex Conditions in American Prisons.* New York: National Library Press, 1934.

Foucault, Michel. *Discipline and Punish: The Birth of the Prison* (1975). Trans. Alan Sheridan. New York: Vintage, 1977.

Franklin, Benjamin. *The Autobiography and Other Writings.* Ed. Kenneth Silverman. New York: Penguin, 1986.

Franklin, H. Bruce. "*Billy Budd* and Capital Punishment: A Tale of Three Centuries." *American Literature* 69, no. 2 (June 1997): 337–359.

————, ed. *Prison Writing in Twentieth-Century America.* With a Foreword by Tom Wicker. New York: Penguin, 1998.

————. *The Victim as Criminal and Artist: Literature from the American Prison.* New York: Oxford University Press, 1978.

Friedman, Lawrence M. *Crime and Punishment in American History.* New York: Basic Books, 1993.

Freud, Sigmund. "Dissection of the Psychical Personality." In *The Complete Introductory Lectures on Psychoanalysis,* ed. and trans. James Strachey, 521–544. New York: Norton, 1966.

Fuller, Margaret. "Our City Charities: Visit to Bellevue Alms House, to the Farm School, the Asylum for the Insane, and the Penitentiary on Blackwell's Island." *New York Daily Tribune,* March 19, 1845. Reprinted in *The Portable Margaret Fuller,* ed. Mary Kelly, 370–376. New York: Penguin, 1994.

Fuss, Diana. "Interior Chambers: The Dickinson Homestead." *differences* 10, no. 3 (1998): 1–46.

Garrison, Tim Alan. *The Legal Ideology of Removal: The Southern Judiciary and the Sovereignty of Native American Nations.* Athens: University of Georgia Press, 2002.

Genet, Jean. "Introduction" to George Jackson, *Soledad Brother,* 1–8.

————. *The Miracle of the Rose.* Trans. Bernard Frechtman. New York: Grove, 1966.

Gilmore, Ruth Wilson. *Golden Gulag: Prisons, Surplus, Crisis, and Opposition in Globalizing California.* Berkeley: University of California Press, 2007.

Godden, Richard. "*Absalom, Absalom!*, Haiti, and Labor History: Reading Unreadable Revolutions." *English Literary History* 61, no. 3 (1994): 685–720.

————. *Fictions of Labor: William Faulkner and the South's Long Revolutions.* Cambridge: Cambridge University Press, 1997.

Goffman, Erving. *Asylums: Essays on the Social Situation of Mental Patients and Other Inmates.* New York: Anchor, 1961.

————. *The Presentation of Self in Everyday Life.* New York: Doubleday, 1959.

Gonnaud, Maurice. *An Uneasy Solitude: Individual and Society in the Work of Ralph Waldo Emerson.* Trans. Lawrence Rosenwald. Princeton: Princeton University Press, 1987.

Grass, Sean. *The Self in the Cell: Narrating the Victorian Prisoner.* New York: Routledge, 2003.

Greene, Roland. "Wanted: A New World Studies." *American Literary History* 12, nos. 1–2 (2000): 337–347.

Gross, Louis S. *Redefining the American Gothic: From* Wieland *to* Day of the Dead. Ann Arbor: University of Michigan Press, 1989.

Guyot, Pierre-Jean-Jacques-Guillaume, ed. *Repertoire Universel et Raisonné de Jurisprudence* (1785). Cited as quoted in von Bar et al., *History of Continental Criminal Law,* 272.

Halttunen, Karen. "Gothic Mystery and the Birth of the Asylum: The Cultural Construction of Deviance in Early-Nineteenth-Century America." In Karen Halttunen and Lewis Perry, eds., *Moral Problems in American Life: New Perspectives on Cultural History*, 41–57. Ithaca: Cornell University Press, 1998.

Hanway, Jonas. *Distributive Justice and Mercy*. London: J. Dodsey, 1781.

Hardt, Michael. "Prison Time." *Yale Review* 91 (1997): 64–79.

Hartman, Saidya. *Lose Your Mother: A Journey Along the Atlantic Slave Route*. New York: Farrar, Straus, and Giroux, 2007.

———. *Scenes of Subjection: Terror, Slavery, and Self-Making in Nineteenth-Century America*. New York: Oxford University Press, 1997.

Haslam, Jason. *Fitting Sentences: Identity in Nineteenth- and Twentieth-Century Prison Narratives*. Toronto: University of Toronto Press, 2005.

———. "Pits, Pendulums, and Penitentiaries: Reframing the Detained Subject." *Texas Studies in Literature and Language* 50, no. 3 (Fall 2008): 268–284.

Haslam, Jason, and Julia Wright, eds. *Captivating Subjects: Writing Confinement, Citizenship, and Nationhood in the Nineteenth Century*. Toronto: University of Toronto Press, 2005.

Hassine, Victor. "How I Became a Convict." In Chevigny, ed., *Doing Time*, 14–21.

Hawser, Harry. *Buds and Flowers, of Leisure Hours*. Philadelphia: Geo. Johnson, for the Author, 1844.

Hawthorne, Nathaniel. *The House of Seven Gables*. Ed. Robert S. Levine. New York: Norton, 2006.

———. *The Scarlet Letter*. New York: Penguin, 1986.

———. "Wakefield." In *Selected Tales and Sketches*, ed. Michael J. Colacurcio, 149–158. New York: Penguin, 1987.

Haynes, Gideon. *An Historical Sketch of the Massachusetts State Prison. With Narratives and Incidents, and Suggestions on Discipline*. Boston: Lee and Shepard, 1869.

Hinton, Laura. *The Perverse Gaze of Sympathy: Sadomasochistic Sentiments from Clarissa to Rescue 911*. Albany: State University of New York Press, 1999.

Holland, Sharon Patricia. *Raising the Dead: Readings of Death and (Black) Subjectivity*. Durham, NC: Duke University Press, 2000.

Howard, John. *The State of the Prisons* (1777). London: Everyman's Library, 1929.

Ignatieff, Michael. *A Just Measure of Pain: The Penitentiary in the Industrial Revolution, 1750–1850*. New York: Pantheon, 1978.

Itzkowitz, Howard, and Lauren Oldak. "Restoring the Ex-Offender's Right to Vote: Background and Developments." *American Criminal Law Review* 11 (1972): 721–770.

Jacobs, Harriet. *Incidents in the Life of a Slave Girl*. New York: Oxford University Press, 1988.

Jackson, George. *Soledad Brother: The Prison Letters of George Jackson*. New York: Bantam, 1970.

Jackson, Bruce. *Wake Up Dead Man: Hard Labor and Southern Blues*. Athens: University of Georgia Press, 1999.

Jackson, Virginia. *Dickinson's Misery: A Theory of Lyric Reading.* Princeton: Princeton University Press, 2005.

Jameson, Frederic. *The Political Unconscious: Narrative as a Socially Symbolic Act.* Ithaca: Cornell University Press, 1981.

———. "Postmodernism and Consumer Society." In Hal Foster, ed., *The Anti-Aesthetic*, 111–125. New York: New Press, 1998.

Jefferson, Thomas. *Notes on Virginia.* In *The Life and Selected Writings of Thomas Jefferson*, ed. Adrienne Koch and William Peden, 173–268. New York: Random House, 1993.

Johnston, Norman. *Eastern State Penitentiary: Crucible of Good Intentions.* Philadelphia: Philadelphia Museum of Art, 1994.

———. *Forms of Constraint: A History of Prison Architecture.* Urbana: University of Illinois, 2000.

Kaplan, Amy. "Where Is Guantánamo?" *American Quarterly* 57:3 (September 2005): 831–854.

Keenan, Thomas. *Fables of Responsibility: Aberrations and Predicaments in Ethics and Politics.* Stanford, CA: Stanford University Press, 1997.

Kennedy, M. Emmett. "The 'King of the Twelve-String Guitar Players.' " *New York Times*, December 27, 1936.

Krupat, Arnold. "Post-Structuralism and Oral Literature." In Brian Swann and Arnold Krupat, eds., *Recovering the Word: Essays on Native American Literature*, 113–128. Berkeley: University of California Press, 1987.

Lane, Charles. "Social Tendencies." *The Dial* 4, nos. 1–2 (July and October 1843): 65–86, 188–204.

Lentricchia, Frank. *Ariel and the Police.* Madison: University of Wisconsin Press, 1988.

Lepore, Jill. *The Name of War: King Philip's War and the Making of American Identity.* New York: Vintage, 1999.

Lester, Cheryl. "Racial Awareness and Arrested Development: *The Sound and the Fury* and the Great Migration (1915–1928)." In Weinstein, ed., *The Cambridge Companion to William Faulkner*, 123–145.

Lewis, Orlando F. *The Development of American Prisons and Prison Customs, 1776–1845.* Albany: Prison Association of New York, 1922.

Libretti, Tim. "The Other Proletarians: Native American Literature and Class Structure." *Modern Fiction Studies* 47, no. 1 (Spring 2001): 164–189.

Lichtenstein, Alexander C. *Twice the Work of Free Labor: The Political Economy of Convict Labor in the New South.* London: Verso, 1996.

Lincoln, Kenneth. *Native American Renaissance.* Berkeley: University of California Press, 1983.

Linebaugh, Peter, and Marcus Rediker. *The Many-Headed Hydra: Sailors, Slaves, Commoners, and the Hidden History of the Revolutionary Atlantic.* Boston: Beacon, 2000.

Lomax, Alan. "Leadbelly's Songs." In *Selected Writings, 1934–1997*, 198–199.

———. "Saga of a Folksong Hunter." In *Selected Writings, 1934–1997*, 173–186.

————. *Selected Writings, 1934–1997.* Ed. Ronald D. Cohen. New York: Routledge, 2003.

MacFall, Russell. "Lomax Finds Treasures in U.S. Folk Lore." *Chicago Daily Tribune*, March 9, 1947.

Markell, Patchen. *Bound by Recognition.* Princeton: Princeton University Press, 2003.

Martin, Robert K., and Eric Savoy, eds. *American Gothic: New Interventions in a National Narrative.* Iowa City: University of Iowa Press, 1998.

Marx, Leo. "Melville's Parable of the Walls." *Sewanee Review* 61 (1953): 602–627.

Matthews, John T. *The Play of Faulkner's Language.* Ithaca: Cornell University Press, 1992.

Matthiessen, F. O. *American Renaissance.* London: Oxford University Press, 1941.

Mbembe, Achille. "Necropolitics." Trans. Libby Meintjes. *Public Culture* 15, no. 1 (2003): 11–40.

————. *On the Postcolony.* Trans. A. M. Berrett, Janet Roitman, Murray Last, and Steven Rendall. Berkeley: University of California Press, 2001.

McElwee, Thomas B. *Concise History of the Eastern State Penitentiary of Pennsylvania.* Philadelphia: Neall and Massey, 1835.

McMillin, T. S. *Our Preposterous Use of Literature: Emerson and the Nature of Reading.* Urbana: University of Illinois Press, 2000.

Melossi, Dario, and Massimo Pavarini. *The Prison and the Factory: Origins of the Penitentiary System.* Trans. Glynis Cousin. Totowa, NJ: Barnes and Noble Books, 1981.

Melville, Herman. *Bartleby.* In *Billy Budd and Other Stories,* 1–46. New York: Penguin, 1986.

Meranze, Michael. "A Criminal Is Being Beaten: The Politics of Punishment and the History of the Body." In Robert Blair St. George, ed., *Possible Pasts: Becoming Colonial in Early America,* 302–323. Ithaca: Cornell University Press, 2000.

————. *Laboratories of Virtue: Punishment, Revolution, and Authority in Philadelphia, 1760–1835.* Chapel Hill: University of North Carolina Press, 1996.

Meriwether, James B., and Michael Millgate, eds. *The Lion in the Garden: Interviews with William Faulkner, 1926–1962.* New York: Random House, 1968.

Michaels, Walter Benn. "You Who Never Was There." *Narrative* 4, no. 1 (January 1996): 1–16.

Miller, D. A. *The Novel and the Police.* Berkeley: University of California Press, 1988.

Miller, Hope Ridings. "Folk Song Curator Relates Saga of Search for Ditties." *Washington Post,* December 20, 1936, B4.

Mills, Nicolaus. "Prison and Society in Nineteenth-Century American Fiction." *Western Humanities Review* 24 (1970): 325–331.

Mississippi Legislature. Joint Standing Committee on the Penitentiary. *Report to the Legislature.* Jackson: Price and Rohrer, State Printers, 1844.

Moore, David L. " 'The Story Goes Its Own Way': Ortiz, Nationalism, and the Oral Poetics of Power." *Studies in American Indian Literatures* 16, no. 4 (2004): 34–46.

Morris, Norval, and David J. Rothman, eds. *The Oxford History of the Prison: The Practice of Punishment in Western Society.* New York: Oxford University Press, 1995.

Morrison, Toni. *Playing in the Dark: Whiteness and the Literary Imagination.* Cambridge, MA: Harvard University Press, 1992.

Murray, Albert. *Stomping the Blues* (1976). New York: Da Capo, 2000.

New Hampshire House of Representatives. *Journal of the House of Representatives.* Sandbornton: N. Howland, for the State, 1830.

New Hampshire Senate. *Journal of the Senate.* Concord: Luther Roby, for the State, 1831.

Newfield, Christopher. *The Emerson Effect.* Chicago: University of Chicago Press, 1996.

Newhall, Eric. "Prisons and Prisoners in the Works of William Faulkner." Ph.D. dissertation, UCLA, 1975.

Ngai, Sianne. *Ugly Feelings.* Cambridge, MA: Harvard University Press, 2005.

Noble, Marianne. "An Ecstasy of Apprehension: The Gothic Pleasures of Sentimental Fiction." In Martin and Savoy, eds., *American Gothic,* 163–182.

Norton, Judee. "Arrival." In Chevigny, ed., *Doing Time,* 22.

O'Brien, Patricia. *The Promise of Punishment: Prisons in Nineteenth-Century France.* Princeton: Princeton University Press, 1982.

Okun, Peter. *Crime and the Nation: Prison Reform and Popular Fiction in Philadelphia, 1786–1800.* New York: Routledge, 2002.

Ortiz, Simon J. *from Sand Creek.* Tucson: University of Arizona Press, 1981.

———, ed. *Speaking for the Generations: Native Writers on Writing.* Tucson: University of Arizona Press, 1998.

———. *Woven Stone.* Tucson: University of Arizona Press, 1992.

Oshinsky, David M. *Worse Than Slavery: Parchman Farm and the Ordeal of Jim Crow Justice.* New York: Free Press, 1996.

Packer, Barbara. *Emerson's Fall.* New York: Continuum, 1982.

Parenti, Christian. *Lockdown America: Police and Prisons in the Age of Crisis.* London: Verso, 1999.

Parker, Theodore. "Thoughts on Labor." *The Dial* 1, no. 4 (April 1841): 497–519.

Patterson, Orlando. *Slavery and Social Death: A Comparative Study.* Cambridge, MA: Harvard University Press, 1982.

Pease, Donald E. "The Global Homeland State: Bush's Biopolitical Settlement." *boundary 2* 30, no. 3 (Fall 2003): 1–18.

Philip, Cynthia Owen, ed. *Imprisoned in America: Prison Communications, 1776 to Attica.* New York: Harper and Row, 1973.

Phillips, Adam. *Houdini's Box: The Art of Escape.* New York: Vintage, 2002.

"Plain truths, addressed to the people of New Hampshire, concerning their state prison, and the management of its affairs" (1834). (Anonymous pamphlet.) Nineteenth-Century Legal Treatises 36686. Woodbridge, CT: Research Publications, 1988.

Poe, Edgar Allan. *Complete Tales and Poems.* New York: Vintage, 1975.

Pollock, Sir Frederick, and Frederic William Maitland. *A History of English Law before the Time of Edward I*. Cambridge: Cambridge University Press, 1895.

Porter, Carolyn. *Seeing and Being: The Plight of the Participant-Observer in Emerson, James, Adams, and Faulkner*. Middletown, CT: Wesleyan University Press, 1981.

Prendergast, Alan. "The Poisoned Pen of Fort Lyon Prison." *Westword*, November 13, 2007, n.p.

Reiss, Benjamin. *Theaters of Madness: Insane Asylums and Nineteenth-Century American Culture*. Chicago: University of Chicago Press, 2008.

Rhodes, Lorna A. *Total Confinement: Madness and Reason in the Maximum Security Prison*. Berkeley: University of California Press, 2004.

Richardson, Robert D., Jr. *Emerson: The Mind on Fire*. Berkeley: University of California Press, 1995.

Roach, Joseph. *Cities of the Dead: Circum-Atlantic Performance*. New York: Columbia University Press, 1996.

Rodriguez, Dylan. *Forced Passages: Imprisoned Radical Intellectuals and the U.S. Prison Regime*. Minneapolis: University of Minnesota Press, 2006.

Rogin, Michael Paul. *Subversive Genealogy: The Art and Politics of Herman Melville*. New York: Knopf, 1983.

Roscoe, William. "A Brief Statement of the Causes which Have Led to the Abandonment of the Celebrated System of Penitentiary Discipline, in Some of the United States." Liverpool: Harris, 1827.

———. *Observations on Penal Jurisprudence and the Reformation of Criminals*. London: J M'Creery, 1825.

Ross, Stephen M. "The 'Lost World' of Quentin Compson." *Studies in the Novel* 7 (1975): 245–257.

Rothman, David. *The Discovery of the Asylum: Social Order and Disorder in the New Republic*. Boston: Little, Brown, 1971.

Rotman, Edgardo. "The Failure of Reform: United States, 1865–1965." In Morris and Rothman, eds., *The Oxford History of the Prison*, 151–177.

Rousseau, Jean-Jacques. *The Social Contract*. In *Basic Political Writings*. Trans. Donald A. Cress. Indianapolis: Hackett, 1987.

Rowlandson, Mary. *The Sovereignty and Goodness of God* (1682). Ed. Neal Salisbury. Boston: Bedford, 1997.

Rusche, Georg, and Otto Kircheimer. *Punishment and Social Structure*. New Brunswick, NJ: Transaction, 2003.

Rush, Benjamin. *Essays: Literary, Moral, and Philosophical*. Ed. Michael Meranze. Schenectady, NY: Union College Press, 1988.

Said, Edward. "Traveling Theory." In *The Edward Said Reader*, ed. Moustafa Bayoumi and Andrew Rubin, 195–217. New York: Vintage, 2000.

Sarat, Austin, ed. *Pain, Death, and the Law*. Ann Arbor: University of Michigan Press, 2001.

Seaver, James E. *A Narrative of the Life of Mrs. Mary Jemison* (1824). In Kathryn Zabelle Derounian-Stodola, ed., *Women's Indian Captivity Narratives*, 117–210. New York: Penguin, 1998.

Sellin, J. Thorsten. *Slavery and the Penal System.* New York: Elsevier, 1976.

Shoemaker, Karl. "The Problem of Pain in Punishment: Historical Perspectives." In Sarat, ed., *Pain, Death, and the Law,* 15–41.

Shulman, Robert. "The Artist in the Slammer: Hawthorne, Melville, Poe, and the Prison of Their Times." *Modern Language Studies* 14, no. 1 (Winter 1984): 79–88.

Smith, Abbot Emerson. *Colonists in Bondage: White Servitude and Convict Labor in America, 1607–1776.* Gloucester, MA: Peter Smith, 1965.

Smith, Caleb. "Emerson and Incarceration." *American Literature* 78, no. 2 (June 2006): 207–234.

Smith, George Washington. *A Defence of the System of Solitary Confinement of Prisoners Adopted by the State of Pennsylvania.* Philadelphia: E. G. Dorsey, 1833.

Smith, Greg T. "Civilized People Don't Want to See That Sort of Thing: The Decline of Public Physical Punishment in London, 1760–1840." In Strange, ed., *Qualities of Mercy.* 21–51.

Smith, Patricia Clark. "Simon Ortiz: Writing Home." In Joy Porter and Kenneth M. Roemer, eds., *The Cambridge Companion to Native American Literature,* 221–232. Cambridge: Cambridge University Press, 2005.

Southern Regional Council. *The Delta Prisons: Punishment for Profit.* Atlanta: Southern Regional Council, 1968.

Spierenburg, Pieter. "The Body and the State: Early Modern Europe." In Morris and Rothman, eds., *The Oxford History of the Prison,* 44–70.

Stowe, Harriet Beecher. *Uncle Tom's Cabin.* Ed. Elizabeth Ammons. New York: Norton, 1994.

Strange, Carolyn, ed. *Qualities of Mercy: Justice, Punishment, and Discretion.* Vancouver: University of British Columbia Press, 1996.

Sutton, Charles. *The New York Tombs: Its Secrets and Its Mysteries.* Ed. James B. Mix and Samuel A. MacKeever. New York: United States Publishing, 1874.

Svaldi, David. *Sand Creek and the Rhetoric of Extermination: A Case Study in Indian-White Relations.* Lanham, MD: University Press of America, 1989.

Taylor, Charles. *Modern Social Imaginaries.* Durham, NC: Duke University Press, 2004.

Taylor, William Banks. *Brokered Justice: Race, Politics, and Mississippi Prisons, 1798–1992.* Columbus: Ohio State University Press, 1993.

Thompson, E. Bruce. "Reforms in the Penal System of Mississippi, 1820–1850." *Journal of Mississippi History* 7 (1945): 51–74.

Thoreau, Henry David. "Civil Disobedience" (1849). In *The Portable Thoreau,* ed. Carl Bode, 109–137. New York: Viking, 1966.

Tocqueville, Alexis de. *Democracy in America.* Trans. George Lawrence. New York: Harper Perennial, 1988.

Tompkins, Jane. *Sensational Designs: The Cultural Work of American Fiction, 1790–1860.* New York: Oxford University Press, 1985.

VanderVelde, Lea. "The Role of Captives and the Rule of Capture." *Environmental Law* 35 (2005): 649–671.

Vaux, Richard. *Brief Sketch of the Origins and History of the State Penitentiary.* Philadelphia: McLaughlin Brothers, 1872.

———. *The Convict: His Punishment; What it Should be; and How Applied.* Philadelphia: Allen, Lane and Scott's Printing House, 1884.

Vaux, Roberts. *Letter on the Penitentiary System of Pennsylvania, Addressed to William Roscoe, Esquire.* Philadelphia: Jesper Harding, 1827.

Vivian, Tim, ed. and trans. *Paphnutius' Histories of the Monks of Upper Egypt* and *The Life of Onnophrius.* Kalamazoo, MI: Cistercian Publications, 1993.

von Bar, Carl Ludwig, et al. A *History of Continental Criminal Law.* Trans. Thomas S. Bell. Boston: Little, Brown, 1916.

Warner, Michael. *The Letters of the Republic: Publication and the Public Sphere in Eighteenth-Century America.* Cambridge, MA: Harvard University Press, 1990.

Wacquant, Loic. "From Slavery to Mass Incarceration: Rethinking the 'Race Question' in the US." *New Left Review* 13 (January–February 2002): 41–60.

Weinstein, Philip M., ed. *The Cambridge Companion to William Faulkner.* Cambridge: Cambridge University Press, 1995.

White, James Boyd. *Heracles' Bow: Essays on the Rhetoric and Poetics of the Law.* Madison: University of Wisconsin Press, 1985.

Whitman, James Q. *Harsh Justice: Criminal Punishment and the Widening Divide between America and Europe.* Oxford: Oxford University Press, 2003.

Whitman, Walt. *Complete Poems.* Ed. Francis Murphy. New York: Penguin, 1996.

Wicker, Tom. *A Time to Die.* New York: Quadrangle/New York Times Books, 1975.

Wiegman, Robyn. *American Anatomies: Theorizing Race and Gender.* Durham, NC: Duke University Press, 1995.

Wiget, Andrew. *Simon Ortiz.* Boise, ID: Boise State University Press, 1986.

Wild, J. C. *Panoramas and Views of Philadelphia and its Vicinity: embracing a collection of twenty views from paintings; with poetical illustrations of each subject by Andrew M'Makin.* Philadelphia: J. T. Bowen's Lithographic and Print Coloring Establishment, 1838.

Willis, Susan. "Guantánamo's Symbolic Economy." *New Left Review* 39 (May–June 2006): 123–131.